Living Islam

Living Islam

Women, Religion and the Politicization of Culture in Turkey

Ayşe Saktanber

I.B.Tauris   *Publishers*
LONDON ● NEW YORK

Published in 2002 by I.B. Tauris & Co. Ltd
6 Salem Road, London W2 4BU
175 Fifth Avenue, New York, NY 10010
www.ibtauris.com

In the United States of America and Canada distributed by
Palgrave Macmillan a division of St Martin's Press,
175 Fifth Avenue, New York, NY 10010

ISBN: Hardback 1-86064-178-4

A full CIP record for this book is available from the British Library
A full CIP record for this book is available from the Library of Congress

Library of Congress catalog card: available

Typeset in Goudy Old Style by Rowland Phototypesetting Ltd,
Bury St Edmunds, Suffolk
Printed and bound in Great Britain by MPG Books Ltd, Bodmin

Contents

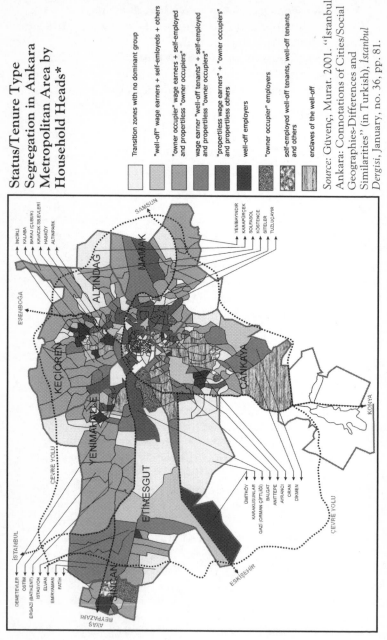

Status/Tenure Type Segregation in Ankara Metropolitan Area by Household Heads*

Legend:
- Transition zones with no dominant group
- "well-off" wage earners + self-emloyeds + others
- "owner occupier" wage earners + self-employed and propertiless "owner occupiers"
- wage earner "well-off tenants" + self-employed and propertiless "owner occupiers"
- "propertiless wage earners" + "owner occupiers" and propertiless others
- well-off employers
- "owner occupier" employers
- self-employed well-off tenants, well-off tenants and others
- enclaves of the well-off

Source: Güvenç, Murat. 2001. "İstanbul Ankara: Connotations of Cities/Social Geographies–Differences and Similarities" (in Turkish), *İstanbul Dergisi*, January, no. 36, pp. 81.

* This map is the decomposition of conventional census status categories by housing tenure types and excludes migrants of the 1985–90 periods. It covers 26,000,000 household heads. For a detailed discussion on the decomposition of employment status and housing tenure categories supplied by general census data see, Güvenç, Murat. 2000. "Mapping İstanbul: Snapshots on İstanbul from the Census of 1990" (in Turkish), *İstanbul Dergisi*, July, no. 34, pp. 35–40.

Acknowledgements

From its earliest stages, I have perceived the process of writing this book as a personal journey on which to examine certain questions that I have asked myself. Throughout this journey I have received support and encouragement from both individuals and institutions. The Social Science Research Council in New York was the first institution to support this project and in this context I owe thanks to John Eade, Ali E. Hillal Dessouki, Barbara D. Metcalf, William R. Roff, Nazif Shahrani and David Szanton. I also owe thanks to the MEAwards Committee of the Population Council for granting me a Dissertation Fellowship and to the Center for the Study of Islamic Societies and Civilizations (CSISC) at Washington University in St Louis, Missouri, where I spent the main part of this fellowship as a fellow researcher. This enabled me to form the theoretical skeleton of this study in a friendly and intellectually rich environment.

For the period of time that I spent in CSISC I would like to express my thanks to Engin D. Akarlı, Tuna Akarlı, Peter Heat, Ahmet Karamustafa, Fatemah Keshavarz and Isenbike Togan, all of whom helped me in many ways and encouraged me by showing a close interest in my project. For the part of my journey I spent in St Louis, I am especially grateful to Engin D. Akarlı and Ahmet Karamustafa who never hesitated to share with me their exceptionally deep understanding and extensive knowledge of Islamic matters. Şerif Mardin, the former Chair of Islamic Studies at the American University in Washington, DC, was another significant person on this journey. During the semester that I spent in Washington, DC, I was privileged to receive his discerning criticisms of my work. His scholarly exploration of the socio-political and cultural parameters of Turkish modernization and the place of religion in it enabled me to start to think about the most basic steps of my study and illuminated my way. I greatly appreciate his encouragement, understanding, and the interest he kindly continued to show in my project, all of which were extremely valuable to me in completing this study.

Colleagues and friends from the Departments of Sociology of both the Middle East Technical University (METU) and Boğaziçi University made valuable contributions to this study with their comments, critiques and suggestions. I would like to express my thanks to Bahattin Akşit, Sencer Ayata and Kayhan Mutlu of METU and Çağlar Keyder, Ayşe Öncü and Nükhet Sirman of Boğaziçi for the confidence they showed in me and my abilities. I was also lucky enough throughout this journey to encounter both old friends and new outstanding people whose friendly assistance was extremely helpful in many ways. Among the latter were Nazan and Michael Mackey in St Louis, and Dr Constance Hendrickson and Yasemin and Tamer Ergin in Washington, DC, to whom I would like to express my sincere gratitude for sustaining me with the comfort of warm friendship, although to them I was at first a rather 'strange traveller'. Some special old friends of mine, Füsun Akkök, Pembe Taşhan Candaner, Aycan Eren, Gül Özyeğin, Nejat Özyeğin and Güler Uluçay-Yüce, in their own unique ways also made very important contributions to my trip. Among them I must particularly thank Gül Özyeğin, a prominent sociologist, who never ceased to give me both her intellectual and practical support whether we were doing our fieldwork, fortuitously at the same time in Ankara, or writing our dissertations in the United States, or when we were apart and could only be in touch with each other by e-mail. I have always benefited greatly from her gifts of reason and rationality which perfectly mixed with a deep sense of humour and feminine understanding. Füsün Akkök, a very special friend, was always there when I needed immediate help or friendship with her exceptionally affectionate heart and the talents of a distinguished psychologist. I am grateful to both Gül and Füsün for their invaluable help, something I know I will never be able to return.

Feride Acar and Ayşe Güneş-Ayata were also extremely supportive in the attempts I made to communicate my ideas on the problems of studying women in Muslim societies in the Gender and Women's Studies Programme at METU. Our efforts to improve our interdisciplinary programme have led to the publication of this book and also another (*Fragments of Culture: The Everyday of Modern Turkey*, I. B. Tauris, 2002) jointly edited by myself and Deniz

Kandiyoti of SOAS with whom we came together in London as a result of our programme's project with SOAS on women and development. The whole process has demonstrated to me once more that women's solidarity can be as pervasive and as important in the professional arena as it is in the personal. For this alone I would like to express my thanks to all three of them.

In the early stages of producing this book, Alex Rooke, Duygu Alparslan Gürkan and Önder Gürkan helped me to overcome the various difficult aspects of turning a manuscript into a proper text and I am extremely grateful to them. I am also grateful to Figen Işık and Mete Tunceri who did not hesitate to offer their exceptional talents and assistance in producing the maps that I have used here in a publishable format. I also owe thanks to Murat Güvenç for allowing me to use his map showing the spatial distribution of social stratification in Ankara, which I believe has helped to enrich the scope of this study. Margaret Owen kindly accepted the task of editing this book and I will always remember her professional skills and personal kindness with admiration. The editorial input of Turi Munthe and Deborah Susman of I.B. Tauris was also invaluable and greatly appreciated.

I would like to express my deepest gratitude to my family for their constant support, patience and affection. My mother, Leman Altınel, and my youngest sister, Zeynep Kayserilioğlu, consistently helped me with my parental responsibilities and encouraged me in my academic endeavours. The place of honour that Sezai Sak-tanber, the father of my daughters and my former spouse, had in this special journey of mine is undeniable and I will always remain grateful to him for the invaluable support he gave to me. From their very conception, at the beginning of the second year of undergraduate education, my daughters Aslı and Binnaz became part of my school life and in return I became known to my school friends as 'Ayşe the mother of twins'. I have always been proud of this and hope that Aslı and Binnaz are also proud of having a 'career mother' despite always having had to share their mother with her books, papers, articles and computer, as well as her students and feminist activist friends. For the joy and enthusiasm they have brought into my life, and for providing me with the driving force to accomplish the writing of this book I would like to extend my most sincere thanks to them.

Finally, I express my greatest thanks to the people, and especially the women, who agreed to become the subject of this study and who generously opened their private lives, their homes and communities, as well as their hearts and minds to me. I wish I could thank them by name but, due to my promise to keep their identities secret, they must remain anonymous. I must say that I feel grateful to them for the trust they showed me in allowing me into their lives and for sharing with me their life experiences and self-narrations. Above all, it is they who made this study possible.

Ayşe Saktanber
Ankara, September 2001

For Aslı and Binnaz . . .

Prologue

This book aims to explore the social practices of what has been described as 'living Islam' both in the course of and in the aftermath of Islamic revivalism in urban Turkey. Therefore, in accordance with the double meaning of the title, *Living Islam*, this book addresses two issues. The first is the claims of some Sunni Islamic activists about what living Islam actually is. The second is the efforts of these groups to create an Islamic way of life in a secular order, thus rendering Islam a living social practice by making the secular transcendental. The main emphasis of this book will be on the latter of these issues.

The ongoing struggle between the secular and Islamic forces in Turkey is like a tug of war. If what Giddens (1991) calls 'life politics', i.e., the question 'how should we live?' constitutes one end of the rope, the question of the status of women in society is the other end. Here, fashionable contrived conceptual tools such as political Islam and cultural Islam have often been employed either to explain the ways in which Islamic activism takes different shapes in the course of political struggle or to differentiate between political endeavours and ordinary religious practices. However, these terms fail to explain the whole picture, at least as it exists in the Turkish context. I argue that the overall effort which motivates Islamic activism in Turkey is to channel what can be described as the cultural into the core of politics, a process that can be called the politicization of culture. Thus, the expression 'living Islam' as I use it here is also closely linked with that process of the politicization of culture.

By the politicization of culture I do not intend to imply that culture is ordinarily immune to power relations and that it has suddenly been politicized by newly emerging Islamic activists in their revivalist endeavours. On the contrary, I argue that such a process of politicization has come about as a way of negotiating between social practices which were thought to be political and cultural. Through these practices, the cultural has been rediscovered, remanipulated and regendered in order to make the expression of what counts as the political much more effective. A space has also been opened where it is possible to make what is unthinkable thinkable and what cannot be negotiated negotiable. At least this is what has happened in the secular social order of Turkish society, where demands for the Islamization of society were rejected essentially by Kemalist state forces and deemed to be serious obstacles to the flow of modernization, progress and thus civilization.

Bhabha argues for multiculturalism, saying that it has become 'a portmanteau term for anything from minority discourse to post-colonial critique, from gay and lesbian studies to chicano – a fiction' (1998, p. 53). Similarly, for Islamic activism in Turkey, culture itself has become a portmanteau-like domain for anything: from discussion of Western domination to moral transformation, from the status of women to free expression of individual rights. Making culture a portmanteau term for the political discourse has also been used to legitimize the fulfilment of an Islamic way of life and an Islamic social order. Such a strategy is possible in that culture has been elevated to an untouchable status in the contemporary understanding of politics and society not only in Turkey but also all over the world. According to this understanding, culture can no longer be the object of illusions of social engineering or of the imagination of social change which do not come into being as part of societies collective will.

I believe that it is this understanding which has also led to a distinction between so-called political and cultural Islam on the part of many observers of Islamic revivalism. By this distinction, everything considered harmful and threatening to the existing social order has been put into the category of political Islam. On the other hand, that which has been considered harmless and tolerable, and, more importantly, unlikely to change in the Muslim 'quotidian', has been put into the category of cultural Islam. To differentiate categories like cultural Islam and political Islam also fits well with the Western (or westernized) view of 'Islam' in that no matter how difficult it is to accept, Islam has a presence, even within Europe and the United States of America, though as an *émigré*, and it continues to assert 'its own' ways of life, ranging

from customs of worship to eating and clothing habits, which
are seldom compatible with Western taste in terms of the ideal
image of what a modern, civilized (read westernized) society should
be.

During the last two decades the paradigm of modernization has
started to be replaced by globalization, and different ethnic and
cultural characteristics of taste and style have not only been greeted
with great enthusiasm, but also seen as enriching aspects of the new
world order (although those things which were tolerated as new
cultural characteristics usually went no further than ethnic food,
music, fashion style or certain forms of art). In this context, it is
quite a painstaking process to distinguish 'innocent' Islamic cultural demands from political, i.e., 'hazardous', ones. For example,
the question of whether veiling is a basic human right for women
as part of their religious beliefs and culture, or whether it is a
political assertion imposed upon them by Islamic ideologies
becomes a complicated issue. Similarly, it becomes highly debatable whether we can approach particular social issues with any
certainty. One such question is whether female students should be
accepted in state schools with their heads covered. Should this be
seen as their parents' right to raise their children according to their
religious beliefs and customs, hence to secure their culture? Or
should it be seen as a violation of the secular code, according to
which no one is allowed to impose religious beliefs upon others?
Many more such questions can be asked. In the last two decades,
various religious associations have been established by Islamic
groups all over the world. Do they serve to disseminate Islamic
political ideologies in the name of meeting Muslims' cultural needs,
or can similar associations and organizations be easily stripped of
their cultural functions and be seen as mere political organizations?
Which outlets for self-expression and sentiment and which daily
habits are actually manifestations of Islamic culture, and which are
politically determined? Which habits and customs should survive
in the name of Islamic culture? Which of them are subject to
change? Which ones endure with time and cross geographical
borders? More importantly, according to whom will these be perceived as cultural or political? Searching for the answers to such
questions within the limits of differentiation between political
Islam and cultural Islam seems to me to be as much making a
political choice as it is the work of Islamic activists. To the extent

one adopts one or the other of these vantage points it becomes a way of imposing a 'positional superiority' over Muslims, in that it shows them which Muslim characteristics are allowed to gain the status of culture, and thus will be tolerated, and which are not.

The answers to these questions are perhaps sought nowhere more eagerly than in Turkey. And that is because, in the Muslim world in general, and the Middle East in particular, it would not be wrong to say that if Sunni Islam is represented by Arab nations, and Shi'i Islam is represented by Iran, then Turkish society represents what we may call 'secular Islam'. In this context, these questions are not, however, asked by the Turkish polity and society in order to try and solve social, cultural and political problems arising from a position caught between the Western–Christian and Eastern–Muslim worlds. They are not asked in order to try and reach a social consensus or open a space for ongoing negotiations between the secular and religious sections of society. Rather, they are asked so that once the answers have been found and 'suitable solutions' applied, the effects of Islamization on society can be forgotten as soon as possible, so that no consensus will be reached, but the problem as a whole will be eradicated.

Throughout all the years in which Islamic revivalism has been on its way to the core of the society, it has been quite difficult, not only for well-educated, urban, modern secularists, but also for ordinary Muslim and non-Muslim citizens of Turkey, to comprehend the reasons for the Islamic challenge. They believed that, as has often been promoted by Turkish public opinion, it could be an unintended consequence of inadequate modernization, manifesting itself in the form of a resurgence of backwardness, ignorance and bigotry. Alternatively, it could be an extension of the dark plans of 'external forces' which, ever since the establishment of the Republic, because of the geopolitical significance of the country, have constantly tried to weaken Turkish society and divide it along the lines of ethnic and religious identity. It is commonly thought that both of these have played an equal role in the emergence of this 'resurgence of obscurantism'.

Therefore, in the face of ascending Islamism, another question is also frequently asked: wasn't it three-quarters of a century ago that the Turkish state decided to side with the modern, democratic, Western world and live at peace with its neighbours, abandoning the expansionist politics of its Ottoman predecessors? With the enactment of the Atatürk Reforms, named after the founder of the Republic, didn't the Turkish state attempt to adapt its overall public life to that of the Western world by completely secularizing the legal, political, economic and social realms? Wasn't it this same state which has been proud of granting women legal and civil rights on an equal footing with men from as early as the 1930s? By the end of the 1940s, with the establishment of the multi-party system, weren't different political groups, including religious ones, allowed to express themselves at the parliamentary level as long as they remained within the confines of republican rule? Despite successive periods of contraction and expansion owing to military inter- ventions in 1960, 1971 and 1980, isn't a democratic parliamentary system relatively secure? This should be the case even if, quite paradoxically, this system is ensured under the watchful eye of the military forces, one of whose fundamental tasks is to protect the country from the 'dangers of obscurantism and ethnic separatism'. Moreover, from the 1980s onwards, haven't almost all levels of Turkish society been opened up to the world? Hasn't this led to a new era of economic and social liberalism that has smoothed the flow of globalization into society? Finally, isn't this the same Turkey that has constantly tried to become a part of the Western world? Now, at the beginning of the new millennium, hasn't Turkey become one of the new candidates for the European Union (EU), making it the first Muslim society, if we discount Albania and Macedonia, to gain EU candidate status?

Under these circumstances, certain questions continue to trouble ordinary secular Muslim and non-Muslim Turkish citizens. What role does a movement like Islamism have in Turkish society when it has chosen to follow a modern, westernized way of life? Why do some girls who get the opportunity to attend university cover their heads and risk expulsion from school, jeopardizing their whole future? If it is merely a manifestation of their faith, should the state authorities be so harsh on them? What kind of life do Islamists want to lead? They also benefit from a modern, democratic, secular system, so why do they want to look and live like Arabs (sic)? Why don't they appreciate the order that the Turkish Republic has created and which has enabled Turkish people to live like other civilized people around the world? Why do Islamists want to go back to the dark ages, when people were suffocated by the religious ignorance fostered by Islamic dogma and corrupt, manipulative clerics?

The aim of this book is to examine the matter from a different perspective. It attempts to determine the kind of questions asked by those who want to make Islam their essential guide to legal, political, cultural and social life in Turkey. Their questions are the opposites of the ones given above, in that they see Islamic religious rules as the foundation of social life and believe that Turkish society lost its soul when it was forced to become westernized. They consider that its roots are to be found in the Islamic world, where once upon a time their Ottoman ancestors were one of its leading forces. In their opinion, Turkish society can only regain its soul through the spread of Islam at all levels of society. By covering their heads women are trying to regain this lost spirit while exercising their rights of religious freedom, an essential part of their basic human rights. Turkey can only attain the status of a democratic and developed society with the guidance of Islam. If other Muslim societies are not just, egalitarian or democratic enough, it is because they have not been able to construct a truly Islamic social order and this failure must basically be attributed to Western intrusions.

Here, it is hardly original to say that the overall motive behind Islamic revivalism, and thus behind all the arguments above, is to bring about a moral transformation. The Turkish form of this moral transformation will enable Muslims to live as *şuurlu* (conscious) Muslims, just as their predecessors did in the *asr al-sa'ada* (*asr-ı saadet*, the age of happiness, i.e., the time of the Prophet). However, it is evident that the way of life that will allow Muslims to live like *şuurlu* Muslims, as it is conceived by Islamic activists in Turkey, still needs to be clarified. It also remains to be explained what kind of social, political and cultural strategies will be created and followed so that such a state of being, i.e., of being conscious Muslims, can be achieved.

In Turkey, as has been argued several times by Mardin (see especially 1989a) the answers to these questions have always come from the specific social sphere to which religion was confined when the Republic was established, that is, the private sphere. As I will also discuss in this book, with the establishment of the Turkish version of a secular regime, almost all forms of religious practice were placed under state observation, with one exception, those which are followed in the private sphere. But in order to supply a realistic picture of the issue it should also be mentioned that with the consolidation of the national television broadcast system in the early 1980s and the establishment of commercial television at the beginning of the 1990s, it became possible for mainstream religion, that is, religion as it is practised in the public sphere by those other than Islamists, to pervade the private sphere via television. However, because alternative pro-Islamist radio and television programmes were also broadcast, the private sphere could still be protected against state interference. Nevertheless, it should not be forgotten that all these broadcasting activities are controlled to a certain extent by semi-autonomous state institutions (RTÜK, the Radio and Television Supreme Committee, for instance, established in 1994). But from the beginning, religion as it is practised in mosques and learnt in state universities, secondary schools and Koran courses, has been regulated and controlled by the state. Traditional religious organizations, in the form of religious orders, which tried to survive in the modern world in spite of strict state regulation and changing social conditions, were either banned or pushed into a state of illegality and hence deemed to be clandestine societies. This was also the case for the various local communities which were sustained by such religious organizations. Only religion as it is practised in the private sphere managed to avoid that strict state control and surveillance and only this religious practice has belonged solely to people's hearts and souls, since it has been left to the guidance of their cultural knowledge and habits. Hence, it is in this same private sphere that the revitalization of Islam as a politicized cultural practice has proliferated in modern Turkish society while also expanding the meaning and the scope of the private sphere. This does not mean that religion has never been experienced by people as a communal activity outside state-controlled mosques. But even gatherings for the purpose of worship and *suhba* (*sohbet*, conversation) among religious orders and groups have in many cases also been subject to state inspection. Yet, the importance of the private sphere in the formation of Islamic activism has been so remarkable that it cannot be ignored. For example, one of the earliest and most powerful pro-religious political organizations in the country, and the first Sunni religion-oriented political party in Turkey, the National Order Party (NOP), first developed from such private sphere gatherings by way of rallying around a religious leader, Zahid Kotku, one of the most influential Nakşibendi leaders. The NOP was established by mainly Sunni Muslim proto-politicians in 1969, giving way to the emergence of the National Salvation Party (NSP) in the 1970s, the Welfare Party (WP) in the early 1980s and the Virtue Party (VP) in the late 1990s. In other words, before presenting their demands publicly in the form of political rhetoric, these people had to create an understanding of an Islamic order of life privately in their dialogues, practices and relationships, while also adapting them to the requirements of the 'outside world'. As Mardin observes, the private practices of Islam have become pervasive in Turkish society as the boundaries of what constitutes the private have expanded (1989a, p. 229). The acceptance into the public sphere of aspects of 'private' Islamic life provided the basis for the rallying call to a new political cause. Here was the first hint of the formation of a civil society movement through which a group of people was trying to create its own Islamic 'ways of operating', in the sense that de Certeau (1984) uses the expression. This group of people was trying to construct its life politics in order to realize their way of life, as they believed it must be. However, these particular types of social action in the private sphere have led to accusations of *taqiyya* (*takiyye*, dissimilation) – the notion that Islamic activists are concealing their real intentions and goals instead of revealing them honestly in public.

Thus, the question of political representation of religious interests has always been intertwined with the question of what I call the public presentation of the self. In the Turkish context, both the political strategies and day-to-day tactics of Islamism became a matter of personalized expression insofar as its social activists had to operate within the strict dictates of a secular order. Islamism has found various public voices and what Göle and her workshop group (2000) call 'new public faces' through civil organizations and party politics, and has gained social recognition in the form of loosely or tightly organized religious orders represented by politico-religious personalities. But no matter how this was achieved, as long as they were known by activities that were labelled Islamist, these activists were always deemed 'perverted' in some way. Thus, only those who gain social recognition on an individual basis, through a perceived compliance with the system, can survive in the public arena. Otherwise, the risk of prosecution and public ostracism is unavoidable. This applies both to political parties represented in parliament, and leaders of powerful religious orders, even though they may be greatly respected by large sections of society and influential political figures. For example, the WP achieved significant electoral success in the municipal elections of 1994 and in the general elections of 1995. In 1994, they gained control of twenty-eight city councils, including Istanbul and Ankara, the largest cities in Turkey. In 1995, they became the leading partner in the coalition government, with their leader, Necmettin Erbakan, taking the position of prime minister. However, that success was not enough to save the party from being closed down by the Constitutional Court in the winter of 1998.

And then Merve Kavakçı, who was elected as a member of parliament for the VP in the general elections of 18 April 1999, was not allowed to take her seat or become a legal member of parliament on the grounds that she covered her head. When she went to take her oath in parliament, she was forced to leave the general meeting hall of the Turkish National Assembly by the insistent protests of other parliamentarians. The reaction against her was especially strong from the Democratic Left Party (Demokratik Sol Parti, DSP) and its leader, Bülent Ecevit, the prime minister of the government formed after the election, which comprised a coalition of the DSP, the Nationalist Movement Party (Milliyetçi Hareket Partisi, MHP) and the Motherland Party (Anavatan Partisi, ANAP).One wonders whether other, socially even less powerful covered women, such as covered professional women, can be employed in state offices or reputable private sector companies. What will happen to others: for example, covered female university students who have to struggle to be admitted into university, especially state universities, and then struggle to survive there? The physical appearance of men is not open to scrutiny as long as they do not wear the clothing of religious codes. However, they cannot enjoy high social status, except in Islamic circles, if they carry the stigma of being an Islamist.

Nevertheless, despite all the pressures at the social, political and cultural levels, these people, labelled Islamists, had to live in Turkish society. They supported their families, raised children, attended higher education institutions, participated in politics, and became prominent in business and the professions and, in the case of the men, as bureaucrats. They travelled between Turkey and other countries, migrating to Europe or the USA either to work

or to study. They established small- or large-scale economic enterprises, ran media companies, founded various civil organizations,
and organized political protests, ranging from the peaceful to the
quite brutal. In short, they managed to carve out a space for
themselves and make their voices heard. But each time they became
too visible or their voices were too loud, they met with strong
opposition from both Kemalist state forces and secularist sections
of society. However, before retreating to the sanctuary of the
private sphere, they forced the Turkish polity and society to
address their religious and cultural identity, their understanding of
democratization and political freedom, and their understanding of
civilization. Of course, as members of this society the Islamic
activists are also forced to ask themselves similar questions. Yet,
above all what they have to do is survive everyday life while still
pursuing their principal goal, i.e., building self-narratives as 'true'
conscious Muslims and creating 'living Islam' by politicizing culture. This, as I have indicated, constitutes the story of this book.

In order to relate at least one fragment of this story I conducted
a field study among people who had come together and created a
space to live Islam as *şuurlu* Muslims. I recount the story of my
entry into this semi-secluded place in Chapter II of this book. I try
to capture and describe the methods of the attempt to build an
alternative, Islamic way of life. This has never been a subject of
inquiry for either Turkish academia or the media. Instead, as
a result of somewhat sensational media coverage or unreliable
individual observations it has been assumed that this is a well-
known area. However, as a sociologist, I believed that the ways in
which these 'Islamists' lead their everyday lives in accordance
with Islamic principles deserved greater attention. I felt that more
detailed inquiry into the social phenomenon of Islamic revivalism
was necessary rather than just asking whether these Islamists could
be conceived of as modern or not. I wanted my inquiry to go
beyond the mere examination of what aspect of modernity they
stood for, especially with respect to covered women.

This study does not investigate either whether Islamic revivalism
can be understood within the hierarchical binaries of political Islam
or cultural Islam, or whether political Islam in particular has failed
or not, as Roy (1994) has argued that it did. Similarly, as a sociologist who is deeply concerned about gender inequalities and sees
them as some of the most fundamental problems in society to

be investigated, without, however, essentializing the issue, I have always perceived those women who cover their heads first as women, before becoming conscious of and distracted by their headscarves. Thus the question of why women are the target of Islamic revivalism and how they came to be the chief actors in the effort to build an Islamic way of life is the central concern of this book.

What I have learned from my fieldwork is that the creation and realization of any sort of Islamic way of life is not possible without the efforts of women. As I argue throughout this book, just as Islamic revivalism cannot be analysed without considering the aspect of faith, so it is not possible to separate the situation of women from the whole process and evaluate it as an adjunct to the more important issues of polity and social order. Especially in a story like the one recounted here, which focuses on living Islam, it is imperative that the account be given of how women become essential to the expression of Islamic ideologies in the quotidian – of how they manage the 'inner space' of social life including the 'domestic' space and at the same time become the public symbol of Islamic revivalism. It is necessary to tell of how they raise children, i.e., younger generations, as 'true' Muslims as well as building their self-identities in the same manner, and devote great effort to extending the meaning of 'private' by devising strategies and techniques, which I call the strategies of containment and resistance, to deal with the secular ethics of modernity. It is these efforts which render Islam a living social practice.

I discuss the situation of women which has always been construed within a framework of paradox, asking, in my terms, whether they are the keepers of Islam or the sources of *fitna*, i.e., social disorder.I try to see how the women that I came across strove to overcome this paradox. I studied them in the particular living space (called *site* in vernacular Turkish) where I carried out my fieldwork. I also try to capture the discursiveness, rhythm and the strategy-generating principles of a given 'quotidian', all of which mark the dialogical boundaries of the making of an Islamic way of life. I argue that, here, Islamic faith works in conjunction with what Bourdieu (1989) calls taste, informing the choices of 'Islamists' and opening for them a space in which they may differentiate their lifestyles from that of people of similar social classes. I take into account the social activities, whether they were culturally given, newly adopted, or even deliberately avoided, of the inhabitants of this living space, and I try to determine how they define the boundaries of an Islamic way of life and strengthen Islamic solidarity. I try, too, to show how this sense of solidarity has been preserved by a certain kind of emotional bonding. This is a trust which reinforces the personal attachment of its members to this living space. It allows them to cultivate a sense of security, which in turn enables them to lead their daily lives in accordance with Islamic precepts despite the strong feeling of resentment that they bear. However, before focusing on that particular 'habitus'and the sense of resentment which is intrinsic to it, I try to demonstrate how the historical roots of political resentment can be traced to the early years of the establishment of the Turkish Republic. This resentment has since dominated the discourse of the opposition which appeared in reaction to the perceived oppression of people with religious affiliations. I argue that this story can be read as the history of the creation of rational individuals in a nation out of the clay of devout members of a multi-ethnic Ottoman society. Moreover, I argue that gender politics in the republican Turkish state played an important role in the formation of a republican identity. The aim in constructing this identity was to create equal citizens in a new Turkish society. The effort to achieve that aim has been constantly challenged by Islamic forces in various ways with various, often controversial, arguments. I try to understand how the women that I interviewed have coped with both of these dominant discourses and ideologies. Here, one of my main concerns was to explore how these women become the 'other' of modern, secular Turkish women. In other words, I try to understand the parameters of the question posed by Nader (1989, p. 324): 'How could images of women in other cultures act as a control to women in one's own society?' I adapted this question to those covered women who are often treated as if they come from a culture that is 'other' in their own society.

Now it seems that the public arena has once more been largely purged of Islamic activists. The Islamic political opposition has again been severely repressed in Turkish society as a result of an ongoing process which was initiated by a series of decisions of the National Security Council (NSC) in 1997. These decisions have become known as the '28 February Decrees' after the date on which they were passed. They were intended to protect the state from fundamentalist militancy, which was seen to be as great a threat to its security as separatist Kurdish terrorism. As a result, the WP was closed in 1998 by the Constitutional Court. The leader of the party, Prime Minister Necmettin Erbakan, then seventy-two years old, was banned from participating in active politics for the next five years. For once, this was not a result of overt military intervention, in that the NSC is a constitutional body composed of civil government officials as well as senior military officers under the chairmanship of the president of the republic. However, before this ban was declared, the VP was established on 17 December 1997 by former members of the WP so that its presence in parliament could continue, now under the leadership of Recai Kutan, one of Erbakan's closest political allies. In the meantime, the ban on headscarves in universities and public institutions began to be enforced much more strictly than ever before. In 1998, the minimum period for compulsory primary education was extended to eight years. This effectively meant the abolition of middle schools (grades 6 to 8), including the middle sections of Imam Hatip schools. The aim was to decrease the high enrolment rates at these schools where religious education constituted the core of the curriculum. Several economic enterprises known to be investments of 'Islamic capital' were brought under tight state control, as were the activities of certain municipalities, the publication of Islamic journals, and certain radio and television broadcasts. Other religious groups not organized as political parties but quite influential in both political and social life, and not necessarily supporters of the WP, were also placed under strict state control. One such group was that of the Fethullah Gülen branch of the Nur community, once regarded as an antidote to the Islamist movement which was supported by the WP but declared to be as dangerous as them. Throughout the first half of 2000, Turkish society witnessed the brutal aspects of Islamic militancy following the destruction of the illegal Hizballah (*Hizbullah*) organization which had been established by non-separatist Kurdish Sunni Muslims. This started with the execution of its leader, following armed conflict with police in the middle of Istanbul, in the well-equipped house occupied by him and his accomplices. The incident was broadcast on all Turkish television channels for several days and nights in the manner of an exciting action movie. Subsequently, Turkish society discovered through close-up photographs published in national newspapers and broadcast on almost all television news bulletins just how violently this group had pursued its ends. It had brutally murdered and buried several of its opponents, including Gonca Kuriş, a former member of the organization who had become known to the Turkish public through television forums and panel discussion pro-grammes. She was a covered woman who chose to make her own individual interpretations of the Koranic verses and be an independent, open-minded voice among Islamists, with the result that she was declared the only true 'Islamist feminist' by the secular media. By the time her corpse was found by the police, she had been missing for several months since being kidnapped in front of her house. This particularly unfortunate case has also been presented as evidence of intolerance by Islamist factions of any women who try to develop independent minds. Implicitly, this bigoted, violent attitude is attributed to all Islamist groups.

Another ongoing social phenomenon which had its beginnings in the second half of the 1990s has continued to occupy an impor-tant place in Turkish public life. Turkish television channels, the secular ones in particular, have organized popular discussion programmes on the subjects of religion and religious belief in regard to the ordinary practices of lay people, especially women. These programmes are usually presented in a question–answer format under the guidance of religiously legitimate popular male academics with a highly modern, secular outlook. These academics have become quite famous for their fierce criticism of others, i.e., of pro-Islamist religious authorities. In other words, Turkish people are being called upon to protect their own concept of religion against that imposed upon them by bigoted Islamists. Thus, people are warned that the Islamists are trying to exploit their religious faith and distort their perfect religion in an attempt to turn naïve believers' love of God into meaningless fear. However, in order to erase that image of both militant and bigoted Islamism, other television channels known to be Islamist or pro-Islamist have put good-looking and fashionably but conservatively dressed presenters (usually women with dyed blond hair and heavy make-up) in front of their cameras to read the news or introduce docu-mentary programs and talk shows.

Despite efforts of Islamic groups to reconstruct their image by trying to adjust to changing social and political conditions, some have clearly elected to carry on leading their lives as conscious

Muslims and, no doubt, will continue to do so. Moreover, I believe that the more they are publicly repressed, the more energy they will devote to developing new sociabilities relating to the private sphere. However, especially in the last decade or so, Islamic groups in Turkey have learned how to organize themselves publicly around civil organizations. They have developed strategies to cope with the criticism directed against them, and have devised their own resistant 'ways of operating' in the course of everyday life. Only time will tell whether the politicization of culture will remain central to their survival strategies in the changing conditions of the current wave of globalization.

At this point, I will not attempt to make ambitious predictions about the future of Islamism in Turkey, but will conclude this long prologue with a short anecdote. It concerns my last encounter with some of the inhabitants of the *site* that I studied, and I hope it will be more revealing than any number of generalized comments or predictions.

One mild autumn afternoon in the year 2000, I was leaving my department building with one of my daughters who had come to visit me from her own university. I heard someone call my name using the polite form of address of 'Ayşe Hanım'. When I looked in the direction the voice was coming from, I was surprised to see one of my interviewees standing in the middle of the main *allée* of our campus. I will refer to her by the pseudonym of Elmas Hanım. Elmas Hanım was standing there with her two adult daughters, who were both beautifully dressed and had covered heads. We embraced warmly and I invited them for a cup of coffee at one of the street cafés next to the tennis courtyards on campus. While we were on our way to this café, she said that she had come to visit one of her nephews who had started studying at METU. She had also hoped to see me. It had been quite a long time since we had seen each other although we contacted each other from time to time through various channels. In the time since we had last met, her elder daughter had graduated from the Faculty of Theology, while the younger one had had to leave university several times because of the headscarf problem before finally managing to finish her degree in the field of chemistry. Elmas Hanım herself, incidentally, is also a university graduate and a teacher. I learned that all three of them were staying at home because no one would employ them as they covered their heads. Elmas Hanım had recently been expelled from her school again and she was waiting for her court case to finish, though with little hope of a positive conclusion. The other two women, her unmarried daughters, had never had jobs despite numerous attempts to find work. The elder daughter was keeping herself busy by doing a graduate course in the same faculty she graduated from, but she said that even there, in the Faculty of Theology, people did not want to see covered women around. Elmas Hanım said, 'Look at us, Ayşe Hanım. Here we are, three educated women, sitting at home, unable to pursue our professions and earn our own money.' She then added, 'But thank God, as always, we find something to occupy ourselves with. We continue to organize reading and discussion groups. We have also formed a new charity group to help needy and orphan children and young girls. We also try to do some embroidery and sell our work, sometimes to help those children, and sometimes to help our-selves.' With a bitter smile, her younger daughter added ironically, 'So it means that we sit at home and prepare our *çeyiz* (dowry)', referring to a well-known tradition of many uneducated young women from modest backgrounds. While we were sipping our coffee, they updated me on the new developments in their *site* – who had moved in, whose sons or daughters had married whom and who had divorced, although this was a rare occurrence. My daughter Aslı and I also gave them our news. While Aslı was talking about her plans for the future, I noticed that these two other talented young women were listening to her with an almost imper-ceptible touch of envy, though this was not ill-intentioned. Although Aslı was talking about her uncertainties about her life as a senior graphical design student, it was obvious that the possibili-ties and choices in front of her were quite fascinating in comparison with their own severely repressed social conditions. I think that Aslı then sensed the same thing as I had. She stopped talking about herself, bringing the conversation to an abrupt end as her voice sank. The three women immediately and enthusiastically expressed the hope that she would realize her ambitions with God's help, mentioning the phrase 'in şa'a allah' (if God wills). Then my three guests cheerfully continued to tell me about life in the *site* and related their observations of the emerging tendency of people to try and be very fashionable. 'You should come and see our new neighbours, Ayşe Hanım,' said Elmas Hanım. 'Those well-off friends of ours have moved to that new villa type of *site*, you know, the one whose construction was going on when you were working with us, but now instead of them we have these new *nouveaux riches* who also claim to be the most *şuurlu* of all of us! So now there is a lot of competition among many of our neighbours to show just how modern we Muslims are. Do you remember the wedding hall at the basement of our block and how unpretentious it was? You should come and see it now; it's like a *gazino* [a big nightclub]. They spent a huge amount of money on renovating it. You should also see the new cars in the parking lots. Now almost all the young women have driving licences.' (However, when they were leaving I noticed that her elder daughter had brought them to the campus in her new car.) She added, ironically, 'Every day our awareness of consumption grows, but some of us still remember to hold the book [the Koran] in our hands.' 'Eh!' I said. 'That was what I was trying to tell you about, I mean about the newly emerging middle class ethos of Muslim people.' 'Up, up', she said, raising one palm upwards, meaning that it was higher than middle class. 'Did all this happen after his family moved abroad?' I asked, referring to the family of one of the most influential religious leaders of the Nakşib-endi religious orders in Turkey. They had been in serious conflict with the leader of the WP on and off for the last two decades or more. Her elder daughter answered, 'No, not just because of that. Because, you know, they were also a model for high living standards. But I guess it is rather because of the times we live in. Consumption is our new faith now, but I think we were left with no other way to express ourselves than through consumption. I think this is also true for the rest of society as a whole. Don't you think so?' I nodded and said, 'Yes, I see your point.' Then she sighed and said, 'So I see no future here for me. I'm seriously thinking of going to live abroad as well.' 'Where would you go?' I said. 'To America', she said, meaning the United States. 'Most of my friends have already gone there', she said. Her younger sister confirmed this, and joined her in expressing a wish to go abroad and live there in freedom. 'Here the system leaves us no other choice than to live at home and be mere housewives', she added. Elmas Hanım cut in, saying, 'What's going to happen, Ayşe Hanım? How long is this oppression of our children going to last?' I said that I didn't know but that we should keep our dialogue alive and continue to talk to each other, and that that was all I could think of for the time being. 'So, we really can expect to see your book', she said. With a deep feeling of guilt, a feeling that has not left me in the last four or five years, I said in a low voice, 'In ṣa'a allah.' The evening following this lucky encounter, I received an e-mail message from Elmas Hanım's younger daughter via my university account. It was sent from her private account and read:

> Dear Ayşe Hanım,
>   Today it was very nice to see you again. We wanted to thank you once more for your hospitality and tell you that we would like to see you again here among us. In the meantime, I hope, *in ṣa'a allah*, that everything will be better for all of us. Whenever you want to contact us, please use this e-mail address. May God be with you. With my best regards.

Whether or not it is through electronic means, what I really hope is that we do not lose contact or lose the ability to keep a dialogue alive with people who think differently from us, and that we try to listen in a Bakhtinian sense to the heterophonies that we produce, that is, if I understand Bakhtin correctly, the ability to hear not only different voices, but also the levels of diversity that can be found in a single voice. I hope that we can develop a responsive and mutual understanding towards people we think are different from us. It was essentially with this aim in view that this book was written.

January, 2001
Ankara

Introduction

Although Islam and the Middle East have been the object of study for a multitude of disciplines over a long time, the proliferation of Islamic movements in the area in the last two decades has given these studies an added urgency. The rise of Islamic movements in the early 1960s which culminated in the Iranian revolution in 1979, and their increasing bid for power in the region as well as some other parts of the world has served to raise fears of a threat to stability and peace on both a regional and a world scale. Furthermore, it has led many social scientists to question not only the tenets of modernization theory, but also the very basis of traditional 'Western' social sciences. The challenges posed by the new Islamic ideologies have caused one of the most influential metadiscourses of modern times – namely that on the dichotomy of East and West – to be questioned in a rather different way, or so it would seem. In this respect, sociological considerations, as well as political concerns, have produced a plethora of studies trying different approaches in order to come to grips with the problem of the new power of Islam in the world.

The present study is an attempt to deal with what has been called the 'revival' of Islam by focusing on a specific model of revitalizing Islam in the capital city of the secular Republic of Turkey. Although the speed of this movement seemed to be slowed down by certain state interventions which were and are heavily backed by military support as well as the support of what we may call the counter uprising of secular forces of the society, it still constitutes a sociopolitical and cultural problem to be solved in the immediate future of Turkish society. Departing from this point, before setting out my problem in its full detail, however, I will try to show some aspects of the contemporary discourse on Islamic revivalism in order to render my case study a meaningfully articulated story, able to find itself a place within the paradigmatic boundaries of the modern discourse on Islamic revivalism as a unique but commensurable sociological 'scriptible', i.e., as a sociologically conducted writerly text which invites the readers of sociology to make their own interpretations and reinterpretations.

I.1. Islam in the Paradigm of Modernity

To begin with it should be emphasized that in the process of reshaping the boundary conditions of the East-West dichotomy in the contemporary world, the Islamic world construes itself not just as a mere reactionary locus of resistance to the age-old Western colonialist and imperialist challenges. It also tries to produce alternative universal ideologies aiming to displace the Western, i.e., modernist, metanarratives which fail to include explanations in their storylines of the demands of a newly globalizing world. Islamic ideologies do not only appear on the world stage by challenging the West as such, but also by questioning the premises of the ideals of modernization in structuring the social world, which have mainly originated in Western societies, as well as confronting the various Western ways of constructing and coding social reality.

However, the other side of the story tells us that besides its considerable achievements, the Islamic world is likely to hold a defensive position in the world. The history of the last two centuries particularly can be read as a history of the ascending superiority of the West, considering the fact that the West had physically and mentally colonized various parts of the Muslim world. Moreover, it should also be kept in mind that the term 'West' is used as a metaphoric sign all over the world to signify the hegemonic power.

Islamic revivalism, however, is not the only challenge which has been posed to modernism and its hegemonic power, the West. On the contrary, a considerable increase in religiosity is a widely observed phenomenon in most parts of the world. Put differently, in the process of the whole world becoming modern – which was marvellously described by Marshall Berman as 'to experience personal and social life as a maelstrom, to find one's world and oneself in perpetual disintegration and renewal, trouble and anguish, ambiguity and contradiction: to be part of a universe in which all that is solid melts into air' (1982, p. 345) – religion is not declining either as a universal force or as a method of providing responses to local problems.

However, it is unlikely that globalization will lead to a lessening of differences among religions as religion continues to increase in strength. Religious fundamentalisms also develop concomitant to modernity through the process of globalization and the condition of post-modernity. Among the various fundamentalist movements, however, what makes Islamic fundamentalism the most threatening of them all for the modern world is its constant challenge to the West by way of its rejection of and assault on both its value systems, which emanate from eighteenth century Enlightenment thought, and the political and scientific cultural representatives of these value systems.

For modernization theory, on the other hand, as Wuthnow (1991) argues, with its major claims of ever-increasing and linear economic development supplied by industrialization and the use of technology, a strong shift from 'tradition', in the form of the displacement of the authority of religion, was seen as inevitable. Moreover, in this scheme of thought secularization was seen as a vehicle to provide norms for rationality and relativism, and hence, with the increasing existence of competing realities, religious doc-trine would not only become less dogmatic – taking on a 'live-and-let-live' orientation – but it would also focus more on happiness in life and less on other-worldly compensations. In addition, because of the contention among competing versions of the truth, 'truth' would become a matter of personal opinion (Wuthnow 1991, pp. 3–4). Other than these particular assumptions of modernization theory, in the modernist paradigm as a whole, including the dis-course of sociology of religion, the power of religion was to be downgraded in modern society only in terms of its institutional power/authority rather than in its cultural aspects (Lawrence 1989, p. 10). Against the dominance of this mental background, for religion in general, I would agree with Lawrence in his contention that 'religion is not just individual commitment entailing personal piety nor group loyalty eliciting ecclesiastical membership. It can also be the corporate public action of religiously motivated indi-viduals on behalf of what they have perceived to be their deepest spiritual loyalties' (p. 82). For Islam in particular, I concur with Al-Azmeh when he argues that 'it should be strongly emphasized that Islam is not a culture, but a religion living amidst very diverse cultures and thus a very multiform entity' (1993, p. 41).

Such a position, however, should not be confused with that through which the orientalist tradition was challenged in its search for an ahistorical Islamic 'essence'. Nor should it be confused with either the stance of the Islamic fundamentalists, which is somewhat parallel to the former in that they claim their own beliefs and practices to be 'Islamic', or the contrary suggestion that there is no one Islam but Islams plural. The last approach was aptly criticized by both Eickelman who called it 'the islams approach' (1987, pp. 19f) and Roff (1987); in its attempts to avoid the traps set by the fundamentalist and orientalist positions, not only was Islamic tradition reduced to an essentialist, ahistoric core, but central, normative tenets of Islam were also disregarded. My own contention with this argument is that, insofar as Islam is seen as a faith possessed of the revelation of God in the Koran, it is true to say that there is one single Islam, through which the condition of being a Muslim has been sanctioned despite the existence of different sects. However, if religion is seen, as Geertz argued, as a perspective like art, science, ideology, law and history, springing from the insufficiency of common sense notions to make sense out of experience in the face of the complexities of experience, which impels men (sic) towards belief, besides other psychological and sociological factors (1968, pp. 93–4), then it is possible to assess religion, and thus Islam, merely as a cultural factor.

My criticism of Geertz's approach and those similar to it, however, does not stem from what I will call a Gellneresque anxiety over post-modern evaluations of modernity, seeing it as an exemplary vogue of relativism (Gellner 1992, p. 3). As Hourani (1980) had already pointed out long before the critique of orientalism became the mark of Middle Eastern studies, 'there is no such thing as "Islamic society", there are societies partly moulded by Islam . . . Before Islam was, they existed, and if Islam has shaped them, they also have shaped it' (p.15). Thus Geertz's pioneering study, *Islam Observed*, showed us how this mutual process has taken place in different ways in two countries as geographically and culturally distinct as Morocco and Indonesia. What I argue, then, is different from the distinctions made between high culture and low culture – that Geertz (1960; 1968) also contributed to, seeing the complexities of religion as a matter of 'sub-traditions'. It differs, too,

from the 'great' and the 'little' traditions of Islam which have served
to a certain extent to integrate the 'folk' culture into the realm
of analysis of dynamics of social change (cf. Eickelman 1987,
pp. 18–19), especially at a time when Islam *per se* was studied within
the overarching essentialist parameters of orientalist tradition as
an ahistorical entity while making the Orient and/or Islam the
'other' of the West and/or the Occident (cf. Hentsch 1992; Said
1987). Such an approach, which I will call binary-hierarchical
synchronization of culture, cannot suffice to explain the ways in
which Islam both informs and is informed by the multifarious
cultural constructions of today's societies. I further argue that in
studying Islamic revivalist movements a distinction should be made
between Islam as a religion and Islam as cultural conduct, in order
to be able to trace the mutually informing reflexivities of the two.
Similarly, in the process of understanding the parameters of Islamic
revivalism as a political movement in the modern world, we should
be able to contextualize its various facets by studying the politico-
cultural workings of a religious ideology in general. For Islamic
fundamentalism in particular, we should also adopt a similar perspective, while seeing it as a moment of ideological praxis which
has emerged as a version of religious ideology along with other
fundamentalist religious ideologies.

Not just in the 2000s, but even in the 1990s, to advocate, as
Gellner did (1992, pp. 10–22), that Islamic fundamentalism should
be seen as an effort to claim the high tradition and culture of Islam
on the part of people coming from the social layers of low or little
culture, not only means misreading modern social structures, but
more importantly, it is also a perfect way of proclaiming Islam *per
se* as the primary cause of Islamic fundamentalism, insofar as the
high tradition of Islam was evaluated by Gellner as its essence.
More importantly he also celebrates fundamentalists –including
those he calls fundamentalists of Enlightenment rationalism – as
'fellow recognizers of the uniqueness of truth' (p. 95). It is actually
possible to trace this attitude to his earlier studies. In *Muslim
Society*, Islam could remain impervious to challenges of modernity
and survive as a non-secularized religion because its great tradition
managed to escape from the blame directed at modern civilization.
Gellner's argument was based on the idea that, unlike Christianity,
Islam was not born within an empire which subsequently went into
a decline that a hostile observer could blame on faith. On the

contrary, Islam was the basis first of an ecumenical empire and then of a number of others which closely identified with the faith and found their legitimization in it. Therefore it had not corroded an earlier traditional civilization nor lived as its ghost, but rather made its own empire and civilization. Hence, 'traditional Muslim civilization' was not, like Christendom, 'the womb of the modern industrial world', and thus cannot be credited or blamed for its totality, nor can the achievement be connected with any sectarian segment (Gellner 1983a, p. 4). Moreover, for Gellner, the dialogue between the folk and the great tradition of Islam is one which was ever closed to the concessions of outsiders and which has taken place within Islam between the orthodox centre – the Great Tradition of this orthodox centre, however, is modernizable for him – and deviant error, as the continuation and completion of the old struggle between knowledge and ignorance, political order and anarchy, civilization and barbarism (pp. 4–5). Thus, when Islam encountered the West – or, as Gellner would probably prefer to put it, Enlightenment rationalism and its modernizing conditions – it not only managed to 'totally and effectively' defy secularization as a 'pre-industrial faith, a founded, doctrinal, world religion in the proper sense', but Muslim countries – which are for him 'under-developed' in the sense of having been 'affected by a deep economic-military inferiority' – managed to escape the hazards of modernity. They did this by 'returning' to their great tradition, 'high Islam', a 'perfectly genuine local tradition', without having been obliged to emulate the West while asking of themselves such questions as, 'Why has the West overtaken us, why is it such a menace to us?' Hence they have seldom solved the dilemma of whether to emulate the West or idealize their own folk tradition (Gellner 1992, pp. 18–20). In this respect, it is not surprising to read that Gellner has tailored for Islam a future in which it becomes a 'constitutional religion', and that for Muslim societies their best possible modernized future is a 'constitutional monarchy', that is, 'a system which retains the ritual and symbolism of genuine monarchy, whilst transferring most of the real business of running society to a more technical, secular and unsacrilized sphere' (p. 91). Although Gellner elaborates upon certain problematic aspects of this idea in the light of Enlightenment philosophy (pp. 91–5), I will not. Instead, I will leave this caricatured picture of 'vigorous Islam', powerful enough to stand before the West by confining itself to its own tenets which by no means will culminate in fundamentalism, and try to focus on a more genuine analysis of Islamic revivalism and, as a specific version of it, Islamic fundamentalism.

I.2. Authenticity and Islamic Fundamentalism

For Choueiri, for instance, although the borders between the terms Islamic revivalism, Islamic reformism and Islamic radicalism must be drawn by their historical conditions of emergence, a subject to which he devotes a whole book, there is still one particular chain of reasoning which links the three to the characteristic of Islamic fundamentalism and marks their fundamentalist constructions, that is, the rejection of secularism (1990, p. 12). But for Esposito (1992) the ideological basis of Islamic revivalist movements can be distinguished in the roots found in the 'rich, long tradition of Islamic revival and reform' (Voll 1982), and, with a search down through the ages, it can be seen that Islamic revivalism came about as a response to the gap between the Islamic ideal and the realities of Muslim life. Thus, the key ideological components of Islamic revivalist movements can be listed as follows: '(1) Islam was the solution; (2) a return to the Quran and the Sunnah (model, example) of the Prophet was the method; (3) a community governed by God's revealed law, the Sharia, was the goal; and (4) all who resisted, Muslim or non-Muslim, were enemies of God' (Esposito 1992, p. 50).

Esposito is known for his scholarly efforts to distinguish Islam, the Muslim world and Muslims from what was seen in the West as an Islamic threat. From this point of view any sign of Islam was construed as an extension of Islamic militancy or religious extremism, as evidence of fanaticism, terror, and the like. Thus he rejects the use of the term fundamentalism, which not only connotes all these negativities, but also addresses a specific moment in Christianity. He therefore generally prefers to use 'Islamic activism' to denote the political orientations of Islamic revivalism (1992, pp. 7–8). This ideological preference, however, despite the likely truth of Esposito's justifications, cannot prevent us from seeing how the key components of Islamic revivalist movements confirm their fundamentalist nature, even in Esposito's descriptions of them.

The case in point here is, then, to be able to show whether Islam constitutes an obstacle for the democratization of those so-called Muslim societies; in other words, can Islam accommodate modernity or not? This orientation has led many pro-Islamic liberal social scientists to produce a discourse that I will call the discourse of accommodation. This discusses to what extent the institutions of democracy and secularization can be established in so-called Islamic societies, so as to maintain the participation of the people in liberal parliamentary politics within the context of a nation-state, whether civil legislation can be passed to realize a freedom of political choice, and also asks whether Islam hinders the development of universal human rights, and the like. The discourse yielded by Tibi (1990), for instance, falls into this somehow apologetic category, whereas other scholars such as Ayubi (1991), Binder (1988), Baker (1990), Enayat (1982), Lapidus (1992) and Piscatori (1986), in spite of some differences in their political stands, tried to understand the ways in which the peculiarities of modern politics in predominantly Muslim countries could be discerned with regard to their Islamic heritages, as well as the impacts of international relations and politics. They have shown that Islamic activism taking its impetus from the movement of nationalism is not inherently anti-Western, but this depends on the degree to which what we may call 'Western capitalist expansionism', the West or westernizing forces, become the most important opponents of Islamic political activism.

On the other hand, if the sole problem of becoming modern is, as Hourani emphasized in pursuing the roots of modernization in predominantly Muslim societies, to be construed as 'the extension of bureaucratic control over the whole of society, and the expansion of urban control over the countryside, the commercialization of agriculture, the beginnings of large-scale industry, the emergence within the cities of classes recognizably the same as in western industrial societies, or the formation of élites educated in a certain way' (1991, p. 99), then all the struggles between secularist and religious forces over the basis of legitimacy of social order are redundant to the history of modernity. These constraints, however, can only supply some conditions of modernity within the process of modernization, but cannot provide an understanding of the ways in which the power structures of modern societies were established and in which their social bases of legitimacy were secured. Esposito was concerned with the matter in a rather different way and argued that the 'enlightened' notion of the separation of religion from politics can amount to the relegation of religion to the stockpile of traditional religious beliefs as an obstacle to modern political, economic and social development. Thus, he claims, this line of thought overlooked the fact that most religious traditions were established and developed in historical, political, social and economic social contexts (1992, p. 200). Moreover, he also argues that secular ideologies have proven as vulnerable to manipulation as religious ideologies; hence, 'Spreading God's will, like spreading democracy, can become a convenient excuse for imperialism, oppression, and justice in the name of God or the state' (p. 205).

Therefore, I will argue that the problem of secularization cannot be separated from the ideological construction of modern state formation processes, nor can it be evaluated as separate from the political ideals of sovereignty. Seen from this perspective, for Esposito, like many other Muslim scholars, traditional Islamic concepts such as *shura* (consultation) and *ijma'* (consensus) are excellent examples of the fact that religious beliefs and laws are the product of human interpretation and the application of revelation (1992, pp. 204–5). Esposito grouped almost all types of Islamic activism, to the extent to which they do not resort to overt violence, under the banner of moderate Islam which was always prone to change and could accommodate itself to the realities and liberal ideals of modernity. For Al-Azmeh it is necessary to make a distinction between Islamic activism and moderate Islam. Modern Islamic revivalism in the Arab (*sic*) world has recently bifurcated – because of radicalism known to have been inspired by Mawdudi (d. 1979) in Pakistan and Qutb (executed in 1966) in Egypt – and thus traditional Islamic concepts such as *shura* and *ijma'* cannot by themselves be evidence of democracy, pluralism and the like. Although 'Islamist modernism' has relied heavily for its political programmes on the possibility, and even the necessity, of 'translatability of traditional texts', in 'radical Islamism', by contrast, such a translation was precluded:

thus, [for the former] *shura* becomes democracy, even parliamentary democracy; Islam becomes a charter for socialism; and the cosmic calamities indicated in the early, apocalyptic chapters of the Koran become premonitions of modern scientific

discoveries. For the radicals, however, Islam is *sui generis*, and is
utterly distinctive; it is therefore totally unrelated to democracy,
especially parliamentary democracy, and any talk of relating it
to socialism is polluting by implication, for the term 'socialism'
is contiguous with communism, and communism is atheistic,
and neither socialism nor democracy occur in the Koran or
salutary tradition (Al-Azmeh 1993, p. 79).

I will quote more from Al-Azmeh (1993) since his study is one of
the works, along with Mardin (1994), which may enable us to
see how the notion of authenticity as the conceptual product of
modernity gains so important a function in the formation of Islamic
revivalism in the modern context, where the ideology of nationalism – from which both the ideologies of secularism and rationalism
also sprang – has maintained the boundaries of social imagination
connected to the sense of social belonging and durability, and thus
the moral conditions of social survival.

In his inquiry essay, 'Cultural Authenticity', concerning the
genesis of Islamic modernism as a version of Islamic revivalism,
Al-Azmeh concludes that:

> revivalism is the axial mode of cultural and political discourse
> and authenticity the sole means of actual access as of moral
> probity; that as a result, historical practice is an act of authenticat-
> ing desires or programs for the present and the future; and
> that this authentication involves references to past events still
> somehow alive at the core of the invariant historical subject;
> events which are repeatable, in the act of breach between past
> and future. Thus parliamentary democracy is presented as a
> simple revalorization of the *shura*, a process of consulting clan
> chiefs in early Islamic times, and rationality becomes a recla-
> mation of a work of Averroes and of Ibn Khaldun, while freedom
> becomes a repetition of Mu'tazilite theological theses on free
> will, and socialism is made to stand in direct continuity with
> peasant rebellions of the tenth and eleventh centuries.
>
> The past therefore becomes the paradigm of a present which
> must be authentic . . . Past and future are unified by their sub-
> stratum, the national essence, going beyond which is akin to
> breaking the laws of the organic nature (1993, pp. 55–6).

INTRODUCTION   11

Actually the notion of authenticity is not peculiar to Islamic revivalism, but is common to other subaltern nationalisms, as it is to
defensive nationalisms and to populist ideologies, and it is widely
used in formal discourses on political and social matters (cf. Al-
Azmeh 1993; Bhabha 1990; Chatterjee 1993). The notion of authenticity is not so much a determinate concept, says Al-Azmeh, it is
rather 'a trope by means of which the historical world is reduced
to a particular order, and a token which marks off social and
political groups and forges and reconstitutes historical identities.
In these senses the notion of authenticity is analogous elsewhere,
doubtless officiated under different names' (1993, p. 41).

As he explains, however, the Arabic term for authenticity is
asala (Turkish *asalet*) which lexically

> indicates salutary moral qualities like loyalty, nobility and a
> sense of commitment to a specific social group or a set of values.
> It also indicates a sense of *sui generis* originality; . . . refers to
> genealogical standing: noble or at least respectable descent for
> humans, and the status of equine aristocrats. . . . Of primary
> importance among these features is the vitalist concept of nation-
> alism and of politics, replete with biological metaphor and,
> occasionally, a sentimentalist populism . . . Thus, the discourse
> on authenticity postulates a historical subject which is self-
> identical, essentially in continuity over time, and positing itself
> in essential distinction from other historical subjects (Al-Azmeh
> 1993, pp. 41–2).

For me what is important here is to see how, through the discourse
of authenticity a return to the *asr al-sa'ada* becomes discussible for
the Islamic fundamentalists – and thus the ability to escape from
'the degraded conditions of today' (Al-Azmeh 1993, p. 42). In
Turkish, the expression 'aslına/özüne sadık kalmak' (remaining
loyal to one's own essence) conveys what Al-Azmeh refers to as
authenticity and *asala* functions in the same way for Turkish
Islamic revivalists. The source of this essence has been sought by
them in the Ottoman past of Turkish people where Islam reigned
as the leading force of a world empire for six hundred years in a
huge geographical territory including the Arabian Peninsula and
the core lands of Islam, with the Ottoman emperors serving as the
caliphs of the Muslim world.

Al-Azmeh also argues that 'a return to pristine beginnings which reside in the early years of Islam, the teachings of the book of God, the Koran, and the example of the Prophet Muhammad' can be legitimized in the course of social action and is necessary to over-come 'the degraded conditions of today'. What should be added to this discussion is that, as Al-Azmeh points out, 'though revival-ism was initially Islamist, . . . it received its most thorough ground-ing in the context of secular Arab nationalist ideology, which regarded Islam as but one moment of Arab glory, albeit an impor-tant one' (Al-Azmeh 1993, pp. 42–3). This constellation of notions of authenticity in the Muslim world came into currency in the second half of the nineteenth century as the beginning of proto-nationalism. In the Arab world, Jamal al-Din al-Afghani (1839–97) and Muhammad 'Abduh (1849–1905) can be counted as the most prominent representatives of this discourse. For the Ottoman world Namık Kemal (1840–88) and, to a certain extent, Ziya Gökalp (1875–1924), can be seen as the Ottoman exemplars of producers of this discourse of authenticity. Here we should keep in mind, however, the fact that the latter had shifted the emphasis from religious revivalism to a romantic nationalism.

My last quotations from Al-Azmeh will be from his essay 'Utopia and Islamic Political Thought'. I will try to trace the uses of discourse on authenticity in today's Islamic fundamentalism. For fundamentalists this discourse becomes a matter of 'activist utopianism', rather than a 'primitivist vitalism', although the two overlap in the sense that the ideal is historically concrete and always immanent, and the task is one of restoration or re-enactment. But what distinguishes today's Islamic fundamentalism from the rather piecemeal moralistic utopia of other Islamic traditionalisms is that here eschatology and past example (the Medinan regime and the prophetic example, which is also the recovery of Adamic order) become utopia when legalism and moralism give way to total political contestation. When these models are activated and valorized, the contemporary form of activist utopianism in Islamic radicalism creates its own programmatic specifications so as to make itself a distinct moment in history. It simultaneously seeks to eliminate history, regarding it as an illegitimate accretion onto the pristine beginning by specifying non-Islam, the *jahiliyya* for instance, as the 'other' of Islam (Al-Azmeh 1993, pp. 95–9). How-ever, depending on which historical world these fundamentalist

movements base their utopianisms on, they may address themselves to different political orders. According to Al-Azmeh, in the
Arabian utopianism, for example, there is no such urge to make
specific political references to state, rather it is very much in
keeping with medieval Islamic habits. But for the Egyptian Muslim
utopianism, state was always important. In fact, 'it seeks immediately to take the state by force, as with the radicals professing
notions like *takfir* [an accusation of heresy or blasphemy]'. Similarly, 'it also seeks . . . to work a rhetorical reconciliation of *shura*
. . . and of liberal political notions with the aim of gaining power'
(1993, p. 101).

From the points discussed so far, the question remains as to
how Islamic revivalism and Islamic fundamentalism can contribute
to our understanding of the modern world. This is a world which
has already come to terms with discussions of post-modernity, the
effort to deconstruct the premises of modernity that came into
being as a consequence of the emergence of new modes of life
sustained by new technical transformations, the latter having perhaps developed more rapidly than those described by Hodgson
(1974) as the activating drives of 'Great Western Transmutation'.
These technical transformations have shaped the perceptions of
humankind by introducing new forms of communication. Through
them narration of the predicaments of humanity took very different
forms, and they became pervasive for most of the world's population. With the introduction of electronic communications, then,
fables, fairy-tales, myths and legends were audio-visualized; reality
turned out to be virtual moments on television shows. Through
the screens of personal computers linked by cyberspace, the realms
of the private and the public have become intermingled, a process
characterized by the anonymity of the flow of information once
the preserve of newspapers and periodicals, and by the subjectivity
of authorship, itself once the domain of the novel.

Thus 'all that is solid melts into air' turned back to earth as
simulacra, the shadows of which have mostly obscured the con-
creteness of famine, local wars, the unequal access of humankind
to the economic power necessary to lead their lives within the
honourable frameworks of human rights. Voyeurism replaced
active participation, survival became a matter of reaching (or not
reaching) the standards of consumption of rich societies. Instead
of deconstructing the hierarchizing and essentializing polar

oppositions of modernity such as mind/body, subject/object, individual/society, public/private, market/state, feminine/masculine, something I see as a necessity, proclaiming the death of not only history and ideology but also the very subject of modernity became a standard way of criticizing it. This was the stance of scholars who live in hyper-modern societies, the domestic backyards of which provided them with an idea of the 'distinctiveness' of culture. This prompted them to defend the rights of these distinct cultures as being the innocent 'other' of might, the victims of modernism, in order to let them survive as they were in the name of multiculturalism or of the politics of difference. Thus, the sense of social belonging was confined to a sense of communalism through which it was thought that people could develop their identities in their own right. Thus they could also be kept distant from the maladies of modern life so that they could have a chance to develop alternatives to modern society, using a sense of creativity that was thought to have been lost long ago due to the homogenizing effects of modernity.

Such 'freedom', however, was not normally granted to other larger 'imagined communities' usually organized in the form of nation-states. Instead, the once sovereign, independent nation-states of the Third World have now been invited to see themselves as tiny socio-political entities, vulnerable in the face of the new capitalist expansionism which deemed it more profitable to divide the world into economically functional regions, rather than to deal with political entities such as these nation-states. The latter have already proven their weaknesses, especially the ones called Middle Eastern countries, by not being able to provide a fertile ground for the development of liberal democratic systems, the sole route to economic welfare. It is implied that the affluence of the oil-rich countries will come to nothing as long as they do not adopt the requirements of democratic liberalism. This I think is true, but what I do not agree with is the way certain Euro-American scholars and their westernized counterparts wrap their self-righteousness in a benevolent but non-analytical humanism. Thus, the way to defeat the double standard in looking at the 'rest of the world', as developed by intellectuals in hyper-modern societies, was to confer upon it the same rights granted to the 'distinct cultures' in their own societies but with the single condition that these nations would also grant the same rights to other communal groups in their own societies, whether formed around race, ethnicity or gender, though they did not show much tolerance for those who rallied on a class basis. This 'if something is good for me it is also good for you' attitude stemmed from the confidence of being on the powerful side, from looking at the whole world solely from their own perspective. In this specific case it involved looking at the world while having been heavily influenced by the effects of their own reflected image, a vista specific to holders of power as well as to cynics and harmless nihilists.

I think that a social movement like Islamic fundamentalism benefits a great deal from the existence of the above kind of mood and, in turn, with its own exclusivism, serves well to strengthen the self-righteousness of Western civilization. Its followers, who have been called both 'Lumpenintelligentsia' (Al-Azmeh 1993) and a 'secondary male élite' (Lawrence 1989), have nevertheless managed to create among Westerners a sentiment regarding Islam which is a 'mixture of fascination and revulsion' (Kepel 1985), insofar as their praxis is associated with Islam as such. The search for social morality in the name of God was not initiated by Islamic fundamentalists, but they and other revivalists have become quite successful in introducing a discourse of moral transformation which has helped to tend the wounds of the long-lasting political powerlessness of Muslims before the hegemonic power of the West. Meanwhile, Westerners feed their egos with the discourse of a globalization attesting to their permissiveness whereby the participation of 'all cultures' in the wagon of humanity through 'different forms and degrees of social participation in the globalization process make a crucial difference to its precise shape' (Robertson 1991, p. 27). The periodization by Robertson, a well known globalization theorist, of global density and complexity can be summarized thus: the germinal phase – lasting in Europe from the early fifteenth until the mid-eighteenth century; the incipient phase – mainly in Europe from the mid-eighteenth century until the 1870s; the take-off phase – lasting from the mid-1870s until the mid-1920s; the struggle for hegemony phase – lasting from the early 1920s until the mid-1960s; the uncertainty phase – beginning in the 1960s and displaying crisis tendencies in the early 1990s (pp. 26–7). There are no contributions by any non-Western culture to this process, although Robertson delineates the characteristics of each phase in fairly great detail; nor is there any sign of European colonialism and imperialist expansionism. Only in the so-called take-off phase does he mention the existence of 'other' societies – the 'inclusion of *some non-European societies* in "international society" ' (p. 27. The emphasis is mine.)

Thus, it seems that in spite of the pervasiveness of the discourse of hybridization in academic circles (which for me connotes the existence of a voluntary 'exchange' and hence cannot always be used to define either the relationship between East and West, or between Islamism and secularism without omitting the power relations between the two or, in Said's term, the 'positional superiority' of the former), the dichotomy of East and West will continue to survive until the majority of Western or westernized intelligentsia realize that only through the heterologous richness of world cultures will a non-exclusivist universalism be created. A vivid picture of how Western culture has been 'copied', 'rejected', 'modified' and thus 'domesticated' by Muslims through Islamic and non-Islamic local themes, thereby creating the modern popular culture of the Middle East, for example, has been provided by Mardin (1994). In this context, I propose to think about what Fischer and Abedi (1990) tell us about the fear of Islam and the Islamic movement's fear of *différence*.

As I have argued, in order to understand Islamic fundamentalism and its mood, it is important to see the ways in which, through the dualistic differentiation of reality construction, the dichotomy of West/East and non-Muslim/Muslim gains so important a function in the construction of power relations – with the result that it constitutes one of the most strategic aspects of reality construction in Islamic fundamentalism, and a way in which Muslim individuals gain their identities. To close this whole argument, it will suffice to point out what Islamic social order might mean relative to the post-modern critique of modernist social orders. This point can also reveal that the contemporary 'fear of Islam' which shapes the common imagination of the Western and westernized world about Islamic revivalism – often without differentiating it from either Islamic fundamentalism or Islam as such – is what Fischer and Abedi (1990) call 'fear of difference and blocking of access to ethics of *différence*'.

Fischer and Abedi point out that this fear can be said to constitute the central point of what is constantly advocated through the rhetoric of contemporary 'politicized Islam' (1990, p.153). However, the same authors hold that without neutralizing, hierarchizing and essentializing the polar oppositions of modernist thought, an ethics of moral pluralism cannot be achieved. That is, it cannot be achieved without reducing the other to the same, while assuming, as Siebers argues (1988), a 'hypothetical sameness that [would] allow us to conceive of different people as being equal to ourselves'. This is understood not in the sense of absolute relativism, however, but in the sense of creating a 'sensitivity to the grounds of difference, so those grounds can be evaluated' (Fischer and Abedi 1990, p.153).

Muslim societies are not the only ones to lack moral pluralism. Yet, through the rhetoric of contemporary politicized Islam, as realized in Iran for example, which insists on the subordination of women while anxiously defending manhood, as well as insisting on the 'eventual erasure of cultural, religious, class and national difference in the name of Islamic universalism' (Fischer and Abedi 1990, p.153), it becomes problematic for the Islamic fundamentalist and other revivalist ideologies to offer a moral pluralism. Therefore, in spite of similarities inherent to both Islamic and Western modernist understandings of universalism, the challenges that Islamic revivalism as a whole poses to the ethics of modernity appear much more threatening than modernist ethnocentrism, sexism and other forms of logocentrism, especially in the absence of flexible democratic political systems where civil society can find favourable soil in which to grow. However, Islam and Islamic political activism are not the only factors to be blamed for the absence of such ground.

Nonetheless, this 'absence' leads some Western scholars to make bitter observations about the Middle Eastern countries and this causes resentment of outside scrutiny by ex-colonialists or superpowers, no matter how correct these observations:

> Like *Coca Cola*, *democracy* needs no translation to be understood virtually everywhere. . . . Only in a handful of Middle Eastern countries, notably Israel and less emphatically Turkey, is there a functioning, participant political system in which people vote regularly and meaningfully, where the freedom to speak freely is protected, and where the rights of the individual are offered significant respect. In many other instances, elections are shamelessly rigged, individual rights are pillaged, and free association is prohibited (Norton 1993, p. 206).

Against this background, the most crucial question for me is to what extent women in Muslim societies can, and will, have a chance to participate in the creation of a democratic system in which they will not be the passive recipients of male-ordered ideals of liberty, equality and fraternity, but where, on the contrary, they will be active participants in reshaping the conditions of political partici- pation, cultural difference, freedom of expression and thereby democracy. This constitutes the most painful part of the attempt through which the place of women has been narrated in Muslim societies and I will focus on this subject in Chapter I.

I.3. Islamist Women: An Unintended Consequence of Turkish Modernization

I argue that the new visibility that Islam has acquired in Turkey, largely as an urban phenomenon, should be construed partly as a reflection of a politically determined social effort to attempt the actualization of a middle class ethos for an Islamic social order, and partly as a reflection of new meanings attributed to the social sphere. This is the sphere which used to be seen as private but which has enlarged its boundaries to cover new areas of sociabilities and hence change its content, and it is this that we may call a process of politicization of culture.

I believe that the sociological formation of these two processes can be read as an extension of two other major social developments which form their basis. First, following Sivan (1992), I will argue that, at least in terms of its practical implications, if (a) the revitaliz- ation of Islam in Turkey today, as in other parts of the Middle East and North Africa, can be interpreted as the response of civil society to the state's failures – 'recapturing the initiative and redrawing the boundaries between the two' – and if (b) this mostly shows itself as a reaction to state practices exercised by the state élite through which the 'presence' of the state has been assured in almost all walks of life', then, I maintain, we can say that the Islamic movement had to create its own intelligentsia capable of replacing the existing 'secular' one. This also includes the need to create other social agents autonomous enough to be able to compete with the state, in both the politico-economic and the cultural spheres, in order to build an Islamic social order. Here, in the Turkish context, the state élite who are, and were, assigned to safeguarding the ideals of the national civic culture become the most important target group, whose professional abilities appear as something to be achieved by the Islamic circles. This civic culture, however, can be conceived of as the extension of an institution-building process. This process involves what we may call a 'national civil religion' that has been enacted by the state, with its 'panoply of heroes, symbols, sacred places (monuments, historical sites), sacred times (holidays, memorial days), and the founding myths' (Sivan 1992, p. 99), as well as myths oriented to the future. Therefore, to be able to detach themselves from the cultural hegemony of the state in most areas of social behaviour, thereby actualizing a moral transformation, Islamic circles in Turkey are in need of creating their own intelligentsia and middle classes, since these are the social agents who will play a leading role in society for the production, dissemination, and consolidation of new models of sociabilities. Only after this has been successfully accomplished does it become possible for the Islamic circles in Turkey today to be conceived of as a social force capable of setting an alternative to the existing social order.

Second, if the overall motive behind the revitalization of Islam can be seen in the reflections of one major question, that is, the question of moral transformation, then to understand this phenomenon it is necessary to ask how the gender identity of women functions as a signpost for that moral transformation. Here, I will limit myself to highlighting only one aspect of this process through which women were vested with the role of organizing inner spaces of social life, that is, the private sphere. This sphere, however, on which I will focus Chapter V, Section 3, is the one to which the very constitution of the republican social order once wished to confine religion, thereby making it a private concern (Mardin 1989a, p. 229). The revitalization of Islam that we witness today has started to flourish from the same sphere. This was not only, as was usually argued, because Islam was a religion which tended to organize all aspects of social life including private everyday life, but also because, as Mardin argues, 'in the contemporary world, the boundaries of private have been expanded and gained new richness and variety, [and thus] religion has received a new uplift from that privatizing wave' (p. 229). According to Mardin, 'private religious instruction, Islamic fashion in clothes, manufacturing and music, Islamic learned journals, all of them aspects of "private life", have made Islam pervasive in a modern sense in

Turkish society, and have worked against religion becoming a private belief '(p. 229).

Similarly, I will also argue that organization of the 'domestic' space, raising children as 'true' Muslims, and making an effort to expand the meaning of the 'private', render Islam a living social practice. That women are the main actors in this area has made them into crucial agents for the daily articulation and reproduction of Islamic ideologies. Thus women, who usually tended to be construed as an adjunct to the more important issues of polity and social order, have become the central focus of Islamic revitalization.

Turkey constitutes an interesting case for the study of the new Islamic movements in that for a long time it was hailed by social scientists, as well as the indigenous élite, as the exemplar of the Muslim secular state. It seemed that the Kemalist reforms in the 1920s had once and for all cleansed the state apparatus from the hold of a backward-looking religious order, and had success-fully oriented society towards the rationalism and positivism that had produced modern industrial nations in the West as the leading actors of modern civilization. The reformers hoped to make of Turkey a nation-state facing the West in which religion, under the tutelage of the state, would be transformed into orthodoxy purified of the more superstitious elements suffocating the masses. Thus controlled religion would no longer constitute an obstacle on the march towards progress since it would retreat to a private world and have authority only over a restricted area of life for a small clientele. This project, which in short amounted to an effort to undermine the political force of religion in society, was part of the new Turkish Republic's modernization, a process which was made up of westernization, nationalization and secularization. Moreover, it was through this project that Turkey's élite hoped to integrate the country with the 'free' capitalist world system.

It was this configuration of forces that made Turkey a special case in the Muslim world, and it is in this context that the new and increasing power wielded by Islamic movements in Turkey from the 1980s becomes interesting. Until the 1980s, the challenge posed to the modernization project by various Islamic loci seemed to be contained by the existing political order. What marks the 1980s and 1990s is the increased popularity acquired by Islamic circles, which has become undeniably visible in all spheres of the Turkish polity, and has led to the ringing of alarm bells among wide sections of the educated urban élite since, apart from the political power Islamic circles have obtained, the Islamic ideologies widely articulated in Turkey today constitute themselves as an alternative to Western-oriented secular modernization, while also attempting to displace the republican discourse of national authenticity.

To be sure the new centripetal Islamic political activities in Turkey have displayed differences in terms of their ideological discourses and political projects, as well as the socio-cultural background of the people mobilized to take part in the actualization of these projects. Islamic movements in present-day Turkey range from the traditional Sufi orders, such as the Nakşibendi, the Rufai and the Kadiri, to religious movements of mainly republican origin (the Nurcu, Süleymancı and Işıkcı) and the autonomous radicals splintered into numerous groups (Ayata 1993a; R. Çakır 1991). These religious centres are further differentiated in terms of their political practice and the various alliances they form with others in their party politics (Ayata 1996). These alliances produce distinct politico-religious groupings that either coexist peacefully or engage in competition for political and ideological supremacy. Thus, for example, the followers of the Nakşibendi order can place themselves within ANAP, the ruling party of the 1980s, or may ally themselves with Necmettin Erbakan's WP and its successor, the VP. Others, as well as some members of the Nakşibendi order, make alliances with different right-wing political parties, but especially the ones in power. Alternatively, they stay out of party politics, yet at the same time become very influential in maintaining the legitimacy of power, as has recently been witnessed in the case of the Nurist Fethullah Gülen and Naim Hoca in Elazığ. But after the 1980s, the tools with which Islamic ideologies were produced in the country altered drastically. This change in the mode in which Islamic ideas could be expressed was in large part due to the possibility of geographical and social mobility allowed by economic growth and the education system (Mardin 1989b). First, Muslims managed to acquire the skills needed to formulate a discourse that, by adapting itself to the reality of a modern developing nation, could attract the attention of people from various levels of society. Second, by tailoring the channels of communication in the country to their own needs, they found the means of spreading their ideas quite widely. Thus the 'new' Islamic force in Turkey appears largely as an urban phenomenon, with its own intellectuals, its own living spaces, and its own alternative models of sociability.

Thus, towards the end of the 1980s, at a time when the call to an Islamic way of life could finally be heard in the very heartland of the urban élite, I asked myself a very simple question: how do people organize their actual daily lives according to so-called Islamic precepts advocating the superiority of the Islamic social order over all others? With this basic question in mind, I tried to locate an urban setting where Islamic ideals guide the lives of its inhabitants. My aim was to comprehend the parameters of lived Islam by seeking the connection between ideology, as expressed in political and media discourse, and the production of Islamic sociability as it developed in these people.

This study, then, is an attempt to explore the social and ideological practices constituting what is described as Islamic revivalism in Turkey today. My aim is to comprehend the message propounded by Muslims by looking at the way they structure their world, ranging from daily life to their intellectual discourse. The two most important areas of Muslim endeavour today are the effort to construct models of an alternative daily lifestyle, and the use of the most sophisticated media channels to develop and spread new ideas, all the time availing themselves of the political power they attained as a means to consolidate their presence in these two areas. The effort to structure daily life according to Islamic precepts also serves to reformulate ideas and produce practical details that will refine the model of Islamic society in the future. In other words, the constitutive activities of Islamic circles in Turkey today are the formulation of a 'counter-society' and the dissemination of their message in thought and deed. In this text, however, I will pay special attention to the position of women who willingly participate in the formulation of an alternative Islamic way of life, and who have paid the greater part of the cost of this social effort, while being marked as not only the 'other' of Turkish women but also, as Islamic women, the 'other' of the 'other'. I examine this specific otherness below. I will try to pursue its aspects throughout this study, and I believe that in so doing I will be able to place the theoretical premises of my case study into the larger scenario of Islamic 'counter-society'.

The covering of women has become the mark of Islam's new visibility in urban Turkey since the 1980s. Women wearing head-scarves tightly framing their faces and covering their necks and bosoms, dressed in long loose overcoats, are now a familiar part of the urban scene, including university campuses. They are usually referred to as Islamist (*Islamcı*) women, or even as 'religionist' (*dinci*), 'backwardist' (*gerici*), 'reactionist' (*irticacı*), 'dark veiled' (*kara peçeli*), 'turbaned' (*türbanlı*) women. Thus in the lexicon of Turkish identity politics, these women constitute a group defined through oppositional terms, similar to such epithets as 'leftist' women and 'feminist' women. The terms 'Kemalist' and 'Atatürkist' women have concurrently gained new political significance, to denote women (often professional élites) who proclaim their allegiance to Atatürk and his principles, that is they speak from a pro-Western, pro-state, secular-nationalistic and gender egalitarian position, against the so-called Islamist women.

Throughout this study I will follow anthropological convention and use the self-referential term, Muslim women, particularly when I refer to women who participated in this study. This will enable me to develop an argument along the lines of what Giddens (1991) has called 'life politics', coupled with what I will call politics of public-presentation of the self.

Giddens uses the concept of 'life politics' to refer to the kinds of political decisions inherent in the ethical question 'How should we live?'; these give rise to the creation of morally justifiable ways of life that promote self actualization (1991, p. 215). He also suggests that self-identity is an extension of the 'narrative of the self', that is the 'story or stories by means of which self identity is reflexively understood both by the individual concerned and by others' (p. 243). Following this line of thinking, it can be argued that the stories through which we respond to the question 'How should we live?' are simultaneously decisions on how to shape our self-identities and how to present them publicly, and involve preferences about the ways in which we enter into social relations and participate in public life. This process, then, entails making preferences according to the stories by which we primarily lead our lives. Such preferences, however, cannot be divorced from power relations and hence are 'political decisions flowing from freedom of choice and generative power' (p. 215).

In the contemporary Turkish context, some people define their self-identities through stories springing from within Islamic meta-narratives[1] and present themselves publicly as Muslims. They sometimes use the term 'conscious (*şuurlu*) Muslim' in an effort to differentiate their Muslim identity from other, by implication, 'unconscious' or 'false' Muslims. Other people, although they may feel culturally Muslim or possess faith, prefer to present themselves primarily not as Muslims, but as, for instance, Turks or Turkish citizens, and to give precedence to different ethical metanarratives in shaping their 'narrative(s) of the self', such as nationalism, humanism, democratic liberalism, historical materialism, feminism, and so on. They often use the term 'Islamist' to refer to the former group, perceiving them as 'the other' in the sense of a repository of imagined opposites, rather than developing reflexive awareness of their own self-identity by coming to grips with such questions as 'How shall I describe myself if they are the Muslims?' or 'How should I live as a Muslim, while giving priority to other attributes of my identity?'

The process we witness here entails the operation of what Bakhtin calls the dialogical principle, which necessitates the existence of the 'other' to accomplish, even if temporarily, the perception of the self as a 'whole', although the self in question is never a whole, but, on the contrary, is always unfinalized since it can only exist dialogically.[2]

As Gardiner points out, for Bakhtin 'this continuous dialogue with the "other", with one's self (inner speech), with the external world – which involves the active construction of relations between diverse phenomena (a process generally denoted as "architechtonics") – is constitutive of human subjectivity as such and represents an inescapable component of any possible creative thought and deed' (1992, p. 73). In the present political context of Turkey, however, the particular relationship between covered and uncovered women does not seem to result in 'responsive understanding' of the kind anticipated in a dialogical relation. Instead, it serves to consolidate the exclusionary attitudes each group develops towards the other.

Names and labels are not the only battleground for power struggles over identities. The body as the site of the 'micro-physics of power' (Foucault 1979, p. 28) also takes its place in identity struggles as the 'inscribed surface of events' (Foucault 1977, p. 148). The physical appearance of the body as arranged by means of dress, hairstyles, posture, and the like serves to present self-identities, thus constituting an indispensable component of 'life politics'.

Physical appearance and dress codes have always been significant as markers of political disposition in republican Turkey. There has never been such an obsession with the physical appearance of any particular group, however, as has been the case with so-called Islamist women. It seems that the 'veil', created in the Western imagination as the signifier of Muslim women's identity (see Ahmed 1992; Lazreg 1988; Schick 1990), has become a means of exploring not only the identity of Muslim women in contemporary Turkey, but also of comprehending the broader parameters of Islamic political activity. Thus 'veiled women', formerly placed in retrospective brackets or seen as reactionist refractions in the flow of modernity, have now acquired sensational news value in the media, and have been drawn into the core of the struggle between religious and secular forces in the political arena, as well as having become a major focus of academic debate on the position of women in Turkey.

Writing towards the end of the 1970s, Mardin observed that the salience of the secularization issue in Turkey has meant that not only has meaningful discussion on the role of Islam in Turkish society been precluded, but also that the resurgence of Islam in Turkey since the 1940s has assumed a variety of meanings according to different vantage points:

> Turkish *laic* intellectuals see it as the victory of obscurantism over science, higher bureaucrats as the disintegration of the fabric of the state and the rise of anarchy, 'fundamentalist' *Sunnis* as a means of establishing social control over the community, clerical personnel in the higher reaches of the General Director- ate of Religious Affairs as a golden opportunity to establish solid foundations for *Sunni* Islam on a national scale, local sect leaders or charismatic sheikhs with their – often inherited – clientele as a welcome opportunity to widen their net of influence, and *Shii-Alevis* as a threat to their religious identity (Mardin 1977, p. 280).

Since the mid-1980s, other points of view have also become salient, most notably the one which sees the position achieved by women in Turkish society under impending threat vis-à-vis the ascendance of Islamic revivalism. Thus, for instance, one of the most frequent questions directed at leading figures of the Islamic movement on numerous televised panels or public forums in the wake of 1994 municipal elections[3] was whether they would cover the heads of all women if they came to power. What is interesting is that this question was often addressed to male politicians by women dressed in fashionably tailored business suits. Attired in clothes signifying their professional status, and hence equal footing with men in a westernized modern world, which presumably includes Turkey, these 'modern-emancipated' women ironically did not see anything wrong with asking men, in this case Islamist men, about the way in which the future of women would be determined in Turkish society. In so doing, they fell back on the position of their predecessors who had to seek men's consent during the pioneering days of the Republic, at a time when women had very limited legal, and no political, rights and were trying to shape their own future social status by attaining civil rights. It can perhaps be deemed legitimate to call upon men to reveal their opinions on the future of women in society, insofar as men constitute the majority of those exercising ruling power. Yet this example also reveals how Muslim women are perceived as the passive recipients of a body of belief given to them by men, rather than as active organizers of that belief.

A broader critical review of the variety of ways in which Muslim women have been portrayed in different discourses – political, journalistic, academic – is beyond the scope of this section. I would argue that such portrayals share a basic common denominator, namely the underlying premise that Muslim women are passive and submissive, rather than active agents in the creation and propagation of Islamic revivalism in Turkey. This association of Muslim women with passivity forecloses inquiry into the ways in which Islamic sociability is produced in the experience of people, particularly that of women, who want to lead their lives according to Islamic principles as defined within a specific political arena advocating an Islamic social order as superior to all others. As I have pointed out here and elsewhere, Islamic revivalism in contemporary urban Turkey is based upon a demand for an alternative moral/social order, an Islamic way of life, thus the politicization of culture. The potential of the Islamic movement as a social force capable of realizing this is contingent upon a politically determined effort to form its own intelligentsia, as well as middle classes, who as social actors can play a leading role in the creation of new models of sociability. It is only through the formation of its own middle class ethos, and its quotidian, that the Islamic movement can become a social force capable of setting an alternative to the existing social order. The distinguishing feature of this alternative order, as embedded within a specific Islamic reason, imagination and memory,[4] stems from the principle of sex segregation which also entails veiling.

To understand why Muslim women, who have otherwise been construed as an adjunct to the more important issues of polity and social order, are deployed in the core of the ongoing power struggles between Islamic and secular social forces in the political arena, it becomes necessary to raise questions about the roles attributed to them, and which they attribute to themselves, in the constitution and reproduction of Islamic life strategies, rather than looking at what Islam means for the position of women.

In this study, I attempt to articulate how the identity of 'conscious' Muslims in general and that of Muslim women in particular is subjectively constituted through reflexive social action in the process of becoming the 'other' in contemporary Turkish society. In so doing, I first of all hope to 'render thinkable' the experiences of women who are not situated within the discourse of modernity. In recent Turkish social science discourse, Muslim women have been construed as representing either the 'dark' side of modernity (Göle 1991, p. 135) or the 'reverse' side of it (Ilyasoğlu 1994, p. 126), and hence as something to be compared and contrasted with the assumed identity of modern Turkish women in general, and Kemalist women in particular. I would suggest that any attempt to explore the identity of women vis-à-vis modernity, be they Muslims or not, is fraught with the inherent danger of rendering them 'objects' of history. My own point of departure will be aspects of what de Certeau (1984) calls 'oppositional practices of everyday life', which are mainly developed by Muslim women in Turkey to cope with dominant discourses and ideologies while, in a Bakhtinian sense, discursively reordering and recontextualizing these dominant texts by juxtaposing them with alternative narratives and texts through the medium of reflexive human action.[5]

Both my information and insight on the subjective experiences of Muslim women stem from fieldwork experience based on an ethno-sociological study in Ankara in a *site*, a type of urban complex. The inhabitants of this *site* have rallied together to create an urban space to 'live Islam' as 'conscious Muslims' in the capital

city of the secular Republic of Turkey. I became involved in
the daily life of women in this *site* as a 'fieldworker', starting in
November of 1989, and continuing, on and off, for approximately
two and a half years. One of my major aims was to explore the
ways Muslim women become crucial agents in the daily articulation
and reproduction of Islamic ideologies and develop various strategies – what I term strategies of containment and resistance vis-à-
vis secular ethics of modernity – in their efforts to build an Islamic
way of life in a secular order, and hence render Islam a living social
practice by also politicizing daily culture.

In this study I also try to elucidate how Muslim women's perception of their own position as the 'other' in the prevailing order
becomes a part of their narrations of the self. They narrate their
own situation as Muslims in terms of having been subjected to
much oppression as a perceived threat to the prevailing social
order, of having been denied the right to express their political
demands and curtailed from actualizing them. Hence a sense of
injury, arising from having been constantly accused of being
obscurantists who prevent society from its onward march towards
progress, is part of the process of becoming the 'other'. But the
meaning of being a 'non-secularized' Muslim in contemporary
Turkish society also implies a certain pride, born out of a sense of
being close to the essential, in other words, a sense of being on the
true path. I will argue that this injury/pride dichotomy shapes the
definitive feature of Muslim women's identity in the process of
becoming the 'other'.

Notes

[1] Here, I quote narratives of different Islamic sects as examples of
Islamic metanarratives since they all assume the validity of their own truth
claims. For narratives and stories I have used local or micro narratives,
which tend to accept that they contain the point of view generally based
on the informant's own experiences. For this difference between narrative
types see, for example, Rosenau (1992, pp. xiv, xxi).

[2] The concept of dialogical principle intrinsic to every imaginable
human relation, act, or utterance – developed by Bakhtin as the core
principle of the actualization of a responsive understanding in any area
of dialogue whether literary, scientific, historical, sociological or daily
ordinary speech – is extensively discussed in a recent work which attempts
to introduce different aspects of Mikhail Bakhtin's work to the English

speaking world. I refer to Tzvetan Todorov's study which tries 'to make Bakhtin readable in our [French] tongue' (Todorov 1992, pp. 94–112). A dialogical relation for Bakhtin is not binary but tertiary. It always includes an addressor, an addressee and a superaddressee (the third). For Bakhtin, 'speakers always shape their utterances not only according to the object of discourse (what they are talking about) and their immediate addressee (whom they are speaking to) but also according to a particular image in which they model the belief that they will be understood, a belief that is *a priori* to all speech' (Bakhtin 1986, p. xviii). Thus, this third (the superaddressee) is with a greater or lesser awareness presupposed by the addressor whose absolutely just and responsive understanding is presumed, either in some metaphysical distance or in a distant historical time. The superaddressee, then, may assume various ideological expressions such as, 'God, absolute truth, the court of dispassionate human conscience, the people, the court of history, science, and so forth'. For a discussion of this in Bakhtin's own words see Bakhtin 1986, pp. 102–31. For a recent study which attempts to show how various cultural and historical typifications of the third operate in different textual contexts in the process of the constitution of the self, see Crapanzano (1992). And for a very insightful critique of Lacanian and Lacanian-inspired post-structuralist theoretical analyses on the constitution of the self, see Elliott (1992).

[3] In the municipal elections of 27 March 1994, contrary to the anticipation of various pollsters, the religiously oriented WP candidates were elected mayor in twenty-eight big cities including the largest, Istanbul, and the capital, Ankara. The total number of municipalities, including sub-metropolitan units, won by the WP was 327, gaining 19 per cent of all the votes cast (R. Çakır 1994, p. 190).

[4] As a general methodological proposition, Mohammed Arkoun suggests that in order to comprehend the formation of any contemporary or historical social 'thought', we should be able to unfold three major components, that is, reason, imagination and memory, by which all 'thought(s)' were informed (1994, p. 60). This text is the Turkish translation of the first part of a series of interviews by his student Hashim Salih, originally published in *Al-fikr al-Islami: naqd wa-ijtihad* (London: Dar al-Saqi, 1991).

[5] For an elaborate discussion of these points, see Gardiner's arguments on 'Foucault and the Problem of Resistance' and '(Re)Theorizing Resistance' (1992, pp. 158–63 and 163–6).

CHAPTER I

A Signpost of Islamic
Revitalization: Women

I.1. Sources of Dissidence

Long before modern Islamic revivalism surfaced in the social sphere, the position of women in Muslim societies had attracted the attention of Western intellectuals who saw it as diametrically opposed to the emancipated position attained by women in Western societies. More recently, this ideologically charged orientalist view has brought its counter-arguments, especially with the development of a feminist sensitivity among Western and non-Western scholars alike.[1] Consequently, it has given rise to a proliferation of approaches which represent an effort to understand the parameters of patriarchal concepts, policies and practices through which the social positions and gender identities of women were generally shaped in Muslim societies.

Keddie (1991) gives a concise summary of the ways in which these approaches can be grouped. According to this, the first major distinction can be drawn between those groups which regard Middle Eastern Muslim women as no more oppressed than non-Muslim women and which, even in key respects, see them as less oppressed than non-Muslim women, and those groups which regard oppression as real. Keddie sees subdivisions in this latter group, some of whom argue that oppression is extrinsic to Islam but instead arises both from indigenous Arabian (sic) patriarchy and foreign importation, while others blame Islam for being intrinsically gender inegalitarian. Finally, there are some who adopt an intermediate position, shifting emphasis away from Islam to economic and social forces (pp.1–2).

The interrelated historical forces in the Middle East have

required social scientists to study the rapidly changing condition of Muslim women against a kaleidoscopic background. The Islamic reaction to the Israeli defeat of Arab armies and the confiscation of Arab land in 1967 and the 1973 oil crisis were part of this, both foreshadowing the Iranian revolution of 1979. It was inevitable that women would be caught up in the defensive and reactionary revivalist movement, motivated as it seemed to be by a moral transformation of the whole people as well as the system.[2]

Despite careful avoidance of the trap of presuming the patriarchal structures of Muslim societies to be reflections of one monolithic entity, and the concomitant display of a considerable sensitivity towards the analysis of these structures in their historical and cultural specificity, it may be safely assumed that the overall tendency in the ways in which the place of women was envisioned in the patriarchal structures of Muslim societies, upon which the basic morality of Islamic revivalism relies, was largely paradoxical. Accordingly, the role of women vis-à-vis Islamic revivalism was construed as being what I will describe as the 'keeper of Islam' versus the 'source of *fitna*'. This paradox basically stems from the way in which the role of women has been analysed and fixed.

In this scheme of thought, then, it is argued that Islamic movements proclaimed women both the 'bearers of culture' and the 'repository of traditions' (Moghadam, 1992, p. 39), and hence women were placed into the core of the gender discourse produced by these movements. But at the same time, women were also regarded as the 'potential source of social *fitna*, that is, disorder and anarchy' (p. 37). The logic behind this conclusion is as follows: if Islamic ideologies supported patriarchal forms of control over women (such as rigid gender segregation, veiling and assignment of men to safeguard family honour through their control over its female members), and if in 'contemporary Muslim patriarchal societies' such exercise of rigid social control was regarded as necessary for women, then this could only come into being as an extension of the perception of women as a potential source of social *fitna*.

Actually basic assumptions of this argument and others like it can be traced from a storyline, the central components of which were brought into social scientific discussion by Mernissi (1975) and thereafter extensively influenced the discourse concerning the subordination of women in Islam. In this account, women's subordination was said to be understood in the context of the way female sexuality was viewed in Islam as arising from the need to regulate the tension between sexual desire and social order. In this framework of thought, it was argued that female sexuality in Islam was seen as something so potent and active that it formed a potential threat to men's dignity, and if it were not regulated, it could give rise to the destruction of the social order which it was man's duty to safeguard (pp.1–14, 20). Within this same scheme, however, women were not the only threat posed to Muslim social order, but they were almost equal to the other major threat, i.e., the infidel, who refutes Islam. This situation was epitomized in Mernissi's widely quoted formulaic statement pointing out the social justification for women's subordination to men in Muslim societies: 'The Muslim social order faces two threats: the infidel without and the woman within' (p.12).

In fact, one way of reading the entire history of the modern Muslim world may be to scan it as a story of a constant struggle to preserve the authenticity of Muslim identity in the face of the impact of non-Muslim, namely Western, intrusions which at many moments turned out to be rather rude forms of both cultural and administrative colonization (cf. Hodgson 1974, Vol. III, Book 6; Stowasser, 1987a). Modern Islamic revivalism, too, which is often identified with Islamic fundamentalism, bases itself on a residual defensive sentiment against the supremacy of the West, aiming at the restoration of a golden and 'purely Islamic' past which accommodates, however, the requirements of the contemporary world.

In this attempt, women were envisioned as the ultimate keepers of Islam,[3] though the boundaries and the scope of their activities should be controlled by men. Women were conceived as the actual organizers of the inner spaces of life, in every sense of the term, which should be carefully protected against any dangers from the outside, i.e., non-Islamic, world.[4] Moreover, insofar as it was thought that in Islam home and family constitute the most important sites of the Islamic community (Stowasser 1987a), these two areas were also construed as the last and most important resorts of an Islamic life against the unwanted interventions of the 'infidel', or, in other words, against the 'Westoxification'[5] of social life in general. Thus, unless the voluntary participation of women in both cleansing and keeping the society away from external contamination was secured, the enterprise would turn out to be a total failure.

Insofar as the confinement of women to the domain of maintaining cultural and biological sustenance, in other words the domain of 'mothering', was seen as necessary in order to safeguard the vital basis of society from non-Islamic, Western intrusions, the problem of defining the gender identity of women became one of the most important moral aspects of Islamic revivalism. Moreover, this understanding functioned as a guiding thread in the formation of gender-political discourses in Islamic movements, for example, those widely observed in Muslim countries such as Iran, Egypt and Algeria. These are the countries where the actualization of Islamic revivalist political projects has reached its fullest expression, often in the form of Islamic fundamentalism.

I.2. The Woman's Place in an Islamic Moral Order

In Algeria women were placed within the confines of the family by the adoption of the Family Code in 1984, in an attempt to pacify the radical challenges presented by the Muslim Brothers, later to be represented by the Islamic Salvation Front (FIS). The family was perceived as a social 'cell' in need of 'protection and preservation' from social ills (Lazreg 1990, p. 777). Moreover, it was thought that these so-called ills might particularly take the form of Algerian women's emulation of Western women and secular Western lifestyles. Corrective propaganda was widely communicated in television programmes, which aimed to teach religion and the role of women in society (p. 776). Consequently, with a strong consciousness of colonial history and also pride in independence, the image of the new woman in Algeria, the Muslim sister, was presented in contrast to the 'other woman' who was certainly a 'caricature of the Western woman' (Cherifati-Merabtine 1994, p. 55). In the case of Egypt, however, Zuhur (1992) argues, 'all the parties involved in the debate over women's status have manipulated women's history'. Thus, she observes, 'the recent history of women in Egypt reflects the issues of nationalism, Third Worldism, anti-Westernism, and self-determinism' (p. 131). Nevertheless, consistently favoured by Islamic revivalists were the sources which supported the idea of Islamic 'family women' who would alleviate 'the influences of Westernization, secularization, and excessive materialism upon her offspring' (pp. 131–2). Subsequently, they opposed family planning and birth control programmes, as well as secular education, and encouraged larger families to increase the size and strength of the *umma* (the community of Muslims), while stressing the paramount importance of home, marriage and family life in the effort of holding Islamic society together. It is this effort which also involves 'disenchantment' with the Western model of women's status that was said to be emulated particularly by the Egyptian feminist movement (p. 88). But according to some observers, both because of its failures in its 'femocratic' policies (Hatem 1991, pp. 7–9) and also because of its own ambiguities concerning gender issues, throughout all the state-building, liberal, socialist and *infitah* (open door) periods, the Egyptian state has often produced official discourses on the women's question which effectively were nothing but 'discourses of deception', taking a conservative stance regarding gender issues without ultimately challenging patriarchal relations or the state's own power bases so as not to antagonize fundamentalist Islamic forces (Badran 1991, pp. 227–8).

As for the case of Iran, the ways in which the Khomeini regime based its oppositional discourse upon a rather harsh repudiation of the Western world, its institutions and world-views, is a subject of which few people in the world are unaware. An immense number of scholarly and journalistic publications, as well as various media outpourings, have dissected Khomeini's Islam. In the meantime, it is argued that in the consolidation of the new regime, through their assumed rejection of Western lifestyle, appearance and behaviour, Iranian women not only became 'the "standard-bearers" of the public face of the Islamic regime' (Afshar 1987, p. 73) but were also called on to provide the happiness of Muslim men in that new regime's process of daily articulation and development. Hence, women were expected to adjust themselves dutifully to the metamorphic swings of a sexual identity which, on the one hand, required women to behave as both shy and retiring persons following Islamic rules of modesty and chastity, and on the other, enjoined them to be always ready to turn into 'lusty lovers' willing to make their husbands' lives happy (p. 78).

In a much cooler fashion, Afsaneh Najmabadi (1991) shows what has been expected from Iranian women by emphasizing the element of continuity between the periods of the Pahlavi shahs and that of post-1979 Iran. For all these periods, she argues, the notion of modesty has maintained the common boundary of women's identity. Thus, the image of the ideal Iranian woman has shifted from 'modern-yet-modest' to 'Islamic-thus-modest' (p. 49). Moreover, in the Khomeini regime, as in that of Mohammed Reza Shah, the problem for women was not expulsion from participation in the labour force,[6] in the sense of experiencing an ultimate confinement to home: rather, as can be seen through a careful reading of Najmabadi, it was a problem of the definition of women's social status, a status that they would be able to gain in return for their participation in public life. Najmabadi's depiction of the ways in which women have participated in public life under the different conditions of both political regimes provides an insight into what kind of position women were supposed to be able to achieve. According to Najmabadi, before the establishment of the Islamic Republic women in Iran were trying to break out of their social definition as the 'symbolic location of social backwardness'. Under the Islamic Republic, although they were still expected to efface this image, this time they had to do it without transgressing the boundaries of social morality, in order not to damage the national Islamic culture. However, with the enactment of compulsory veiling it was no longer possible to be modern and at the same time remain modest and authentic (p. 70).

Except for compulsory veiling, this situation also obtained in Algeria and Egypt. In none of these three Muslim countries were women removed from either the public or private aspects of economic activity, but, as I conclude from my reading of both Najmabadi and Lazreg, women could only obtain an elevated social status and respectable public image as long as they stayed within the boundaries of that notion of modesty. More importantly, within these boundaries women were not expected to compete with men on an individual basis: rather, they were supposed willingly to support them in public life without undermining the moral fabric of Islam.

In Malaysia, too, one of the 'remote' corners of the Muslim world, Ong has observed that Islamic revivalism based itself on values similar to those discussed above, which in this context were seen finally as the 'Arabization of Malay culture' (1990, p. 269). This found support, however, insofar as it was seen as a reaction to both colonial and post-colonial Western influences in the society. This reaction has also overlapped, to a certain extent, with the 'Look East' policy of the state introduced in the early 1980s to enforce discipline in modern institutions. An effort was made to draw attention to the similarities of Japanese and Malaysian 'morals and ethics' in terms of the 'communal spirit' of Japanese enterprises being similar to Islamic kinship values (p. 265). However, Islamic male authority over the family was undermined in the process of mobilization of the female labour force to participate in national development projects; this aroused a strong reaction from Islamic forces. The state met this protest by launching an Islamization campaign of its own, promoting, for instance, images of the 'ideal mother' in Islamic programmes on television, who, as a devout Muslim mother, would put her husband and children before anything else. It should be added that this policy was also congruent with a need for population growth on a national scale (p. 272).

Although in all those societies gender inequalities were highly intensified through the actualization of new revivalist Islamic policies, the collaboration of women with the movement was not encouraged by suggesting that Muslim women were the source of *fitna*. Sources of *fitna* were the 'other' women who did not profess faith in Islam due to their failure to behave according to the Islamic code of modesty. Therefore through new Islamic revivalist ideologies, not only was the image of women drafted into the locus of one fixed identity but also the meaning of Islam was severely fixed and homogenized.

I.3. Paradoxical Boundaries, Shifting Meanings: Women in Islamic Ideologies

Once the problem is set within the confines of a paradox there remains little room to elaborate upon the congruity of meanings. However, meanings are not only changing but also fluid. They may transgress the boundaries of discourse, sometimes deepening the cleavages, and sometimes even bridging them. In this respect, I will argue that it is through the discourse of modesty that the revivalist Islamic ideologies try to surmount the paradox in front of them, i.e., the way in which they perceive the social position of women as the 'keepers of Islam' or the 'source of *fitna*'. Insofar as the notion of modesty was conceived as one of the most approved cultural values (in contrast to arrogance, extravagance, indecency, and the like),[7] and insofar as it was believed that, by adopting Islamic precepts, modesty would be attained almost effortlessly (in other words, Islamic faith was seen as the guarantor of possession of this attribute), the notion of modesty imposed upon women as a definitive attribute may be appreciated as a blessing, rather than seen as a repressive idiosyncrasy.

Nevertheless, this situation has often been interpreted as a consequence of a rather calculating attitude on the part of women. Thus, some observers have advocated that women, especially the young ones, were likely to see the restrictions imposed upon them as a small price to pay in exchange for the security, stability and respect that, through the actualization of Islamic ideologies, they were promised (cf. Azari, 1983; El-Guindi, 1981). However, it is also possible to think of women's acceptance of these restrictions while taking into account different aspects of that attitude. For example, as Abu-Lughod rightly points out, it can also be argued that 'as far as people perceive moral standards less as norms than as values, for the individual to achieve these standards becomes a matter of self-respect and pride rather than an obligation' (1986, p. 237). Thus, from this point of view, the notion of obligation or price is removed and women are instead pleased and proud to accept Islamic values, which they do not perceive as restrictions.

Regarding the specific paradoxical nature of Islamic ideologies, I also argue that, as in the case of many other paradoxical situations, there may be a positive outcome. Not only does it thrust people into a state of confusion but it may also provide them with some mental space for developing practical philosophies to carve a niche for themselves in the realm of subjectivity and to perpetuate their sense of personal authenticity. In other words, paradoxical situations may provide an opportunity for people to find intermediary ways to explain to themselves the conditions under which they can operate. Moreover, they may figure out what sort of strategies they can develop to survive in existing conditions without, however, having to face much contradiction in the ideals they have opted for. This struggle to resolve apparent contradictions, in fact, may be said to constitute the basic principle of pragmatism in the sense of finding practical ways to solve problems. Even the followers of radical ideals have sometimes had to resort to just such struggles to be able to cope with the ambiguities of predominant or hegemonic discourses and policies. Moreover, following Harding (1986), if we can also argue that even the analytical categories should be unstable in the sense of allowing us to redefine the relationship between knowledge and power (cited in Caplan 1988, p. 17), why then should we not see that this may also be valid for Islamic ideologies? To observe the existence of a paradox is one thing, to attribute an explanatory power to it is another. The existence of a paradox does not necessarily attest to the inconsistency of an ideology as such, but it may signal the existence of rifts from which new and potentially beneficial paths can be found.

With this perspective, then, it may not be sufficient to pose the question as to whether new Islamic ideologies contain certain paradoxes on the 'question of woman' or not. Rather, it should be asked how they manage to sustain the collaboration of women in the formation of moral standards set for them, despite the paradoxical characteristics they display. And instead of taking social merits such as respect, security and stability as given and self-explanatory, we should ask why some women see certain ends as so rewarding that they try to make them come true. Otherwise, it is difficult to understand why other women, especially those who see the promises of Islamic ideologies as misleading and deceptive, instead prefer to follow strategies such as risk-taking, competition, assertiveness, and the like, seeing them as necessary for their self-actualization.

Does this mean that notions such as security, stability and respect are worthless to these women or does it mean that they just want to attain them through different channels? Or much more probably, is it that they want to change the very definitions of these concepts, asking questions like 'security for what?', 'stability under which conditions?' and 'respect from whom?' Here, what we need to see is that all these questions are also worthwhile for women who support Islamic ideals. We should consider the fact that instead of receiving a set of beliefs given to them by men in a passive way, they measure these ideological messages and policies against their personal knowledge of Islam (though they may attain it either through their immediate environment or as a consequence of a well established political campaign). Then they might compare those beliefs with both their personal experiences and cultural histories, weigh their positions in society with respect to power relations, and develop coping skills for both self-management and public adjustment, thus seeing how far they can change their conditions of existence under given circumstances. This is one aspect of what Kandiyoti (1988a) calls 'bargaining with patriarchy'. It is from this point that we can avoid thinking of the 'cost' women are likely to pay for internalizing the idea of being the source of *fitna* as a self-inflicted condition for reasons such as bearing a 'false consciousness' or having masochistic tendencies.

The other side of the paradox – being the keepers of Islam – should also be questioned. As I have tried to show, women were seen as the keepers of Islam by being vested with certain social roles mainly to be performed within the boundaries of a specific space, namely the house, where women were often thought of as being kept busy with child-bearing and household chores, as well as being a place where cultural roles and values were transmitted by women, especially to the younger generation.

I.3.1. The Symbolic and Actual Meanings of Home in the Islamic Imagination

Home is a kind of space, the symbolic meaning of which transgresses the walls of an actual house. For example, Douglas argues that 'having shelter is not having a home, nor is having a house, nor is home the same as household' (1991, p. 289). She goes on to argue that: 'Home is located in space, [but] it is not necessarily a fixed space... [it is] a space under control' (p. 289). It is a way of 'organizing some space over time' (p. 294). In addition, for Douglas, what makes that space home is the solidarity it provides. She also argues that home should be approached as an embryonic community.[8] Nevertheless, the concept of home as 'a kind of space' which provides solidarity for the survival of an embryonic community entails a question also posed by Douglas: 'What makes [this] solidarity possible?' (p. 294), a question which I think is also applicable to the notion of 'house' in the Islamic imagination. Although it is argued that, unlike home, house implies edges (Rykwert 1991, p. 54) so does the notion of solidarity, by bringing in its wake concepts of norms, rules, policies, precepts, and the like, even though these are concepts intended to provide fellowship, unity and harmony. Therefore, what Douglas suggests in order to understand 'home' can also refer to 'house' in the Islamic environment.

According to Campo, for instance, in the Islamic imagination, house constitutes one of the key metaphors which help Muslims to place themselves on earth as well as in the hereafter, and it links together major components of belief and its practice (1991, p. 7). Therefore in Islam even the most profane connotations of house as a part of domestic discourse have always included the notion of sacrality. In addition, in Islam, starting from the Ka'ba as the house of God on earth, which also constitutes the central locus for the congregation of all Muslims living in this world, *Dar al-Islam* (House of Islam) was conceived as a kind of space where Muslims rule and the law of Islam prevails.[9] Furthermore, in the hereafter Muslims find their 'final house', paradise, a 'house of peace' in the realm of the blessed for the pious (p. 24). Likewise, the actual houses of Muslims, in the sense of living space functioning as a home for the survival of the embryonic community (here read family – as in my formulation derived from Douglas) also reflect the sacrality which was embodied in those broader notions of house in Islam.

In the process of domestication in Islam, however, 'a great part of a house's sacrality depends on the reputation of its female occupants' (Campo 1991, p. 37). In this process women were not the keepers of the house in the sense of being its rulers, but in the sense of being keepers of its sacrality, unity and harmony. These are what makes a house home, 'a kind of space' for holding people together while cultivating a sense of Islamic solidarity. Although the ultimate ruler of the House of Islam is certainly God, men as the earthly representatives of God are also the rulers, i.e., in vernacular terms, heads of Muslim houses. But without women, as I have shown, a house can never be a home, nor can its permanence be maintained.

There is no need to mention that home is not always a living space in which people receive protection, love and care. People may also experience restriction, hatred and neglect within the boundaries of a home, though all the historical and sociological evidence shows that such negative occurrences are more likely to affect women than men. God, in His image of the powerful householder who looks after His people should in return be respected, loved, served and obeyed – synonyms for worship (Campo 1991, p. 9) – and men are second only to God in receiving those services of nurture and comfort as well as obedience. As I will argue in Chapter VI, Section 4, in the context of the Islamic discourse on gender complementarity, insofar as women were thought of as having been created with the innate qualities of motherly mercy and affection, they were also expected to give rest and comforts to men, who in return were expected to take care of women. More important among the benefits that men gain through the medium of the merciful nature of women, men can learn how to love, that is, they can be helped to appreciate divine cause and grace, and thereby be helped to approach God.[10] This constitutes the ultimate aim of Muslim strivings while trying not to stray away from the correct path.

Hence, it is this gift of motherly qualities that makes women indispensable for the survival of Muslim men, and also responsible for the sustenance of Islamic life. Likewise, motherhood places an immediate personal responsibility on women to raise their children as faithful Muslims, again with motherly love and affection enhanced by their piety. This specific attribute of women, however, not only perpetuates their being acknowledged as the keepers of Islam, but also entails both the mystification and romanticization of their compliance in 'mothering', while reducing their indispensability to dependency. This helps us to come to grips with another question in understanding the status of women in Muslim societies, a question formulated by Stowasser: 'Liberated Equal or Protected Dependent?' (1987b).

Nevertheless, insofar as sexual difference is construed as intrinsic to a conceptual framework of gender, indeed to the condition of being in this world, to bring this difference into balance in a non-hierarchical way appears one of the most difficult problems in all cultures.[11] Likewise, stereotypes that sustain sexism usually stem from the ways in which sexual difference has been construed. Muslim societies, however, are not the only societies where sexism underscores the social structures in which gender relations are embedded. Nor are new revivalist Islamic ideologies the only ideological constructions which univocally advocate the necessity of 'mothering' and the importance of 'family' for the survival of society. If this problem were peculiar to Muslim or Eastern societies, there would be no explanation for the emergence of feminism in the West. Thus, instead of isolating Muslim societies and the ideological discourses flourishing from within the cultural experiences of them, we should try to grasp similarities between Islamic and non-Islamic Western discourses, as well as differences, which are all embedded in the overarching parameters of modernity.

I.3.2. Mothering in the Discourse of Modernity

I think the realm of sociology provides an appropriate source in which to look at the hegemonic Western modern discourses of family and society. Here, I will take up Yeatman's (1990) argument to clarify my point. She argues that through sociology, a discipline which was strategically attached to modernist conventions, and particularly through structural–functional analyses, the 'social' was differentiated into distinct but mutually dependent functional parts of the whole – such as the polity, the occupational system, the educational system, family life, and so forth – which also entails ascribing to them a status of relative autonomy. However, for Yeatman, this emphasis on the plurality of life spheres should be evaluated as the reflection of democratic respect felt for the exist-ence of plural viewpoints. Making all functional spheres equally necessary, modern theories of functional differentiation displayed a horizontal integration which made all equally participant in the assumed hierarchical order of social agents. Family life was drawn into this order, where it was made responsible for the primary socialization of individual agents (p. 282). Therefore, 'mothering' also appeared as a very important function for the survival of modern society. According to Yeatman, ' "mothering" and "primary parenting" are distinctively late modern ideas and values. They presuppose the development of the idea of childhood, and of the construction of "home" as an effectively oriented relational setting differentiated from the extra-domestic, and thus public, settings of an impersonal market and bureaucratized state' (p. 291).

Here, the similarity I am trying to point out between the main-stream conceptualization of home and family, characteristic of sociology, and the conceptualization found in Islamic discourse, highlighted by contemporary revivalist Islamic ideologies, is obvi-ous. To be sure, as Stowasser points out, differences arise between those 'ideal paradigms' in that they give directives to the Islamic understanding of women and family which actually reflect the ongoing social changes and/or stagnation of the social order in the Islamic world (1987a, p. 264). There is no need to add that ideal paradigms concerning women and family prevalent in Western thought have also been influenced by the social changes and/or stagnation of social order in the Western world. Yet, having seen the similarities, we should also ask how the moral demands put forward by Islamic ideologies differ from those of their 'late-modern' parallels, in a context where home and family are seen as the foundations of Islamic society, and 'mothering' has become the most indispensable function performed for the survival of these foundations.

One way of answering this question may be to say that, for Islamic ideologies, it is always women who are responsible for 'primary parenting'. In this articulation, women are rendered prisoners of their anatomy as a result of an irreversible restriction imposed upon their gender identity. This, however, would be immediately denied by the women I interviewed. They would assert that, according to Islamic rules, they are not obliged even to nurse their own children, or to look after them. It is the fathers who are responsible for maintaining services necessary for childcare. If women look after their children, it is not because Islam commands them to, but because they want to preserve their inborn quality of motherly mercy. What is conveyed here is the existence of a space for subjectivity: Muslim women are able to draw a distinction between a normative obligation and a personal commitment, verbalizing it in Islamic terms.

Nevertheless, it can still be argued that it is this approach of Islamic ideologies towards home and family, with the foundational and thus vertical integrity it assumes between different functional parts of the society, which differentiates it from others which assume a horizontal integrity. At the same time Islamic ideologies maintain a relative autonomy which in turn entails a certain amount of plurality. But insofar as these pluralities rallied around one type of authority, that is, the authority of the social, it also renders their legitimacy contingent with that of the whole, i.e, the social. Thus, the assimilative character of these conceptualizations can also render this enterprise univocal. Moreover, in the modernist realm of dualistic ordering of reality such as subject/object, mind/body, masculine/feminine, adult/child, public/private, individual/society, market/state, and so forth, power relations were similarly structured according to basic modern authority relations, such as men and women, parents and children, market and state. We should also remember that in this framework what was conceived as

individual freedom was the shift of the individual from one term
to its opposite, and back again, something which was designed for
the mastery of this world by possessive individuals (Yeatman 1990,
pp. 287–8).[12]

1.4. Islamic Revivalism as the Stimulus for the Study of Women in Turkey

Writing about the predicaments of women under the rubric of
Islam is not as common in Turkey as it is in other societies with
predominantly Muslim populations. The social status of women
in Turkey vis-à-vis Islam was problematized around the axes of the
question of emancipation or liberation. Although the 'emancipated
but unliberated' social status of women constituted a point of
agreement (Kandiyoti 1987; Toprak 1990a), the point of emphasis
shifted from the specific impact of Islam, as embedded in patriarchal conservative structures through which the liberation of
women was restrained (Toprak 1990a), to the functions of patriarchal structures peculiar to local characteristics of cultural control
(Kandiyoti 1987).

One reason for not taking Islam as a starting point for the
evaluation of women's status in society arises from being critical
of tautologous approaches that assume Islam is a unitary ideology
from which the construction of women's gender identities can be
spontaneously understood in any given Muslim society (Kandiyoti
1987; Ertürk 1991). The other reason, and I think much more
important than this rightly adopted methodological approach, was
that in Turkey the state controlled Islam to the extent that it was
not considered influential in giving directives to social life in general
and people's socially determined personal orientations in particular. Thus, under the protective umbrella of the nation-state's controlled secularism, Turkish social scientists were able to put an
analytical distance between themselves and religion in terms of not
taking Islamic thought and culture as a frame of reference. In
addition to that, due to Turkey's particular historical past – specifically in terms of never having been administratively colonized
by the West – Islam did not necessarily constitute a source of
authenticity in the process of shaping a new contemporary identity.
Nor was there an explicit hostility towards the West in society,
other than an often self-inflicted and rather vague inferiority com-

plex (being an underdeveloped or developing semi-Westernized country) going hand in hand with a superiority complex (having a long historical past saturated with stories of independence and sovereignty before both East and West). Thus, Turkish social scientists, having acquired their individual identities in this realm of politico-cultural mentality, have often taken advantage of being able to make a choice between lending their loyalties to either Western ideals of liberty and equality, or to Islamic ideals of fraternity.

Given this background, which was mostly instilled with pro-Marxist theoretical discourse, women in Turkish society have long been studied within a particular framework of social change in which transition from rural/traditional to urban/modern social structures constituted the backdrop to the social picture.[13] These studies saw women as part and parcel of social development and looked at their situation in respect to relatively autonomous, mutually dependent parts of the social whole such as economy, polity, education and family life. However, along with a considerable increase in feminist sensitivity, this 'women and' understanding in women's studies has gradually been replaced by a 'women in' attitude, in an effort not to undermine women's importance in the transformation of social structures.[14] On the other hand, religion remained something which belonged to tradition, something to be eradicated on the way to modernization (i.e., social development in this scheme of thought), despite its being a social factor which undoubtedly played a great role in the ways women's daily lives and local discourses were conducted and in informing social structures and policies effective in the formation of women's status in society. Even when 'sex roles' began to appear as an important part of social structural analyses alongside class, income distribution, level of education, family type, and so on, how those sex roles could have been affected by religion, namely Islam, and moreover by different versions of Islam, was not taken into account.[15] For years, Mardin alone called Turkish social scientists to task for conceiving of religion merely as a residue of a backward-looking past. He tried to show how religion worked as an ideology as it survived in popular culture, starting from his well known study *Din ve Ideoloji* (1969), which pushed the paradigms available to him to their limits.[16] Likewise, when, within the parameters of patriarchy, the place of women became an analytical category in which to search for the construction of hierarchical differentiation in various areas of sociability between men and women, religion's possible role in the formation and legitimization of patriarchal structures and practices did not evoke significant curiosity.

Except for Mardin's pioneering works, religion in Turkey has not occupied an important place in sociological analysis aimed at the exploration of cultural aspects of social processes.[17] Yalman (1969; 1979) and Vergin (1985) were among the few who studied different aspects of religion in the process of social change without, however, being obsessed with the traditionalizing effects of Islam. Up to the1990s, except for *Islam in Modern Turkey* (Tapper 1991), there was no significant collective attempt by Turkish social scientists to study different social and cultural aspects of religion in modern Turkish society.

This void might be interpreted as due to the paucity of anthropological studies of Turkish society. However, as early as 1949, at a time when the first wave of debate on Islamic revivalism was under way, Paul Stirling (1958) was trying to understand through his fieldwork experience in Turkish villages what kind of reconciliations villagers were making between their religiously informed customs and newly introduced secular codes. It is possible to observe similar attitudes in the work by Thomas (1952) and Reed (1954; 1956), this time among 'modern' Muslims. A comparable path was also followed by Fallers (1974a; 1974b) and Magnarella (1974) in an effort to understand how people living in provincial towns of Turkey tried to bridge the gap between secular and religious ideologies in their daily life.[18] Later on, it was observed by Tapper and Tapper (1987a) that in the context of rising Islamic revivalism such an attempt might well culminate in a headline reading 'Thank God We're Secular!' In the 1970s, for Fallers and Fallers (1976), religion was not something to be skipped in the attempt to explore sex roles and the ways in which those roles had been differentiated in the different social layers of a provincial Turkish town. And Delaney (1991) provides a recent example of someone for whom – in the course of studying gender and cosmology in a Turkish village society – 'the embracing context of Islam' as well as the place of Islam in people's cosmology has to be seen as one of the most important factors to be taken into account.[19]

The strange omission of religion in exploring various layers of cultural tissue, and the ways in which meanings and symbols of

religion have changed in Turkish society, have also found their
reflection in women's studies, although with a single exception.
Toprak stood alone for years in trying to show how religion could
be operative in the formation of the social status of women in
Turkish society, though she mainly concentrated on how the omission of the influence of religion in women's issues handicaps the
understanding of the lower status of women in the public realm
(Bingöllü 1979). Subsequently, various studies, devoted to understanding the relation between women and Islam, have focused on
the role given to women by Islamic dogma, in addition to several
etiquette books teaching women religious behaviour and conduct.[20]

In this respect, one can safely wonder whether a Western
observer such as Marcus (1992) would ever have attempted to
understand the importance of Islam in the construction of gender
hierarchies in Turkish society if she had only read the material on
women in Turkey, especially that written up to the 1980s by female
Turkish social scientists. In the event, she started her exploration
of women in Muslim societies, including Turkey, through the
literary texts of orientalist traditions.

Only after the second half of the 1980s was religion, under
the guise of Islamic revivalism or fundamentalism, discovered as
something which could be operative in the process of identity
formation. This time, however, the construction of gender identities through Islamic ideologies became the locus of sociological
inquiries which concentrated on women, treating the problem as
if it were exclusive to women and unconnected with the gender
identities of Muslim men. It has been argued that in the 1990s, not
only in religious but also in ethnic, linguistic, cultural, regional and
local movements, identity politics started to occupy a central place
in both Western and non-Western agendas alike (Toprak 1994, p.
293). But because fundamentalist politics in Turkey has focused
on the gender question while aiming at redefining the social status
of women, the gender question (as connected to identity politics)
has become the distinguishing mark of the movement. Thus, accordingly, it was also argued that if the movement had been stripped
of this concern, 'little would remain to separate it from other
contestants for power' (p. 295). This gender identity, however, was
thought of as differentiated from others as long as it was veiled. In
other words, those women who became participants in Islamic
activism were brought into the discussion mainly because of their

action of 'veiling'. Thus, the limited number of books which were published on the subject came out with titles such as: *Örtülü Kimlik* (Veiled Identity, Ilyasoğlu 1994) and *Modern Mahrem: Medeniyet ve Ortunme* (Göle 1991; translated into English as *The Forbidden Modern: Civilization and Veiling*, 1996).

I.5. The Status of Islamist Women in Turkey Today: An Unresolved Puzzle

In recent social scientific discourse the identity of 'Islamist' women has been almost exclusively described with respect to different expressions of modernity. However, Göle's study (1991), a distinguished one in the area of the project of Turkish modernity, which extended the search for the parameters of Islamic revivalism in Turkey, is worthy of further detailed mention. For Göle, the 'veiled bodies of Muslim women' who form the 'dark side of modernity' have not only signified the protest of Islam against Western modernism but, by means of the new visibility that veiled women have gained in society, have also brought that dark side of modernity into the light of day (p. 135).

This idea of defining veiled/Islamist women as people who come from the darkness of modernity is closely associated with the idea developed by Anderson in *Imagined Communities* (1990) in order to understand the emergence of nationalism, and of the very notion of nation. For Anderson, the eighteenth century in Western Europe not only marked 'the dawn of the age of nationalism' but also 'the dusk of religious modes of thought'. It was this 'century of the Enlightenment, of rational secularism [that] brought with it its modern darkness' (p. 11). This darkness, however, emerged out of the 'ebbing of religious belief' since, for Anderson, the extraordinary survival of various world religions attests to their imaginative response to human suffering: 'the great merit of traditional religious world-views has been their concern with man-in-the-cosmos, man as species being, and the contingency of life . . . which naturally must be distinguished from their role in the legitimization of specific systems of domination and exploitation' (p.10). Hence, according to Anderson, with the ebbing of religious belief nothing makes fatality more arbitrary than the disintegration of paradise, and nothing makes another style of continuity more absurd than salvation. What, then, was required was a 'secular transformation of fatality into continuity, contingency into meaning' (p. 11). He continues his argument with the aim of showing how the idea of nation was better suited to this end than religion. Thus, for Anderson, the darkness of modernity was not religion *per se*, but it was something that came into being with the attempts made to deconstruct religion, which amounted to the disintegration of paradise, the absurdity of salvation, and was one of the important consequences of the rational secularism of modernity.

What, then, do these veiled women bring into the light of day? Do they remind us of the inadequacies of rational secularism in maintaining answers to the existential questions of mortal human beings? Or do they just remind us of the failures of nationalism? Whatever the answer, insofar as Göle equated veiled women with the failures of modernity, her attempt turned out to be a precise way of making veiled women not simply the 'other', but rather the opposite of the positive qualities of modern society. This is because, as well as placing them on the 'dark side of modernity', she also sees them as its representatives. In a much more optimistic way, instead of thinking of veiled women as the carriers of darkness into the brightness of modernity, as it seems Göle might also think, we can hope that, on their way back home, they will carry the light of modernity to enlighten the darkness of their restricted spheres of private sociability. Moreover, according to Göle, the enthusiasm that Islamist women have shown for participating in public life should be construed as a success of Kemalism, which was strong enough to drag those selfsame dark bodies into the light of national public life and provide them with opportunities to prepare themselves to become a part of it.[21]

Ironically, it was Göle who argued that, through relying on the principles of this understanding of Kemalism, veiled women were sent back to their privacy – that is, they were not allowed to cover their heads in public institutions, and were thereby unable to follow their professions. Perhaps that is why Göle insistently counterposes veiled woman with national Kemalist woman[22] instead of pursuing convergencies as well as divergencies, despite both having been exposed to this society while living in it as women. This does not mean that she ignores the critical attitude of veiled women towards male oppression. However, the particular examples she uses for the struggle of veiled women in displaying the hypocrisies of any patriarchal social order, including an Islamic one, debated in terms of feminism, do not come from this particular 'dark side'. She discusses the debate which took place in the daily *Zaman* in September 1987 on the question of women's rights (Göle 1991, pp. 119–28). It supported the basic arguments of feminism and displayed a capacity for harnessing elements of Marxist and liberal as well as Islamic discourses, and was led by three well-educated young women whose political identity had been shaped within the Ülkücü (Idealist) youth groups of the extreme-right Miliyetçi Hareket Partisi (Nationalist Action Party). More importantly, these women were at least ambivalent about whether they should adopt the Islamic dress codes of modesty or not. They are of course on the side of women who cover their heads in public. However, of the three, one has never covered her head, humorously saying, 'I prefer to be as I was when I came from my mother and I would never cover my head', and the second has covered her head on and off, and her ambivalence has culminated in the decision to uncover her head (personal communications with M. Gülnaz and T. Tuncer). The third, whom I never met, was also said by her friends to be an 'open' woman. All three possessed a sincere faith and were practising Muslims, yet could not be considered among the women who were called Islamist by Göle, nor did they associate themselves with them. Nevertheless, the debate they created has entered into the discourse and will continue to be a part of it, but it cannot be taken as an example of how to understand the inner dynamics of the movement. Instead, their protest should be assessed as the challenge of some nationalist Muslim women vis-à-vis male-ordered Islamic revivalism: this is a point which becomes extremely important when we come to think of what would happen if Kemalist women, somehow strongly nationalistic and anti-imperialist, were to place themselves in league with religious concerns.

However, for Göle veiling does not attest to the total submissiveness of women, inasmuch as it provides some women with an opportunity to participate in public life. This is exactly what Hoffman-Ladd argues concerning the veiling of Egyptian women: 'Most of these women who wear *hijab* do not intend to relinquish their right to enter the public realm, but create their inviolable private space by means of their dress, which protects them from harassment, desexualizes their contacts with men, and proclaims their respectability' (1987, p. 43). This 'inviolable private space' created by adopting Islamic dress-codes of modesty was what Göle (1996) called *modern mahrem*, the 'forbidden modern', a space which was created by (the dark side of) modernity despite modernity. In this framework of thought, the bright side of modernity, the public, a space which pertains to men, becomes a place where women can come and go depending on the permissiveness of men, without considering how those 'visits' change the boundaries of public and private and of men's and women's respective positions in society. During such 'visits' women may be wrapped either in a veil or an attitude of 'comrade-in-arms', or in the guise of 'phallic woman', to be able to benefit from that light, i.e., the civilization created by men. For Göle, the major problem of modern civilization was to what extent it would make women visible in the realm of men.

This understanding of women vis-à-vis modernity, i.e., women as the 'object' of modernity, is not inherent to modernity as such; it is the interpretation reached by Göle through her reading of women's place in the construction of modernity. Göle would not have suggested the conceptualization of veiled women as the dark side of modernity had she not seen women as its 'object'. However, for 'the transformation of prejudices into objects of study', in the sense that de Certeau argues as one of the preliminary steps of writing history, a break with those prejudices is first required in order to render them thinkable (de Certeau 1988, pp. 33–4). After all, how we read cannot be separated from where we read. The analytical distance that Göle tries to put between her place and the place allotted to women by the discourse of modernity disappears to the extent that she also objectifies veiled women as the 'dark side of modernity'. Göle's account also places her in the perspective of modernity. In this way of reading modern civilization and/or modernity, Göle is here consistent with her statement that her subject was not the question of women (1991, p. 9); she takes women as a significant study subject as far as they reflect the civilization of men.

In the case of 'Islamist' women, however, by way of veiling, women not only constitute the dark side of modernity (Islam in the modern world in Göle's reading) but also become the 'other' of the 'other', i.e., the 'other' in relation to Kemalist women. Although we cannot be sure whether Kemalist women represent the 'bright side of modernity', we can guess, however, from what we know about the experiences of women in Turkey: they were allowed to stay on the bright side of modernity much longer than veiled women, the latter returning to their privacy, a place imagined by Göle as a 'hidden continent'. This continent was a site in which the relationship between men and women and modernism took place (Göle 1991). However, to be able to 'discover/analyse' this continent (and thereby 'read/write' its history) and the inner dynamics of the Islamic movement, Göle insightfully suggests dis- cussing the ways in which 'Islamist' women themselves conceive of religion and their social movement, though her investigation into their 'social action' was only based on a series of group discussions. Nevertheless, the importance of social action in the analysis of this hidden continent is explained in Göle's terms as follows: 'History has been written on the borderlines of the tension between the subjectivity of social actors and the evolutionary rules of social structures' (p. 81). And in the realization of the history of modernity, 'Islamic bodies came out with a different semantic while resisting to enter into the spiral of modernity' (p. 134). Nevertheless, once Göle's highly metaphorical conceptual frame- work is accepted, her attempt to grasp the discourse of privacy as part of the project of Turkish modernity, though a 'hidden conti- nent' in her imagery, becomes a very illuminating text about men's adventures on the way to modernity in which women were side- lined as reflections of men's identity.

Far from Göle's metaphorical ability and her imaginative capacity which was impelled by the enlightening brightness of modernity to unfold different aspects of a discourse of identity, for Ilyasoğlu, to be able to explore the identity of veiled women, it was revealing enough to associate 'twists of the body' with 'features of self-identity' (1994, pp. 67–8). An identity actually maintained the status of identity as long as it was veiled. Without offering any theoretical framework, she asserts that her attempt should be construed as a dialogue with the veiled women. At the end of this enterprise what she suggests is seeing the élite Islamist women (they actually become élite at the end of the study though they were called working veiled women at the beginning) as the representatives of a 'reversed modernity' or a 'self-modernization' which, in any case, should be regarded as 'their own version of modernity' (p.126).

Whether the identity of veiled women represented the dark side of modernity or a reverse form of it, it was construed as something to be compared and contrasted with an assumed identity of modern

Turkish women in general, and Kemalist women in particular. For Acar, however, what should be taken into account was not the Kemalist women's identity *per se*, but what Kemalism had promised to women and failed to deliver adequately (1990, p. 70; 1991, p. 282). This approach also reflects the 'emancipated but unliberated' debate on the position of women in Turkish society. On the other hand, for Acar, the way of life proposed to Islamist women through Islamist women's magazines was a contemporary creation to the extent that what was 'traditional' in Turkish society was neither homogeneous nor dominant and widespread in any one form. This specific construction, however, emerges from the confrontation of Islam with the secular world (1991, p. 287). Following Mardin (1989b), Acar argues that this new form also relies heavily upon items which are strongly anchored in the daily life of Turkey, even though for her the reconcilability of some of them with Islamic principles is debatable (Acar 1991, p. 300). Nevertheless, regarding the restricted roles assigned to women, Acar is sceptical of the concepts of pluralist democracy and human rights invoked by those magazines (especially by *Kadın ve Aile*, and *Bizim Aile*), on the grounds that they might be merely the tactical utilization of the resources and tools of secular culture as an extension of the survival strategy developed therein.

In her study of *Kadın ve Aile*, Arat also contends that the ideology espoused by this journal is inherently restrictive in many respects. Nevertheless, for her, though 'ironically', the journal can also provide opportunities for the enrichment of secular Kemalist culture. The evidence is the encouraging attitude of the journal towards women's acquisition of 'a taste of public life', guiding them into many communal activities, opening debates on individual human rights, making them aware of other Muslim women at the international level, and exposing its female writers and editors to the public realm and personal autonomy. Moreover, for Arat, the magazine's search for alternative ways of life can also be channelled to a liberating end (1990a, pp. 21–3).

What Arat does not mention, however, is that one of this magazine's most prominent women, who actually initiated its publication, is an ex-citizen of the United States of America and took her well-known Turkish name after she married a Turkish gentleman and converted to Islam at a time when she was mature enough to make a choice between different life orders. Her conversion was completely her own choice. To be sure, her country of origin does not make a difference either to the faith she possesses or to the ideology she holds. But I believe that if the personal background of other 'Islamist' women counts towards the way in which they have participated in the 'movement' and towards the shaping of their demands and future orientations, then the experiences this woman had while as an independent, assertive female member of a highly modernized society could also have had an effect on her contributions and on the line followed by the magazine, especially in the development of the trends linked by Arat to progressive ends. Similarly that the 'Western medium' of the magazine stemmed from its 'resemblance [to] . . . relatively conservative Western women's magazines, in terms of the issues they dwell on and their general appearance' was something which also caught the eye of Acar. However, she attributed it to the tactics of Islamic revivalist movements using characteristic Western resources or norms while blaming Western lifestyles as evil and dangerous (1991, p. 288).

The overall tendency in explaining the endeavours of Muslim women to create an alternative Islamic life and a social identity can best be summarized by Toprak's analysis (1994); here this effort was seen as part and parcel of a 'search of the marginals for respectability of status, and indeed for a redefinition of status hierarchy', and yet 'the turban and the long coat as "uniforms" serve the function of the blue jeans which women of these traditional backgrounds are most likely not allowed to wear. Both forms of dress are oblivious to status and class distinction' (p. 303). The distaste that jeans aroused in conservative sections of society when they emerged as a symbol of youth protest has been exchanged for the approval they have received from almost all sections of Western or westernized societies once they ceased to be the symbol of one particular ideology, that of the working class. In the Turkish context, the extent to which the 'turban' can be tolerated is an interesting question for the future. However, the image projected by jeans was always polysemic and its 'adherents' could always search for new 'faiths'. But it seems that once it is worn with a faith, the 'turban' starts to denote a meaning which conveys a sense of irreversibility because of the particular characteristic of the 'faith' lying behind it. Thus, it can be argued that this sense of irreversibility makes the turban/veil/headscarf the stamp of a specific otherness, an otherness which seems unlikely to be eradicated simply by upward mobility.

Notes

[1] For a very well articulated examination of East-West critique of gender relations, see Nader (1989). For criticism of Euro-American social science paradigms, including feminist ones, in which women in Muslim societies are studied, see Lazreg (1988).

[2] For example, Baker argues: 'For the last two decades, political debates in Egypt, and throughout the Islamic world, have centered on the question of the moral purpose of ruling power' (1991, p. 47). In an earlier account, the rise of the Islamic movement and its take-over of state power by 1979, i.e., the Islamic Revolution in Iran, was analysed by Najmabadi (1987) as a paradigmatic shift from a material transformation of a backward society to the moral purification of a corrupt society, the overall move being seen as an effort to realize a moral transformation.

[3] I derive my formulation of 'keepers of Islam' analogously from Hale's (1987) identification of the Nubian women of Sudan as the 'keepers of culture'.

[4] The same understanding was also true for other early anti-colonialist movements whether Islamic or not. See, for example, Chatterjee's arguments based on Indian and Bengali anti-colonialist nationalist movements (1993, pp. 116–57).

[5] 'Westoxification' (*Garb-zadegi*) is a term which was introduced into the literature of Islamic revivalism by Iranian ideologues and used during and after the revolution to indicate the harm from westernization to the 'health' of Muslim society. See, for example, Fischer and Abedi (1990, pp. 202, 208, 210). For how this concept was employed to depict women's identity in Iran, see Najmabadi (1991, p. 51). In Najmabadi's usage the term is translated into English as 'Westoxication'.

[6] See, for an example of analysis which is both quantitative and qualitative of Islamic ideology and women's employment in Iran, Moghadam (1988).

[7] For the operation of various versions of the notion of modesty, see Abu-Lughod (1986, chapter 4).

[8] Douglas also argues that if approaching the home as an embryonic community 'sounds platitudinous it is because many sociologists think of the community as modeled on the idea of home'. She continues her argument as follows: 'This relic of nineteenth-century romantic enthusiasm has been a stumbling block in sociology, where it is assumed too easily that the survival of a community over many vicissitudes does not need explaining. On this line of thought both home and community are

supposed to be able to draw upon the same mysterious supply of loyal support, and further, their inner sources of strength are unanalyzable: thanks to a kind of mystic solidarity, home and small local community are supposed to be able to overcome the forces of fission that tear larger groups apart' (1991, p. 288). This view originally appeared in M. Douglas, *How Institutions Think* (Syracuse: Syracuse University Press, 1986, pp.21–43).

[9] I have taken this definition of *Dar al-Islam* from Lewis (1991, p. 73).

[10] At this point I should mention the importance in Islam of the ability of Muslims to be able to approach God and of the 'means' which provide that approach. For example, Schimmel shows that in many Sufi traditions love was praised as the highest possible state in approaching God and was even seen as superior to gnosis. In spite of some differences among them, Sufis were certain that 'nothing is dearer to God than that man loves him'. Schimmel gives the following prayer ascribed to the Prophet as a good example of the importance of love in Islam: 'O God give me love of Thee, and love of those who love Thee, and *love of what makes me approach Thy love*, and make Thy love dearer to me than cool water' (1986, pp. 130–1, my emphasis). The prayer is quoted from Farid al-Din Attar, *Tadhkirat al-awliya*, ed. R. A. Nicholson, 2 vols, London: Luzc,1905–7.

[11] For an extensive critique of theoretical approaches in which culture and society were perceived as male phenomena, see Rogers (1978). This does not take into consideration cross-cultural variations dependent on behavioural and ideological differentiation between the sexes and thus does not address the issue of how power imbalances are usually constructed in favour of men. For a voluminous critique of how the problem of sexual difference constitutes one of the core elements of contemporary feminism in Western societies, see Rhode (1990).

[12] Yeatman (1990) argues that 'the central motif of the modernist model of individuality is private property, [that is,] individuality resides in ownership of property, in what Macpearson calls "possessive individualism"' (p. 287).

[13] For a different approach which suggests classifying the development of women's studies in Turkey in three parts, e.g., Turkish village studies, modernization and feminism, see Arat (1993).

[14] Compare two major bibliographical compilations on women's studies in Turkey: Aren (1980) and S. Çakır, (1992).

[15] See, for example, the volume edited by Kağıtçıbaşı (1982). Here religion is understood to be 'community religion', a part of the traditional socio-cultural context (pp. 9–10). But this form of religion has not been taken into account in the sex role studies concerned here.

[16] Among various of Mardin's seminal works devoted to understanding the relation of religion and the social and personal construction of reality

see his edition *Cultural Transitions in the Middle East* (1994). This attempts to understand the ways in which Western culture has been 'domesticated' by Islam through 'folk themes', leading to the creation of modern popular culture in the Middle East as I have described in the Introduction, Section 2.

[17] In the 1990s, when she was pointing to religion as an accommodating mechanism embodied in the everyday practices of people and folk culture in the process of social change, Kıray noted: 'Although very much discussed in recent social science literature, explanations based on field research on changing religious practices in the urban environment in Turkey are rather limited' (1991, p. 7). However, I should add that in the realm of political science a fair amount of studies can be found that focus on the role of religion in Turkish politics. See, for example, Heper (1981), Toprak (1981), Sunar and Toprak (1983) and Sarıbay (1985a; 1985b).

[18] The specific impact of religion as embedded in cultural norms, values and customs was emphasized in a limited number of studies of Turkish society. See, for example, Dubetsky (1976), Karpat (1976) and Meeker (1976).

[19] For specific religious rituals and their relation to the formation of gender identities, see also N. Tapper (1983; 1985), Tapper and Tapper (1987b), and Olson (1991).

[20] See, for example, the section on 'Women and Islam' in Aren's bibliography of women's studies (1980, pp. 71–4).

[21] For the legal status that Turkish women could obtain after the establishment of the Turkish Republic in 1923 and the impact of legal and educational reforms on women in modern Turkey see, for example, Abadan-Unat (1991).

[22] For a similar critique, see Ayata (1993a).

CHAPTER II

Story of the Field: 'They'll never let you in'

II.1. The Field

I undertook fieldwork for this study from November 1989 in Ankara. The main part of the research was completed by the end of 1990, but some subsequent parts of it were added up to the end of February 1992 and I also made some additional visits to the field in the early months of 1993.

My fieldwork took place in an urban complex of a type usually called *site* in Turkish, an adaptation of the French *cité*, a term applied to a multi-ethnic suburban residential area composed of high-rise apartment buildings of poor construction quality and inadequate urban facilities. In the Turkish context, however, the term is used variously. A *site* may be a residential area composed of high-rise apartment blocks of modest quality and social environment, or an area designed for middle and upper-middle classes. The latter may contain well designed high-rise apartment buildings or detached houses ranging in size from moderate to large villas, or a combination of both, offering an environment where these classes somehow isolate themselves from the common disorders of the urban crowd and lead a decent life. The neighbourhood in which I carried out my fieldwork was located in a densely-populated outlying district in the north-west of Ankara, nine kilometres from the downtown area. The district contains many of the socio-economic and cultural facilities typical of metropolitan life but in a rather peripheral way. Urban planners in Turkey refer to this kind of development as *apart-kondu*, the analogy being drawn with *gecekondu*, unauthorized squatter houses, but indicating high-rise apartment blocks built without planning permission and initially unlicensed. Once licences were granted, however, the area emerged as one of Ankara's highest density residential districts, the inhabitants being mainly middle and lower-middle class.

The *site* in which I conducted this research forms quite a small part of the neighbourhood once the whole population is taken into account, but it is also one of the more well-established and neatly constructed parts of the area. The inhabitants are identified by their neighbours as 'closed', 'religionist' or Islamist people, and are recognized by their appearance which is in accordance with the orthodox Muslim codes of contemporary Turkish urban people: women wear large headscarves covering their necks, shoulders and bosoms, and long loose overcoats; men wear moustaches or the moustache and beard typical of religious Turkish men, and formal, simple suits with or without neckties.[1] The inhabitants of this *site* are not the only residents of this district known for their religious allegiance. It is quite common to come across people of a religiously conservative type as well as all sorts of other middle and lower-middle class urban people. Nevertheless, since it is known that the inhabitants of this *site* rally around a living space deliberately organized so that they may live in accordance with Islamic codes, they are distinguished from the others and provided with an identity as members of a specific Islamic community.

This image of strong religiosity is also manifested in the name of the *site*,[2] which is also formally registered as its postal address. Most important of all, as I will try to explain below, this *site* gains its religious reputation from some of its more famous religious families, who come from a very well-known branch of the Sufi Nakşibendi order, and other families who formed the higher ranks of the WP, now the VP. Thus, people who live in this *site* are no doubt conceived of as 'religionist' or Islamist, if they are not labelled as religious fanatics, reactionaries, obscurantist, fundamentalists, etc., but never simply as Muslims. The strength of their religiosity is also demonstrated by their calling themselves 'conscious Muslims' (*şuurlu Müslümanlar*), as distinct from 'false' (i.e., secular) Muslims.

This sentiment of 'otherness' that I try to delineate is the underlying feature of the identity of 'Islamists' in that it creates an image of a highly secluded people who have something to hide, or at best wish to protect themselves from other sectors of society. This appears to threaten the existing social order and engenders suspicion regarding the legality of their social activities; and the aura of mystery which it arouses deepens the social distance between so-called secularized and non-secularized Muslims. The social stigma thereby attached to the people called Islamists is usually supported by a collective memory of both the distant and more recent political history of republican Turkey, as well as by the worldwide media images of Islamists as extremists, fanatics and terrorists.[3]

I was also told that the *site* was one of the more important bastions of Islamic fundamentalists, a place where Islamic rules dominate the life of the inhabitants in a rigid way. This should be understood in reference to the political atmosphere in Turkey before the military intervention of 1980. In those days highly polarized right- and left-wing radical groups proclaimed certain areas of urban settlement to be under their control as their 'liberated zones', and did not allow people belonging to opposing groups to enter these districts. The *site* where I carried out my research could not be compared with such zones but access could be difficult because of its highly suspicious attitude towards secular urban élites.

This *site* is composed of: five high-rise apartment blocks with approximately seventy apartments in each block; one mosque; a place annexed to the mosque designed to be used as a slaughterhouse during the sacrificial feast of Bayram; one small building originally built for Koran courses; ten dormitory-like apartments for university and lycée students (one for males and one for females in each block and usually designed to host ten students in each); a large meeting room used for social occasions, such as wedding ceremonies and seminars, in the basement of one block; one teahouse for males near the mosque; one nursery school for nearly thirty children organized in an apartment; one playground for small children; several open areas for the young; one supermarket (which became a seven-storied department store two years after I started this research and moved to nearby the *site*); and finally some open places used as parking lots.

In the late 1960s, a group of people came together to establish a construction cooperative with the goal of building a living space that would allow them to 'live Islam' as 'conscious' Muslims. The group included the founding fathers of Milli Görüş (National Vision), which is a shorthand description of the politico-societal project of Necmettin Erbakan's WP, some of the leading figures of the Zahid Kotku branch of the Nakşibendi order, and some of the followers of these two movements. Organized around this cooperative, they extended their living space into various social organizations, ranging from *awqaf* (singular *waqf*, charitable endowment) to youth and women's organizations. After coping with many economic and psycho-sociological difficulties, they finally managed to complete the whole *site* in 1985. This place should not be conceived, however, as the domain of a closed community under the politico-religious leadership of one branch of Islam. It constitutes a living space in which highly conservative Sunni Muslim families with various religious political affiliations but a similar Islamic world-view lead their lives.

This particular *site* constitutes a sociologically significant object of study as an exemplary endeavour to establish a model of an Islamic 'counter society', in which the production of Islamic sociability as developed in the experience of Muslim people can be observed, as well as an Islamic imagery upon which such a model of the Islamic way of life can be founded. But I propose that this 'field' should be conceived of as a 'laboratory', rather than as a representative sample, enabling us to comprehend the ways in which the ideal of living an Islamic life has been attempted in thought and deed in an urban context, specifically in Ankara, the capital city of the secular Republic of Turkey.

II.2. Entering into the Field: Prejudices, Opportunities and Coincidences

The method I employed in order to be able to enter the field was no less strategic than the other ethno-sociological methods which made this study possible. After I had been informed of the existence of this *site*, I started to look for people who could give me reliable information about it. There were many people identified with their Islamic political affiliations who could attest to the existence of such a *site* founded by 'Islamists', but none of them knew much about it, or seemed to be willing to be part of even such a preliminary inquiry. Others, however, who wanted to help me, had to face the difficulties of overcoming the thick layers of seclusion.

I had learned well enough from previous research experiences that, in any ethno-sociological study, finding a 'correct entry' to the field helps to solve more than half the problems of the actual research. Nevertheless, after spending several months in a series of unsuccessful efforts to find someone who would initiate contact and mediate between me and the inhabitants of the *site*, and after having heard nothing but comments such as 'You won't be allowed to do that kind of research', 'They won't let you into their private circles' or 'They'll never let you in', I finally realized that I had to present myself without relying on anyone else. In other words, I had to find my own ways of explaining myself to the people living in the *site*. But at the time I reached that conclusion, I could not even find out the address of the place; I was not even sure of its name or the district in which it was to be found.

At this point, a series of unexpected coincidences facilitated my entry to the field. The stories of these coincidences, later on, became very important for the people who agreed to be inter-viewed, persuading them that the aim of my research was purely academic. The way I gained entry was also perceived as an indicator of my personal dedication in carrying out this research; the fact that I was directed by nothing other than my academic intentions cultivated a sense of trust. I will first briefly describe the important stages of this process of 'entry'; second, I will show the way in which the highly suspicious attitude of the inhabitants of the *site* towards the secular urban élite emerged as an imperative for the design and the scope of the research.

When I was actually doing my research some of the most fre-quent questions addressed to me concerned how I had heard of the existence of the *site* or how I had learned about the people living there. I usually answered this sort of question briefly, relating the actual stages of the process of entering the field. The details of my story, as I told certain key persons in my research sample (and who often told this story to the others, sometimes in my presence), are as follows.

At the time when I became interested in the revitalization of Islam in Turkey, I aimed to conduct field research in order to investigate the meanings, symbols and practice of Islam constructed and operated as a set of cultural means regulating the everyday life of people in an urban context. I wanted to research these points at the level of the *mahalle* (quarter), the smallest unit of urban settlement, which in many cases holds various people of different social origins together, not only space-wise but also to some extent identity-wise. Hence, I started to make preliminary investigations for an appropriate place of study, especially among the quasi-urbanized *gecekondu* areas of Ankara. Finally, I decided to focus on a specific area for a pilot study, an area peculiar for its physical proximity to the highly prestigious settlement areas of Ankara, and also for its having displayed a rapid change from a *gecekondu* area to a new apartment-like settlement, as well as for the mixed nature of the population, composed of highly politicized Alevi and Nakşi-bendi people. After three months, I concluded that research could only be made possible by teamwork if it was not to be designated an ethnographic investigation requiring the employment of com-pletely anthropological techniques of investigation (namely making a long-term participant observation, and entailing actually living in the field for a period of time).

The causes of my failure to carry out research in that specific area can be explained by a series of socio-phenomenological obstacles. These obstacles range from the highly polarized religious character of the population to their conditions of existence, which create a sense of insecurity. This insecurity stems from the way they per-ceive their social situation as being open to threat from the urban élite, usually viewing 'newcomers' as a menace to the order of their previously established city life. Furthermore, those who participate in research which aims to investigate their private beliefs and attitudes suspect they might jeopardize the very delicately estab-lished networks of social control upon which they build their strategies of survival.[4] I must add that, as I was told later, the fact that I was a relatively young female researcher from the Middle East Technical University also created an obstacle to building a relationship of trust, especially for Nakşibendi people who had had many unpleasant political experiences in the recent past with people from the same university. Particularly before the 1980s, the students of my university had a reputation for being exclusively left-wing revolutionaries with a political rhetoric proclaiming any religious affiliation a sign of backwardness or ignorance which should be immediately removed. Of course, the reasons for my failure could be expanded upon, but these were the most important ones, at least from my vantage-point.

Although I believe I learned a great deal from this experience, when I decided to give up my attempt and leave that particular place, there was one phrase that I have always kept in my mind as a summary of my research endeavours. It was said to me by a woman from this *mahalle* while I was trying to convince her to be one of my interviewees. After I had explained to her why I was carrying out this study and what my aim was, she gazed at me and said, 'I see, you are going to fill a book and you need my help.' This was exactly what I needed; I was still suffering from a lack of help and material with which 'to fill my book'.

One day, while I was with my professor lamenting all the difficulties I had had in the field, and telling him desperately how I wished I could have found someone who would at least tell me the exact location of the so-called bastion of the Islamist people in Ankara, there was a loud knock on his office door and the door opened before an answer could be given. A short, provincial-type middle-aged man stood in the doorway with a large smile, and greeted my professor with a heavy eastern Turkish accent. My professor was visibly shocked. Pointing at him, he exclaimed, 'That's him, that's him. He is the guy you wished to find all along.'

This gentleman and my professor were close friends from their years of graduate study at the University of Chicago, though they had not seen each other for more than ten years. After the gentleman had graduated from the Faculty of Theology in Ankara, he wrote a master's thesis in Chicago on the philosophy of Christian theology and, without finishing his PhD, returned to Turkey and lived in his native town, teaching English in an Imam Hatip school. He had finally decided to complete his PhD in the Faculty of Theology in Ankara, and thus had come to visit his old friend.

At the end of a nice, lively conversation, I was finally provided with some preliminary information about the *site* where I conducted the present field study, including its exact name and the name of the district within which it lies. However, the gentleman had no acquaintances among the people who lived there, nor did he think that he could find any, but he promised to help me as much as he could. In the following days, I participated as the only female member in a few of the informal discussion groups organized by him and other academicians from my university's Department of Philosophy and from the Ankara University Faculty of Theology. Topics ranged from human rights in Islam to the philosophical foundations of Islamic knowledge. In addition, the gentleman became a generous source for the exchange of many basic books on Islam. Nevertheless, apart from encouraging me by saying I was qualified to carry out my research, he could (or would) not help me to find someone who would provide me with an entry to the *site*. He and his friends also seemed to agree with the people who continued to tell me repeatedly that the inhabitants of the *site* would not let me in because of their highly secluded nature.

I also tried to get the help of certain studious young participants in our undergraduate programme, whom I trusted and who were also known for their religious affiliations, but the result was no different from that of my previous efforts. All this convinced me that no one wanted to take any 'responsibility', even for merely introducing someone wishing to do research on the so-called Islamist people, particularly in this *site*. This was quite understandable in the political atmosphere of Turkey at the time.[5]

The professional side of my identity, however, had constantly told me that the inhabitants of the *site* could not be as secluded as was claimed, since they adhered to a legally established political party and also to a very well-known and powerful branch of the Nakşibendi order: both of these were struggling to gain the religious leadership in the country's political arena by proclaiming themselves, though through different channels, capable of solving the problems of society, which were apparently caused by its having strayed from the path of Islam for the sake of westernization. This was also evident from their political stance as delineated in their several publications: they constantly argued that Islam was quite compatible with the requirements of the contemporary world, while severely criticizing the moral aspects of the Western version of modernity.

Earlier experiences were also helpful. As an undergraduate I had prepared a term-paper which was a content analysis of the newspaper *Milli Gazete*. It was then the voice of the NSP and continued to be so for both the WP and the VP. The people who worked there were sensitive about the way in which they were perceived by others. Their frequent questions about how I saw them, whether I found them different from other intellectuals or not, and so on, were still fresh in my memory. This was heavily connected with the stigma attached to them: they were labelled backwardists, reactionaries, obscurantists, and the like. I had gained the impression that Islamic activists were keen to express themselves properly as 'true progressives' to secular people, in order to rid themselves of any such stigma of backwardness marking their social identity.

These perceptions led me to examine my current position from a theoretical standpoint that I shall describe here, since it contributed significantly to my continued approach. I started to read the process I was going through while trying to get enough information to enter the field as one of signification through which, in a Barthesian sense, the production and reproduction of a myth was realized. For Barthes, as Heck (1980) explains, any process of signification consists of a plane of expression (signifier) and a plane of content (signified), and the signification is the relation of these two planes. Any system of signification operates on a two-tiered level. The first system of signification is called 'denotation', and the second 'connotation'. Accordingly, for instance, when the word *gerici*, 'backwardist' (signifier) has the content of the concept, 'a person who is opposed to progress or development' (signified), the relation between the signifier and signified gives us the signification, a person who advocates the protection of the status quo against progress and thereby contributes to the prevention of society's progress. At the second level, this system of denoted meaning can become the plane of expression, or the signifier of the second system. Thus, following my example, it can be argued that in the context of the Turkish Republic's westernization movement, the word 'backwardist' becomes the signifier of a specific sign: 'religionist' at the connotative level, i.e., on the second plane of expression. 'Connotative meanings' on the other hand, as Heck says, 'are defined by lexicons or sub-codes which are used in specific groups or with reference to a more delimited domain'. For Barthes, myths are also generated in the same way as connotation: 'The difference between myth and connotation depends on the amplitude of the lexicons from which the concepts are drawn' (Heck 1980, pp. 124–5). According to this, the connoted meaning of 'backwardist', for example, was drawn from the lexicon of an identifiable sub-group, the early republican westernizing reformists who at the same time formed the bureaucratic-military élites of the society. Then how does a connoted meaning drawn from the lexicon of an identifiable sub-group become a meaning which operates at the mythical plane of expression? In Heck's words:

By contrast [to connotation], myth seems identifiable with the lexicon of very large groups, if not of the society as a whole. Myth therefore differs from connotation at the moment at which it attempts to universalize for the whole society meanings which are special to particular lexicons. In the process of universaliz-ation, these meanings, which in the last instance are particular to certain lexicons, assume the amplitude of reality itself and are therefore 'naturalized'. Thus we might say, *myths are connotations which have become dominant-hegemonic* (Heck 1980, p. 125).

Thus, when the word 'backwardist' connotes a meaning of religious opposer to progress and development, two concepts also associated with westernization and modernization, and when this meaning is shared by large sections of the society, even if their ideas and interests conflict with the reformist élites, then 'backwardist' signi-fies the same meaning, i.e., 'religionist', for these large groups of people. Therefore a word such as 'backwardist' operates at the level of myth. In other words, it then belongs to a mythical, i.e., dominant-hegemonic, plane of signification. Thus, we immediately recognize its denoted meaning. As Coward and Ellis argue:

The connotation leans on the denotation; there is a perpetual to-and-fro movement between them so that they appear as a natural unity. The connoted myth is successful exactly when it 'goes without saying', when it confirms an established position from doubt or attack, when it universalizes history by saying, 'That's the way it must be' (1979, p. 28).

I argue that 'the secluded nature' of Islamist people is also seen as 'the way it must be'. Hence, this idea of their seclusion is seen as natural by various people who stand for different political positions such as social democracy or liberalism as well as Islamism. Although the emphasis of their explanation for the phenomenon may vary regarding their assessments of the extent to which state oppression leads Islamic activists (the people with religious political affiliations) to develop such an attitude of seclusion, it is important to note that people who approach 'Islamist' people with this kind of prejudice contribute to the reproduction of a myth of seclusion – as was evident in my experience. This situation, by and large,

entails the perpetuation of the sense of 'otherness' for people who
have religious political affiliations.

I should now mention another, though a second-order, coincidence which facilitated my entry to the field. I was married at the
time to a person who, due to his deep interest in music, knew
almost everybody in town selling good quality hi-fi. One of these
shopkeepers had once been a member of the youth organization of
the banned NSP. My husband noticed that there was a poster
hanging on the wall of his store containing major parts of the
speech of Necip Fazıl Kısakürek to youth. My husband conveyed
my 'problem' to this shopkeeper, with whom he already had a
friendly relationship. The shopkeeper gave him his card, advising
him to tell me to see the general coordinator of the WP, adding
that this was a person who would have access to almost everybody
with even the smallest Islamic reputation in town. When I asked
myself whether I would ever have thought of resorting to a person
of authority, in order not to endure the difficulties I had encountered in conducting my research, my answer was no. For I believe
that any sociological research designed to get information from
actual people must be based on their consent and voluntary participation. Therefore, I had always hesitated to do something which
would impose myself on the people whom I wanted to research.
But now I decided to take my chance.

In the following days, my husband's friend called the party
coordinator on my behalf and told him of my situation and made
an appointment for us, i.e., for me and my husband. Neither I nor
my husband knew whose decision this was; my husband simply
informed me that his friend had told him the coordinator had
invited both of us. At that point I was not opposed to the idea,
since I thought that this might be a sign of politeness on this
person's part, rather than any kind of conservatism. After all, it
was my husband who had initiated this relationship. I was a married
woman and in this society it is traditionally accepted that a husband
should escort his wife if she goes to meet a man she does not know,
even if this was a professional meeting. This is especially the case
in Islamic circles, so I decided not to violate their 'rule'. But my
biggest justification in taming the feminist side of my identity was
consideration of the fact that my husband happened to be the
mediator between me and these two gentlemen.

Before going to the appointment, I decided to write a research proposal specifically prepared for this meeting.[6] It was an ethical sort of proposal, as well as a sociological one, consisting of three sections. First, I briefly described the aim of the research. Second, I wrote a piece in which I declared that I would keep the identity of interviewees concealed, and never let anybody else use my raw data, nor would I use this data except for academic purposes. In addition, I also guaranteed that I would not let the interviewees have information about each other, and that information would be gathered from each interviewee separately. Third, I gave a profile of the area of my quest, exemplified with sub-headings. Finally, I did not neglect to write my open academic address on top of the proposal. With this proposal, I was hoping to make clear that I intended to carry out this research within exclusively academic orientations, and not within the prevailing interests of the secular Turkish media, which usually approach 'Islamist' people with a certain amount of prejudice and bias and the aim of displaying what they term the hypocrisy or ignorance behind seemingly religious political efforts to realize an Islamic social order.

At the meeting, which took place in the party building, we were very kindly received. I repeated the points written in my proposal orally. The coordinator listened to me very carefully and told me that the members of his party had great respect for my university and its members, and that he personally believed in the virtue of sociological knowledge. I said to him that many people had told me the inhabitants of this *site* would not allow me to carry out research among them due to their highly secluded nature. He agreed that this might be the case since they would be afraid of being the inadvertent cause of any harm to Islam. After all, he said, we are all human beings and we make many mistakes, and our mistakes could be attributed to Islam. In his opinion, that was why Muslim people would hesitate to take part in such research. I tried to assure him that this would not be a hypothesis-testing type of study and that I was not inclined to judge the value of Islam through the practices of certain Muslims.

During the meeting my husband did not participate in the discussion, except during informal conversation, the aim of which was actually to get information about us. I deliberately use the term 'us', since there I was seen as a member, and a mother, of a respectable family, rather than just a female academic researcher. From a Muslim point of view being married with children is more important than anything else for a woman. My social position also 'proved' that I was a woman who was capable of carrying the responsibility of a family while trying to make a career. However, I do not want to speculate on whether I would not have been taken seriously if I had not been married. The point I am trying to make is that my social position as a wife and mother inevitably played an important role in facilitating my acceptance as an eligible person.

As the concluding point of our meeting the coordinator told me that he personally would like to help me. First, however, he had to consult with his friends on the matter, then he would let me know whether my request would be received favourably or not. At that moment a delay, if not a refusal, seemed inevitable to me, and I must admit that I was not particularly hopeful. But just as we were about to leave, there was a knock on the door and two prominent columnists from a daily newspaper unexpectedly arrived to visit him. From the way he introduced them to us they appeared very close friends. My host seemed really surprised at the timing of their visit: one of the columnists lived in the proposed area of study. The host proudly told me that this man's wife was the most suitable person to help me with my project since, in addition to her other social qualities, she was a university graduate. All of us were very pleased at this coincidence and our meeting continued for some time more so that I could explain my situation to the newcomers. Then the one who lived in the *site* told me to call him after two or three days by which time he would have told his wife about my request.

Three days later, when I called him at his office, he gave me his home number so that I could speak to his wife, saying that she would decide whether to assist me or not. The next day, I called his wife. She was polite, discreet, but assertive, and told me that her husband had informed her of my situation, and it seemed that he had found my case worthy of consideration. She also thought it would be worthwhile listening to me and she would like to meet me. She invited me to her house for the next afternoon.

II.3. The First Encounter

On 21 November 1989, I went for the first time to the *site* which was later to be my research field. Although the part of the city where the *site* was located was unfamiliar to me, it was not difficult to find, even though it was not on a main street. It was neither unusually protected, nor surrounded by high walls with a control gate. It was encircled by low cement walls topped with loose barbed wire which marked the borders of the *site*. In Turkey even children's playgrounds may be surrounded with barbed wire, so its existence here should not be understood as the overcautiousness or over-protection against outsiders which barbed wire often symbolizes. It may, however, be indicative of a certain understanding of aes-thetics, or more correctly a lack of it, but not necessarily of an understanding of an ascetic life.

At first glance, the *site* looked just like other ordinary, middle-range *sites*, which are to be found in many urban settlement areas with similar socio-economic backgrounds, and had a rather neat appearance. This should not, however, be understood as meaning that the *site* was of first-class construction quality. The only note-worthy physical difference distinguishing it from similar *sites* was the existence of a mosque located just across from the front entrance, though without a minaret. But a person approaching from the side entrance, as I was later to do, would not even notice that there was a mosque there. In subsequent years many *sites* appeared, especially in large cities, with a miniature minaret on top of one of their apartment buildings, but having a separate mosque was not common for a middle-range *site*.

Because I had not yet been given permission to carry out any research there, on the first occasion I did not want to examine every corner, but on my third visit there, on 26 November, I satisfied my curiosity somewhat by taking a short walk round when I arrived. The apartment blocks were painted in pale green and located more or less so as to form a crescent towards the middle of which a mosque was erected. Inside the block I entered, the apartments were located around a large octagonal courtyard whose roof was an angled dome made of glass. Since the blocks were twelve storeys high, the existence of this 'courtyard' gave a cold, distant feeling to this inner space, even though there were big green plants hanging casually from some floors. The sense of rising emptiness made one think that a monumental kind of impression, largely achieved through height, had been attempted at the entrance of the building. As I would see later, the same architectural design was repeated for each building block.

My first impression was that the purpose of this design, with both the blocks and the apartments inside them arranged in a circle, was in order to strengthen the sense of gathering around one thing or one idea. This settlement pattern may also be functional, in that the people on one floor could see the door of each apartment on that floor from their own door, and so none of them would 'turn their backs' on one another. This situation might also strengthen the sense of neighbourliness. Later on, I would learn that my early speculations corresponded very well to the 'real' imagery of both the founders and the architects of the *site*.

In the house to which I had been invited, a woman wearing an Islamic headscarf received me. She was the lady I was supposed to meet. She first introduced me to her children, then took me to the room in which she received guests. It was evident from everything that she had prepared her house and herself for a formal guest, and I really enjoyed her hospitality, as I always did in the following days and months.

During our meeting, especially when we were discussing my project, she made sure her oldest daughter was with us. She was about seventeen, attended the lycée section of an Imam Hatip school and seemed to be a dignified, highly articulate young person. She was also covered but seemed more outspoken than her mother. A feeling of empathy immediately developed between the daughter and me. The mother was not timid in communicating her opinions, though she had a very polite style, and she seemed, as one would expect for a woman of her age and social status, experienced enough not to reveal her feelings rapidly to a person whom she was meeting for the first time. I was not expecting to meet someone as perceptive as she was in comprehending the requirements of undertaking an ethno-sociological study. She was, however, very careful to try and make it clear that she would never want to be part of anything which could inflict even the smallest harm on Islam; it was her belief that the open-heartedness of Muslims has often been abused by people who want to use the good intentions of Muslims for their own purposes.

As a conversation opener, she first wanted me to tell her the aim of my study in detail, through which academic stages it would proceed, and by which channels I had arrived there, and how I had met her husband. On this last point, she was no less careful in learning the details than with the others. She was so quick to understand the sociological aim of the study, and to put it in its correct context, that I felt very comfortable in assuming that I could thoroughly convey my message.

She insistently underlined the point that the people in the *site* had nothing to hide, and that all they wanted to do was to 'live Islam'. They wished to be counted among the *sahih* (true) creatures of God, as conscious Muslims. They would therefore be pleased to help in the realization of a scientific (in her own terms *ilmî*)[7] study that, in her belief, would also be approved by God. They would never give their consent, however, if this study were to harm the Muslim community at large, or give rise to distorted views of the Muslims of that *site* in particular. In this respect, I tried to assure her that I would stay within the boundaries of sociological methods of study, and make an effort to apply the ethics of the profession.

I told her truthfully that I could not anticipate all the possible results of the study, but that she should have no doubt that I would show the maximum loyalty to the principles of impartiality at every stage. I also underlined the point that no one should expect a sociological study to praise the groups it studies, or to censure them. This study, however, would inevitably be filtered through my perceptions, which meant it would include my interpretations, reflexivity, and so on. But by and large, its realization would depend on my capacity to utilize sociological knowledge and insight. In this respect, I told her that in the process of data collection, for its reliability and validity, I would also need the collaboration of the interviewees, for example, in allowing me to use a tape recorder and in giving honest answers to my questions without maintaining a sense of suspicion. She promptly objected to my proposal that I record the interviews, for 'Muslim women would definitely reject letting their voices go out', i.e., they would not wish to be heard by strangers. I told her that I would be the only person who would hear the tape recordings but she persisted in her objection. I did not press the point since I thought insecurity might arise in many different ways, including the possibility that somehow particular voices might be recognized by others.

Another issue I wanted to make clear was that I was well aware of the responsibility she would assume in agreeing to assist me by helping to convince people to take part in this research: she would be the person introducing me to her community and initiating relationships between the inhabitants of the *site* and me. Besides, in the event of discontent over the way in which the research proceeded, she could jeopardize her reputation as a trustworthy member of the community.

She subsequently asked me, though apologizing a great deal, whether I possessed faith. I asked her to be more specific, so she asked whether I believed in God or not. My answer was positive. She wanted to learn how I believe in God. I once more asked her to clarify her question. She said what she wanted to know was whether I knew the five pillars of Islam. She herself recounted them, and immediately added that, of these five, the most important of all was *shahada* (*şehadet*, witness), which includes acknowledging the books God gave, the existence of His previous messengers, and believing in His oneness and that the Prophet Muhammad was His last messenger. I said yes, I believe that there is no God but God, and that Muhammad was His last messenger and I also believe that in the history of humankind, people must have experienced all the other revelations. She again apologized for asking all these questions but, as she hoped I would understand, she had to know what type of a person her community was dealing with, so that they could know how to express themselves. I assured her that her situation was very well understood, but that she should also know that I have a strong belief in the fact that none of God's creation, save He, has the right to intervene in the relationship between Him and me. She seemed to appreciate this point, and added that it was not for us to decide who was His true, *sahih*, believer or who was not. After that, she also made a comment about the way in which I had been raised, and her assessment was correct in that my religious identity had been shaped within the principles of secularism.

In the meantime, her younger sister, also covered, came in from shopping and joined us, and this led us to make some womanly small talk about rapidly changing women's fashions and rising prices while having our tea. It was impossible not to see how the younger sister showed respect for her older sister's opinions on matters social as well as religious. It seemed to me that, along with her authority in religious matters, this woman held an exalted social status not only in the eyes of her family but also in her community due to both her personal and professional qualifications.

My host also seemed impressed by my persistence in pursuing

a career after marrying at quite an early age and raising my children without quitting my education and job. She seemed really interested in this subject and asked me various detailed questions about how I had managed to achieve this, telling me she also wished to obtain her master's degree. She made me tell her about my master's thesis, which surveyed the role of children's picture books in Turkish as one of the important agents of socialization and studied them in terms of authority relations, gender roles, and the physical and social environment around which the narrative content of the stories was featured. Since this survey also covered religious children's picture books, my opinions on the subject aroused a deep interest in her. I think this also allowed her to make some preliminary assessments about the way in which I approached socio-religious matters and what I meant when I talked about the necessarily critical nature of sociological thinking.

All the conversation at this meeting should be construed as supplying the constitutive elements in building a mutual trust between us, enabling her to make a positive decision about my entry into the social milieu in which she lived. In other words, during this meeting both of us experienced an example of what Giddens calls 'fateful moments', in which 'the consequential decisions have to be taken or courses of action initiated' (1991, p. 243).

Towards the end of this meeting, we discussed the possibility of utilizing the techniques of random sampling in order to be able to collect data through in-depth interviews. She displayed a realistic grasp of this technique after listening to my explanations of what it would entail. She thought it would be very difficult to persuade every member of the households falling into the sample to cooperate because not everyone would have the same attitude towards the significance of such research or towards contributing to it. In her opinion, this might cost me a lot of time. As time passed, too, the possible defensive attitude of some might create a sense of discontent among the rest of the inhabitants, although their approach to the project might be positive at the beginning. She pointed out that people are very often hesitant to respond to even the most 'sterile' inquiries, such as marketing polls (seeing them as a burden), and that the families in this *site*, with their conservative nature, would not easily accept the idea of opening even some part of their private lives to an outsider. She added that this attitude would not be confined to Muslims but, as I should well know from my earlier experience as a sociologist, such indifference to the value of social research is common in many segments of society.

I did not doubt her sincerity and I was more or less in agreement with her judgements on the subject. But before telling her that there was another legitimate way of composing a sample, which is the technique I later applied (usually called the 'snowball' technique, through which a sample can be taken by going from one interviewee to another depending on a reference system formed by the participants themselves), I had to be sure that her primary intention in suggesting that I try to form my sample out of certain people who would be likely to consent to an interview was not to control each step of my research. That this was not her intention was evident from her careful assessment of her own capacity to collect a sufficient number of people to form an adequate sample. She suggested that she should be the first interviewee, so that it would be easier for her to explain it to the others. We made an appointment for a few days later, 24 November 1989.

When I was about to leave she asked her daughter to accompany me in case my unfamiliarity with the area prevented me from finding the bus stop. Her daughter seemed quite willing, telling me that since she was accustomed to the neighbourhood, it was no problem for her to go out in the dark. On the way to the bus stop she cheerfully told me how lucky she thought it was particularly for young girls to live there, and how her school friends fancied life in the *site* because of the harmonious relations between neighbours, the outcome of their common understanding of Islamic life. Not fearing the molestation of strange men was her first example of the comfortable life they enjoyed there – a suitable subject as we passed through badly-lit narrow side streets to reach the main one. In her opinion, people of this neighbourhood generally, not necessarily people from the *site*, knew from these girls' appearance where they were from and what type of lifestyle they had chosen, something for which almost everybody showed respect.

She also gave me some examples of the customs the inhabitants of the *site* had invented and developed while leading their lives so as to become true Muslims. These were points on which I would later have the opportunity to make my own observations during the course of my research, and which I would be able to incorporate into my analysis of the efforts that these people made to create an Islamic way of life.

What this little walk taught me was that one could learn a great deal from even the smallest encounter with the inhabitants of this place, and thus I had to record every moment of my presence in the field. As was the case in this conversation, every dialogue might very well provide some information about the way in which situational explanations could be maintained. More important, as Bourdieu (1989) argues, these might be seen as reflections of the 'strategy generating principles' produced and reproduced by a group of people to form a commonsensical world, in which 'harmonizations of agents' experiences' are 'orchestrated' according to an achieved consensus on the meanings of the practices in that world. These, however, as Bourdieu stresses, should not be conceived as 'the products of a genuine strategic intention but transposable dispositions which enable people to cope with the unforeseen future and the ever-changing situations while transforming the past effect into the expected objective', namely 'habitus', in the sense Bourdieu proposes the term, through which 'the dispositions of those [practices] can be traced as embedded in the aspirations and world-views they express'.[8]

On my second visit to the family's house on 24 November, I was received with warm kindness and joy. The whole family, apart from the father, was there, and except for the questionnaire on demographic data, we could only complete part of the interview but had a great deal of fun. The mother especially seemed very interested in the questions and enjoyed pondering while trying to answer them, which provided her with an opportunity to review the family's lives and pursuits in constructing an Islamic way of life.

Having my first experience in a friendly and unceremonious atmosphere helped me greatly in making up my mind as to how to proceed in the following days, in the sense of seeing which questions were to be abandoned as redundant, how I should articulate certain questions during the course of an interview, which subjects I should approach with a certain sensitivity so as not to irritate people, and so on. At the end of this meeting the mother invited me to a wedding ceremony due to take place in the common room of the complex two days later, on Sunday, when she thought she would be able to introduce me to some other women. This would be better than trying to see them separately and arrange appointments with them one by one. I gratefully accepted this invitation: along with the opportunity to participate in a wedding ceremony, a chance for an invaluable observation of a very important cultural ritual, I might also be able to start assembling my sample.

That Sunday we met at their apartment late in the morning to go to the wedding, which would be held at 11 a.m. At the wedding, as the mother had anticipated, I was able to arrange appointments with five women who already seemed well informed about me and my project. Instead of asking specific questions, they just let me know which day would be suitable for them and gave either their phone numbers or addresses.

It was quite a busy day: after the wedding my hosts decided to take me to a play that afternoon in a cinema building in the same neighbourhood. It was called *Kara Geceler Efendim* ('Dark Nights, Sir', an allegorically transformed version of the phrase, 'Good night, sir'). The play was directed and chiefly performed by Ulvi Alacakaptan, a talented young man of the theatre. The nephew of a prominent republican lawyer, he had been known as a leftist and had then converted to Islam after the 1980s. After the play, I went back to my hosts' home: they had invited me for a Sunday snack but this turned out to be almost a feast, the first of many. As it was Sunday, the father was also at home, and he participated in our conversation and the part of the interview we had not been able to finish on the last occasion. When I left their apartment late in the evening, still without having completed the interview, I had to refuse their invitation to stay and continue our conversation, not necessarily just to finish the interview, because I had to fetch an Indian anthropologist friend from the railway station.

That night, I had to decide on the technicalities of research in terms of data collection, and register the data I had already obtained through making some participant observations, a half-finished in-depth interview, and a completed questionnaire. Because I was not allowed to use a tape recorder, I would have to use notebooks for the interviews, which led me to develop certain techniques for the arrangement of data recording and to improve my writing speed. I would have to pay great attention to not skipping anything in order to be able to capture interviewees' explanations in their own words, as well as their ways of expression, since these constitute and display the most important elements of a specific discourse.

In the following days, I also backed up my data collection by tape recording my experiences, observations and impressions when I returned from the field, so that I could immediately register the emotional, as well as the factual, side of my experiences. Nevertheless, I must say that there were times when emotional fatigue discouraged me from recounting my experiences in this way, and I would leave them to 'cool' until I recovered as much as possible and put them together in written form.

In the following twenty-eight months, I intermittently continued my research depending on the tightness of my teaching schedule (along with the other time-consuming requirements of academic activity) and, more importantly, the political developments dominating the public agenda in Turkey which deepened the cleavages between the secular and Islamic sections of society and affected the attitude of would-be participants in the research.[9] Here, I must also mention the importance of the Gulf War of 1990–1, which placed new social pressures on Islamic activists the world over and augmented the reservations of the inhabitants of this *site* as well.[10]

Personal dispositions as well as objective societal conditions sometimes hindered the progress of the research. I met with unopened doors in spite of having an appointment and I had to deal with people who pretended they would be interviewed but cancelled the appointment the day before.

Similarly, my own attitude of remaining faithful to my principles meant the loss of an opportunity to broaden the size of my sample. For instance, I was told that I had been criticized for not joining in the prayers when we were in the mosque, and for not even opening my hands to say 'Amin' (Amen) during *tefsir* (*tafsir*, Koran commentary) studies. In this context, I was trying to demonstrate that I was not there to worship, but to carry out research. Except for the times when the Koran was recited or we were in the mosque, I did not cover my head. This, however, did not constitute a point of criticism since, as people gladly told me many times, I was seen as respectful enough towards them and their way of life, though without compromising my own identity. They neither expected a woman to cover her head if she did not wish to do so, nor did they have a policy of exclusion for uncovered women. A woman wearing a mini-skirt or a low-cut blouse, however, would never be taken seriously – as would also be the case with many of conservative outlook in Turkey.[11]

My strategy for preserving my identity was quite simple and can be summed up in one word: openness. First, I always gave true information about me and my family, as well as my academic life. Second, I tried to be open as far as I could in communicating my ideas and opinions on any subject when asked. However, I also tried to remain true to my position of participant-observer and interviewer by refraining from imposing my own values and ideas on others, especially in the course of interviews. It did not prevent me, of course, from sometimes asking questions which they found controversial.

Nevertheless, after a while it became common knowledge that I saw the secondary position women usually occupy in almost all social systems as open to question. In fact, my discontent concerning the position of women in society was told and retold, together with an anecdote about something which had happened after a session of *tefsir* study. After having spent long hours on the details of the fourth sura of the Koran – 'Nisa' (Women) – in a very crowded room ringing from time to time with small children's screams, a few women remained and started to make additional comments on the subject. One of these women, a very well educated preacher, began enthusiastically to explain to me how the wrongdoings of men against women would be punished by God. When she maintained that misogynists would be turned over to suffer in His Hell, I sighed quite tiredly and said, 'Amin, inşallah' (Amen, if God wills), without having given much thought to my words. My unexpected reaction made the women burst into laughter and I realized what I had said. Later on, that little story was recalled in various circumstances as a sign of my sincerity on the subject: with them I never said 'Amin' after any prayer, except for that 'specific one'.

The extent to which I set the limits of my policy of openness was determined within the boundaries of my habit of always addressing adults with the polite Turkish second plural person pronoun *siz* (you), without making any distinction in terms of age, sex and status, and suffixing their names with the courtesy titles of *Bey* and *Hanım* (Mr and Mrs). Likewise, I myself was always thus addressed. I sometimes observed that this made some women query the friendly relationship established between us, but they showed respect for this tacit agreement, which came into being as a consequence of the efforts that I made to stress the researcher side of my identity.

There was another issue which emerged as crucial during my attempts to carry out this research. This was the need to comprehend the parameters of prevailing power relations in the community, through which diverse actors played roles in different capacities. However, that this could set obstacles in enlarging the research sample came to my knowledge only after I had observed that the differences in prestige in which the notables of this *site* were held affected the type of power they exercised regarding the determination of the scope of activities and also the attitude of the inhabitants toward 'outsiders'.

II.4. Contesting the Status of Prestige among the Community Élite

I noticed that the conflicting levels of prestige among the élite of the *site* were due to differences between those who were among the inner circle of the Zahid Kotku branch of the Nakşibendi order led by Esat Coşan and those whose prestige had been attained through an articulate religious education and their social and political involvement in the formation of an Islamic way of life, without necessarily being an adherent of the order. Although people who constituted the latter group usually owed their political allegiance to the WP, this did not prevent them from showing veneration to that religious order or others, nor did it inhibit their adherence to it or similar orders. However, since the legitimacy of their prestige was not contingent upon a spiritual perfection attained through the Sufi *tariqa* (*tarikat*, path), they could only claim legitimacy for their religious authority on the basis of those aspects of religion which provide guidance for Muslims in leading their social lives according to Islamic precepts. In other words, their religious skills fell short of a claim to guide Muslims on the esoteric paths of Islam which lead to attainment of the ultimate truth, and nor would they ever intend to make such a claim.[12]

But this group among the élite could make the voice of Muslim people heard in the country's political arena through access to the vehicles of parliamentary politics, whereas the notables of the religious order exercised political power by being morally influential in the larger echelons of right-wing politics.[13] Nevertheless, the former have always been criticized by the latter for aligning themselves with the opponents of Islamic politics in the course of parliamentary life and for straying from the path of Islam by becoming part of the secular parliamentary political system.[14]

In the context of the *site*, people who were from the inner circle of the religious order seemed more likely to display inward-looking behaviour in their attitudes towards outsiders than the politically identified groups. The reasons for this are manifold, but the important point here is that since my entry to the field was through people who did not belong to this inner circle, the important affiliates of the order might have thought that their authority was being undermined and their pre-eminence over the other members of the community denied. Whatever the reason, women belonging to the inner circle of the order tended not to agree to be interviewed.

This became clear after I had been introduced to this group by a woman who had already been interviewed, despite being an adherent of the order, and who was the daughter of an ex-deputy of the banned NSP. Following the rules of snowball sampling, she took me to a reception held by one of her friends where I could meet with women who might consent to being interviewed. There I felt like an intruder, someone demanding something precious (their privacy) without offering anything equal in return. The hostess and her guests were circumspect in their attitude towards me, especially those who had closer affinity with the higher ranks of the order than the lay adherents. Of course, I was not in a position to determine exactly who was who at the beginning, but during the course of the meeting – either from their explicit assertions or from their implicit attitudes – the social status and identity of almost all were revealed. I do not mean to suggest that this meeting did not provide me with a very rich source of information, or that I was excluded from participating in some very useful arguments and friendly conversations, but rather that in the end I was not successful in persuading these women to become interviewees for my research.

The very first explanation these women gave as a reason for their unwillingness to collaborate was the amount of time the project would require from them. Other objections poured forth simultaneously at this point, as if they were building some kind of totem to maintain the argument. Some women clearly stated that, as dutiful housewives and pious Muslims, they would prefer to spend their time on their families and religious duties, instead of wasting it on something which was inconsequential for them. For others, the likelihood of being recognized, hence failing to protect the privacy of their family lives – something of sacred importance for them – was the main objection. The necessity of obtaining the consent of their husbands, and their possible disagreement, was another objection that some of them used. Generally, they did not hesitate to say that they saw no point in participation in the project. In fact, they seemed sufficiently prejudiced against it to imply that it might even harm them. In this respect, some of them recounted the treatment of Muslims by the media and the way in which they had suffered certain experiences as a result of being open-hearted to all. As one young and well-educated woman indicated, however meticulous I was in reflecting reality, others could easily use my results in a distorted way to blacken Muslims.

While these arguments were being put forward, one fairly young woman (who held the most venerated position due to her family ties) did not explicitly confront me, but mostly kept her silence, except to show the occasional gesture of approval – nodding or joining in the others' collective mumblings with one or two words such as 'yes' or 'sure'. However, as could be expected from a person of such status, she was the one to put an end to our debate. She said that although she also saw no possibility of personal participation in the project, she would of course like to have me as a guest at her receptions, and, if I liked, it would be their pleasure to see me at more of their gatherings and public meetings. She added that, in the meantime, 'some of our sisters' might like to think about the subject again, and would let me know whether they agreed to my request.

By saying these things, first, she confirmed her position of exalted status through her benevolence, to the extent that she treated me as a guest; she did not show an attitude of total exclusion, and observed the rules common to both the Turkish and Muslim traditions of hospitality. Second, she affirmed an image of fair patronage in setting her clients free to make their 'own' decisions. Although she might have been completely sincere in her intentions, the message she conveyed was inevitably read as disapproval, insofar as what she did and would do was seen as something to be followed as a model.[15] Her attitude of 'setting the others free', and the extent to which her overall argument was built upon the excuse of insufficient time, prevented any controversy between the women who had already agreed to be interviewed or who were would-be interviewees, and the others who rejected the idea. Thus the former would not be suspected of acting in a way which threatened the harmony and the security of their shared ideals of living Islam as true Muslims in the same living space.

By emphasizing the time constraints, the group of women who refused to be interviewed were able to convey their message by implication: this project could be seen as something not worth spending time on, and anyone spending time on it would either kill or fill that time with nonsense. In this argument, consciously or unconsciously, time played a central role in the expression of their sentiments: time is a concept open to almost all kinds of association with life itself. Both are used interchangeably to indicate the state of existence or, in other words, the state of occupying a place on earth. As Lakoff and Johnson (1980) argue, time is a concept which is metaphorically conceptualized in terms of space and it is space that shapes the ways in which we will live our natural experiences. I argue that time is also intrinsic to our natural experiences, insofar as they are embedded in space as bounded by time.

Using the metaphorical potentials of the concept, it was possible to understand that, by spending time on the project, these women would be allowing someone to intrude on their life space, and that this, through the non-constructive use of time, might count as losing a piece of life. But the waste of time as such was not the only point at stake. Even worse was the implication that by filling it with something potentially harmful, a piece of their life would be tainted. Here, the question to be asked was, of course, where this feeling of contamination came from. The answer came as a result of later experiences acquired in the field. At the time it was just something I sensed, and not without feeling humiliated.

The fear of contamination is an issue which parallels the effort of building up a true Muslim identity. This is an effort which entails a moral purification which should not be hindered by any non-Islamic, primarily Western, intrusions. Although this is valid for all 'Islamic' people, regardless of whether they are members of a religious order, those attached to religious orders pay much more attention to it as a consequence of the necessity of observing rules set by their spiritual guide. The more they devote themselves to religious duties, the more they can preserve their concentration on religion, which enables them to improve their spiritual development. This includes avoidance of collaboration with faithless people as far as possible, a practice more easily observed by women than men, who, in their position as family breadwinners, are supposed to be in close relation with the outside world.

The tendency to seclusion, which sometimes conflicts with the behaviour and activities of other 'conscious' Muslims, is tolerated insofar as it is perceived as one of the requirements of Sufi studentship (Schimmel 1986). Yet, this difference in attitude, which indicates the existence of potentially different world-views, may constitute a point of conflict among those who call themselves conscious Muslims, even if it is ultimately perceived by them as a slight one.

What is of interest here is that none of the women explicitly mentioned the worry of prosecution. The state can theoretically accuse them of violation of the Criminal Code, which prohibits, amongst other things, participation in the rites of a Sufi order. They behaved instead as if they had no sense that they were doing anything illegal that might disturb the public peace and the order of society, and were simply fulfilling the requirements of their religion. To refer to the possibility of prosecution would, of course, be to cast doubt on their behaviour and they thus avoided all mention of it, preferring instead to refer to the framework of the state's unjust treatment of Muslims.

In this specific instance, the women's argument for not helping in my project was based on 'lack of time', but they also revealed, through their reference to the harm which they thought this project could cause, a feeling of suspicion. In sum, their objection to taking part in my project was built on multifaceted arguments covering many aspects of Muslim people's discontent with their perceived conditions in this society. Here one of the most crucial points is why some of them assessed the project as a new threat while others did not. In this respect, I will go on to argue that the fact that they held different views concerning the relations they should have with secular people closely reflected the group dynamics of the inhabitants of the *site* as a whole: they aimed to build their social status on different forms of authority relations.

When I left the reception, however, I was full of mixed feelings about the reasons for being rejected, blaming myself more than anyone else, and thinking that I had not prepared myself for such a rejection. My warm acceptance at the beginning of the research by a few women who had kindly agreed to be interviewed had led me optimistically to expect the rest of the research to continue in the same fashion. I felt strongly that I had to be more assertive and put much more effort into persuading these women than I had done so far. Of course, at the reception I had not merely limited myself to observation – on the contrary, I had tried to make my own points – but ultimately I did not want to be in the position of forcing them to change their minds. I tried to understand why and how such an attitude of resistance had emerged. Yet, on the hour-long bus journey home, I was really worried this meeting might determine the whole future of my project and put an end to it.

A few days later, I called the lady who had provided my entry to the field to let her know what had happened at the meeting as well as to talk about the other appointments she had arranged for me. It seemed that she also found the women's attitude of rejection surprising, but she made sure to treat it as calmly as I was trying to do as I told her about the situation on the phone. Although I avoided being judgemental, I did not hide the fact that I was sad that some of the women had treated my project as something potentially harmful.

Over the next few days, I was able to accomplish two more interviews. Towards the end of the second, my initial contact came to join us since the woman I was interviewing was one of her close friends. I knew that that night Esat Coşan[16] would come from Istanbul and give a sermon in the mosque. Since I was menstruating I would not be allowed, according to Islam, to enter the mosque and I felt I should let her know my predicament. I did this because of my preference for not abusing the beliefs of the women who trusted me and to show respect for their rules of religious observance and their way of life. As a result, I was able to learn what kind of arrangements these people had made in order not to exclude women from important events when their physiological situation hindered their participation.[17]

For those specific situations, and probably for other reasons too, a public address system had been installed in one of the apartments for simultaneous broadcast of sermons from the mosque. This apartment belonged to one of Esat Coşan's close relations, the young woman of high status whom I had met at the reception a few days earlier. On the way there, my last interviewee decided to join some other women going to the mosque. When the lady (my initial contact) who was taking me to the meeting tried to insist on her coming with us, she replied that it would be better for her to join the other women because she did not want to put the owners of the apartment to any trouble, thus avoiding any pretence that she was a good friend of the people in the apartment. Although it was said that these meetings were open to every woman, her attitude made me think that not all women felt free to knock on the door, but rather just those who felt sufficiently close to these people.[18]

When we arrived the door was opened by the woman whom I knew from the reception. Although a fleeting expression of surprise passed across her face, when she saw that I was with the lady who had initiated my entry to the *site*, she invited both of us in and my companion told her why we were there. She said she was pleased to have us and took us to the room where women were gathered to listen to the sermon. Other women whom I knew from the reception were there and they too seemed surprised to see me, and greeted both my friend and me in a cool manner. When the sermon finished the women inquired after each other's and their families' health, and my friend explained briefly to everybody why we were there in particular and told them about my presence in the *site* in general. She also explained to them why she had agreed to help me in my project and how she thought that certain 'serious academic projects', such as mine, could help people to see that Muslims' only aim is to serve Islam and their only wish is to gain the blessings of God. She said she thought that Muslim women had a responsibility to explain themselves to those who do not know their real conditions of existence, their aims and intentions, in order to prevent the unfounded rumours circulating about them, especially with regard to why they cover their heads.

On account of her professional role she was quite accustomed to talking convincingly to the women on any subject, but this time she realized that her task would be harder in light of the pre-determined ideas of these women which made them unyielding in the defence of their position. I observed her falter slightly as she took further steps to try and convince them, using a humorous style to describe her reasons for participation in the project.[19] This might have helped ease the atmosphere, but unfortunately it did not work. But she was contained enough not to show defeat. She behaved as if her intention were merely to use this opportunity to explain why she had agreed to help me and to let more women hear about the project. The primary purpose of our visit had indeed been to listen to Esat Coşan and I had had no idea that she would talk about my project and defend it in front of everyone. This time I deliberately did not talk much, except when I thought that my explanations were necessary. I saw no use in restarting the whole process, observing that the same women were recalling the same arguments; moreover, I have never liked to be seen as a pushy person who imposes herself on others despite their explicit reluc-tance. In addition, it was my companion, not I, who decided to initiate the conversation.

When we were leaving, a middle-aged lady, who had so far stayed quite still, came over to us. This was a gesture towards my friend to show that she was still respected in spite of her divergent views on the subject in question. She kindly inquired as to my friend's family's health and asked after all her children one by one, recalling their names, asking how school was going, as well as how her husband's business was, and so on. This was more than just the formalities usually shown to a guest. Her attitude towards my friend was different from her attitude towards the others, who would have been very glad to be exposed to her interest due to her special affinity with Professor Coşan. It was clear that she wanted to show that she valued my friend and her efforts to disseminate the message of Islam. She also assured my friend that she should always know that her efforts were very much acknowledged by the present company, and that they always prayed for women like her who humbly devoted their lives to the service of God. Then she turned to me and quite softly said that she was very pleased to meet me and that, although these ladies did not want to be interviewed, their doors would always be open to me as a guest. It seemed that she was trying to make amends for any problems I may have had due to my earlier rejection. Since this happened in front of many women as they left the apartment after the meeting, her behaviour almost functioned as a restoration of my credit.

On the way back to my friend's apartment, we did not make any comment on the meeting. However, as we were about to part, she quite openly said, 'Now I understood what you went through at that reception, since I think this evening I also experienced the same feelings you probably experienced when you were rejected.' The tone of her voice was so sympathetic that no one could miss that she really was quite sorry. She also added that I was right when I commented that the refusal might have been a result of having done something wrong in terms of undermining the authority of the inner circle of the *site*. It seemed that she agreed with me when she said, 'I guess we were expected to ask them for permission before commencing the research. Now I am afraid we were perceived as having been unruly in bypassing them.' 'Anyway,' she said, 'everything will depend on the will of God, and if He closes one door, He opens another, and no one other than He knows what is auspicious for us and what is not.' She also reminded me that if she had not believed that I was sincere in my comprehension of the conditions under which certain believers in this country lead their lives and how they try to follow the rules of Islam in their everyday life, she would not have agreed to help me. After all, she said, she had decided to help me for nothing but the mercy of God, and we had nothing to trust other than a hope for His blessings in trying to pursue the accomplishment of any project. As a last point she warmly thanked me for having faced all this with a certain understanding and for having preserved my attitude of respect to all of them, and for not having made this situation an issue. I told her that it was my job to thank her for the trust she showed me and my project by seeing it as worthy enough to be defended. And I immediately added that, after all, this experience would constitute one of the most important parts of my research, and that I would incorporate this whole process into my analysis. She laughed and said, 'Nothing can prevent you making observations, can it?' and added, 'So I will try to get used to it and look at the matter from your perspective. I hope you will also become able to see things from our perspective and, with the help of God, none of us will stray from correctness when trying to accomplish this study, nor do anything wrong which will blacken our reputation.'

From then on, I continued my research with the women who had willingly agreed to be interviewed, including one young newly-wed who belonged to a rather prosperous religious family from a historically significant city in the Marmara region whom I had met at the reception. Through her, I also interviewed a friend of hers. Thus the end result of the reception was not as unproductive as I had feared in terms of forming the sample. In addition to other experiences I had at the *site*, the reception provided me with an invaluable opportunity to observe incidents of controversy at the personal level, the existence of which is usually denied by these Muslim people.

In what follows I will describe the methods and research techniques upon which this study was based and the way in which I conducted the rest of the research, and also how the study expanded into new areas of participant observation, something that I had not initially planned.

II.5. The Fieldwork, Methods and Strategies

Considering the specific context in which the research was to be carried out, as I have tried to explain, the use of relevant sociological and ethno-sociological research techniques emerged as an important issue. I decided to employ a multiplicity of techniques that included a survey questionnaire, in-depth interviews, focus group interviews and participant observation.

The survey questionnaire and interviews took the family as the unit of study, and I applied them to twenty-five families (out of 300 households). These families were inevitably chosen by snowball sampling due to the highly suspicious attitude of the population towards secular people. Although interviews were mostly carried out with women, the questions and issues covered all the family members, which accounted for 120 people, and in most cases teenage daughters of these women also participated in the interviews. Additionally, I usually encountered the husbands and had the opportunity to talk with them on the matters covered in the interviews. However, men interviewed only made up 20 per cent of the sample. These were mainly highly influential members of the community.

The survey questionnaire provided for data on the demographic characteristics of the sample such as age, sex, place of birth, marital status and marriage, family type, educational and professional status, migration patterns, and also the past and present socio-economic conditions of the families.

In-depth interviews, which tended to last between five and seven hours, were designed to explore the extent to which Islam determines and shapes the present and future aspirations and expectations of these people, as well as the ways in which Islam gives direction and organization to both their daily lives and various sorts of sociability. The issues which constituted the framework of the interview covered the organization of home life and division of labour in the family (both between spouses and between parents and children); cultural formation of relations of intimacy, family-planning, education and child socialization; patterns of book, jour-nal- and newspaper-reading, and television-watching; recreational and social activities; ways of using urban spaces; patterns of forming relationships with various social institutions; neighbour patterns; and the nature of worshipping practices. The interview also covered the views of the participants on many political and economic issues, such as the government's economic and social policies and the general state of politics in Turkey. How they saw their present and future situations in the society, and what kind of difficulties they faced while trying to realize an Islamic way of life in a secular social order, also constituted other important aspects of the interview.

In focus group interviews, I tried to organize open-structured discussions of the more general but critical issues of expected life order. Depending on the attitude of the participants, these interviews could turn out to be a loosely ordered conversation or a tightly organized discussion session on a specific subject. In sum, four focus group interviews were undertaken to gather information on various subjects: one was with only six adult men, one was organ-ized as a mixture of adult women and young girls (total eleven), and the other two were with adult women (six and eight). These groups also included people who did not live in the *site*, but who had close relationships with the inhabitants and shared the same ideals.

Participant observation constituted the most strategic aspect of this project, in terms of both acquiring information and experience of the various areas of sociability and gaining the insight necessary to follow their local discourse. In this context, I participated in several social and religious activities, such as attending Islamic theatrical performances, wedding and engagement ceremonies, seminars (either open to both men and women, or women only), and joined periodic reception days for women, some activities of the Association of Ladies' Voices (Hanımların Sesi Derneği), women's *tefsir* studies, and the Koran courses taught by female preachers who lived in the *site*. I participated in a series of *kandil* celebrations (five Muslim feasts, celebrating the Prophet Muham-mad's conception and birth (Regaib and Mevlud), the secret night he first received God's revelation (Berat), his night ascent (Miraç), and the 'Night of Power' (Kadir Gecesi)), which were organized in the largest mosque of the city (Kocatepe Cami) by the most influen-tial female preachers in Ankara. These celebrations, bringing together around five thousand women, are very important social activities. The content of the sermons is particularly noteworthy for the dissemination of Islamic ideals, the preachers themselves referring to the gatherings as occasions for *irshad* (*irşad*, a term used to mean teaching the right way, offering guidance on how to act, and the like). I visited a private school well thought of among Muslims in Ankara, established in order to give a specific formal secondary level education in line with their religious ideals. This was the most popular Islamist private school, a boarding school for primary and secondary education, used not only by 'Islamist' but also by migrant workers, working in Germany for example, who want to be sure that their children are protected from the undesirable effects of modern urban life and learn their religion and customs. There I also had the chance to attend one of the first fashion shows at a time when it was not yet public knowledge that they were being organized in Islamic circles.

Finally, for the other important aspect of the project, I surveyed a series of literary publications, television programmes, and movies on video in order better to evaluate the discourses that partly shape the imagery of the inhabitants of the *site*. Phone calls and a number of friendly visits also served as important means to deepen my understanding of the way in which the people I studied think and behave in different circumstances and the ways in which they look at both themselves and the world in their quest to cultivate a separate identity (different from other Sunni Muslims who adopted the code of secularism) and, so they claim, to live Islam as 'conscious' Muslims.

Notes

[1] As Esposito argues, although there is an ongoing debate about the rule of Islamic modesty, which actually takes its final shape according to customary practice in Muslim societies (all of which have brought their own interpretation to the subject throughout history, especially with regard to the veiling and seclusion of women, and adopted different norms as their customary laws), the prevailing practice in any specific culture tends to be seen as unalterable. In contrast to such ideological assertions, however, even within one Muslim country, there have always been different groups who advocate different codes of Islamic dress as the most convenient one according to Koranic prescriptions (Esposito 1991, pp. 98–9).

For recently adopted diverse styles of Islamic codes of modesty in modern Turkey see, for example, Olson (1985, p. 161).

[2] I do not give the name of the *site* here in order to protect its identity.

[3] For instance, as I have shown in the Introduction, Esposito argues that calling Muslims Islamic fundamentalists opposed to any possibility of secularizing Islam (since for them Islam is an entirety in which the mundane and the divine cannot be governed separately) is an extension of a Western view arising from an orientalist ideological standpoint through which Islamic activists are shown as extremists, fanatics, terrorists, etc.; see 'Contemporary Islam: Reformation or Revolution' (Esposito 1992, pp. 7–24).

[4] For example, in her study of various groups of *gecekondu* people in Ankara, Güneş-Ayata observed that the problem of social control appeared an important subject for the construction and maintenance of social identity. She argues that the various patterns of solidarity developed in *gecekondu* areas (depending on patriarchal, ethnic and religious customs and the effort to protect economic interests) become a crucial issue for the *gecekondu* people where protecting their privacy is concerned since they mainly build their strategies of survival upon it. Therefore they avoid talking about their privacy with the motive of preserving their sense of solidarity, which is acquired through different channels of social control. Thus protecting both their own and their neighbours' privacy becomes the most important manifestation of that solidarity (1990–91, pp. 89–101).

[5] Turkey has witnessed a series of assassinations, most of which were said to have been carried out by extremist Islamic groups. Professor Muammer Aksoy, an Atatürkist professor of law, was killed in January 1990; Çetin Emeç, the coordinator and chief columnist of the liberal rightist daily *Hürriyet*, was killed in March 1990; and Turan Dursun, a former religious officer and a writer known for his rather harsh pro-Marxist criticisms of Islam, was killed in September 1990. Professor Bahriye Üçok was killed in October 1990. She was one of the rare female professors of the Faculty of Theology, Ankara University and a prominent figure in Turkish parliamentary life. The social tension between secularist and Islamist due to these assassinations reached its apex in 1993 with the murder of Uğur Mumcu, on 24 January. He was one of the most prominent columnists in Turkey and his proficiency in political matters was acknowledged by every faction of the Turkish polity and society. Last but not the least was the murder of thirty-seven people in the upheaval during the Pir Sultan Abdal Festival celebrated in July 1993, in Sivas.

[6] See Appendix I.

[7] Tapper and Tapper argue that the term *ilm*, which denotes religious science and knowledge, was replaced by *bilim*, that is, secular scientific knowledge, in the education system of the Republic. For a discussion of

the difference between *ilm* and *ma'rifa* (one refers to theoretical, scientific, analytical knowledge learnt from a text by memorization, the other to personal, practical and holistic knowledge derived from experience and intuition) and how they both differ from *bilim* in the republican Turkish context, see Tapper and Tapper (1991, pp.71–5). For a general discussion on the subject see Eickelman (1978).

[8] Bourdieu develops this argument in *Outline of a Theory of Practice*, first published in 1977. See Bourdieu (1989, pp. 72–95 passim, and notes 1 and 2).

[9] See note 5.

[10] The eruption of the Gulf War served to increase the social pressures felt in Islamic circles, who saw it as the start of the US intervention in Islamic activism in the region. For an analysis of the impact of the Gulf War on Turkish foreign policy see, for example, Sayarı (1992).

[11] For example, during interviews or attending social activities and the like, I never wore my hair down, but made sure it was tied back in a pony-tail or more frequently a form of knot. When people from the *site* came to visit me at my home, I wore it down as I usually do since I did not want to give a false impression of my usual physical appearance. As for my way of dress, I preferred to wear long loose skirts (not unfamiliar to my style), but never my jeans in their presence since wearing trousers in public places is one of the most unwomanly things for women in Islamic circles. Females, especially young girls, sometimes do wear jeans in their home environments but usually do not go out wearing them even if they cannot be seen or noticed under their long loose overcoats. These were the basic efforts I made in order to achieve an acceptable appearance in their eyes. They were aware that I was trying to take care to be respectful of their moral codes and I believe my efforts were positively evaluated. Besides, I was trying to avoid distracting them with my appearance, which could have disturbed both their and my concentration in the course of interviews. There were even moments when women made kind comments about my clothes or expressed their compliments, and we exchanged information about where something could be bought which would appeal to their tastes without being objectionable in terms of the rules of Islamic modesty.

[12] For a detailed discussion of the rules of adhering to a religious order see, for example, Schimmel (1986, pp. 3–23).

[13] This is a point which is extensively discussed by some observers of Turkish political life. See, for example, Ahmad (1991, pp. 3–22), Acar (1993, pp. 225–32), Mardin (1989b; 1991a) Sarıbay (1985a; 1985b), Toprak (1981).

[14] Çakır gives detailed information about the emergence of a dispute between the leading cadres of the WP and the Esat Coşan branch of the

Nakşibendi order before the 1991 national election as well as its historical roots. Esat Coşan is the son-in-law of Zahid Kotku who led a branch of the order. Upon his death an offshoot of the Zahid Kotku branch formed around Coşan. Although, as is very well known, the members of the leading cadres of the WP, especially its leader, Necmettin Erbakan, were both inspired and supported in their entry into active politics by Zahid Kotku and owed their moral strength to him (since this entailed their recognition by large portions of religious sections of the society), they did not follow Esat Coşan. See R. Çakır (1991, pp. 18–54 and 214–25). Before the 1980 military take-over a similar dispute appeared between the NSP, which was also under the leadership of Erbakan, and various religious orders including the Nakşibendi, and this dispute is said to have been highly costly to the party later, leading it to lose a considerable amount of voting support, particularly in Eastern Anatolia. For this point, see Sarıbay (1985a).

[15] It should be noted that a person having a kinship tie or a close affinity with a *wali* (*veli*, saint, friend of God) or *shaykh* (*şeyh*, spiritual guide) is not automatically granted authority to exercise power over others, and similarly there is no necessity for others to heed the words or follow the behaviour patterns of this person. But as was evident in this case, insofar as these people show themselves to be mindful of their social positions and manage to gain the respect of others, their words and deeds constitute a model for others since they are already perceived as blessed persons, and their ascribed status is something to be admired by the lay adherents of the order.

[16] At the time Professor Esat Coşan (d. 2001) lived in Istanbul. He was the leader of the Zahid Kotku branch of the Nakşibendi order, which is known to be based in the Iskender Paşa Camii in Istanbul where Zahid Kotku once lived and was the imam. Since Coşan's relatives lived in this *site*, it was possible for the inhabitants of this complex to encounter him and to enjoy the privilege of having him in their mosque to give a sermon. When this happened, it was common to see hundreds of people from different parts of Central Anatolia come to Ankara in order to listen to him.

[17] In Islam the first condition of being able to perform any prayer is the necessity of being in a state of canonical purity, i.e., having performed one's ablutions. Without performing ablutions, no one is allowed to pray, to read the Koran, to perform the ritual prayers five times a day (*namaz*) or to enter a mosque or other holy places. Micturation, excretion, sexual relations and menstruation are the main reasons for the loss of purity, requiring the renewal of ablution. Therefore, since women cannot perform their ablutions during menstruation, this prevents them from performing all their religious duties. In other words, during menstruation, as well as

during the childbirth period, they are excused from their ritual obligations and to break this rule is a sin. As can be seen, since ablution is a matter of personal responsibility, trust is seen as essential for relationships between Muslims; no one inquires about others' ablutions, except for parents and elders who feel themselves obliged to ensure the compliance of young people with the rules of religious obligations.

[18] It should be remembered that this type of gathering is arranged mainly for a specific reason and aims to provide an opportunity for women who cannot attend the mosque because of their physiological situation (see note 17). However, the real reason why the women of the religious leader's family listened to the sermons from home may have been simply that they preferred the comfort of home to the crowded mosque.

[19] For example, in her explanation of why she had agreed to be interviewed and help me in my project, the necessity for Islamist women to express the belief underlying veiling had been one of her main points of emphasis. This issue is the most sensitive point of controversy between Islamist and non-Islamist people, and much vulgar criticism has been directed at Islamist women for covering their heads. To indicate the need to illuminate people on that subject, and at the same time pointing to the ignorance of their opponents and teasing them, she said, 'We should tell them we cover our heads because they are not infested with lice.' This, however, only led to a display of meaningful smiles, revealing the women's bitterness about the subject, and did not provoke them into proving the reverse, even though this would obviously be the last reason for them to cover their heads and anyone who believed it would seem ridiculous. The term *bitli* (one who is infested with lice) is often used to insult people: this 'joke' shows how they perceive their treatment in the society at large and how insulting and humiliating they find it.

CHAPTER III

The *Conscious* Muslim:
A Sociological Profile

III.1. Selection of the Study Group

In sociological study both the general principles governing the inquiry and those which become operative in the uses of methodological techniques in any particular case directly affect the decisions concerning the selection of the study group. The questionnaire I used in this study was designed to elicit demographic information (see Appendix I) from a group selected by 'snowball sampling' and covering twenty-five families. Although the chief informants of this inquiry were women, both the questionnaires and the interviews aimed to acquire information about the whole family. Despite the general tendency of sociological inquiry to use men as the main source of information, taking them as the head of the household, I deliberately chose women and took them as my chief informants and interviewees.

Behind this preference there lies a series of assumptions which form the logic of this study. First, I argue that any sociological study taking the family as its unit of analysis should resort to knowledge of women, since women are the main agents of the formation and organization of everyday family life.[1] Second, one of the major hypotheses of this study is that the visibility that the revival of Islam has gained in Turkish society is mainly shaped around its efforts to make an Islamic lifestyle alternative to that based on westernizing principles. Its main social target in Turkey is the transformation of the prevailing secular ethos upon which the structure of everyday life relies and women therefore become the active organizers and carriers of this ideal rather than being passive recipients of a body of belief given to them by men.

Women, as I argued in the Introduction, are the main actors in the task of rendering Islam into a living social practice, and this gives them a crucial role in the daily articulation and reproduction of Islamic ideologies. Thus they are of crucial concern in this research. Third, looking at the matter from this perspective, I also argue that these so-called Islamist women turn out to be the symbol of the movement of Islamic revitalization for both Islamic and non-Islamic circles. They must therefore be considered as the chief representatives of the movement by any study which aims to understand the parameters of living Islam and the production of its sociability as developed in the experience of Islamist people.

In this study, therefore, not the biologically determined gender identity of the researcher but the nature of the study necessitated the selection of women as the informants and the interviewees in the study group (although the study does not limit itself to the social conditions of Islamist women). Selection by a woman of female informants is usually assumed to be a natural consequence of Islamic rules on sex segregation which entail minimizing the contact between strange men and women. From my experience in the field, I believe that this would probably hold true in the case of a male researcher aiming to conduct a study of the private lives of Muslim people. He would probably not be allowed to get in close contact with Islamist women without the surveillance of their husbands or fathers, and it would be impossible for him to make participant observations by attending certain women's activities in order to find out about, for instance, their intimate relations. Conversely, I do not think there would be a serious problem for a female researcher aiming to collect her data through conducting interviews with male Islamic activists and observing the various forms of male sociability if she managed to be accepted as a credible person. That a woman may participate in certain male gatherings and hold discussions with them as long as she is seen as suitable and knowledgeable enough to discuss social and religious matters with them is true in Turkish Islamic tradition in general, and in the Republic of Turkey in particular. This was evident from my experience of being able to conduct interviews with five men: we talked about many subjects and covered various dimensions of relations between men and women, including love and intimacy. I also arranged an interview with a focus group consisting exclusively of men.

Credibility on the part of a female is also required for her to participate in women's religious gatherings. Here, being female does not guarantee acceptance as a participant observer among women if the would-be observer does not hide her true identity as a researcher, something I never did since I felt it contravened the ethics of sociology. In some gatherings, then, I was as alone as if I were in the middle of a crowd of men, especially while I was taking my notes when hundreds of women were praying, crying, and so on. The women I interviewed, and the other men and women I contacted in various circumstances throughout this study agreed with these findings. More importantly here, women perceived themselves as the main actors in the mission to actualize an Islamic way of life.

III.2. Components of an Habitus

III.2.1. Family and Marriage

The typical structural characteristic of the families which constitute the core units of this study was that they were almost exclusively nuclear. This accords with the family type which predominates in the typology of family in Turkish society.[2] Out of twenty-five families, only one of them was extended in any real meaning of the term in that one of the married sons was living in his father's house with his pregnant wife. Two families included grandparents, but merely to care for them in their old age ('transient extended' family).[3] Three families constituted conjugal couples who could not have children but two of these households cannot be identified as 'single' families[4] since in one a teenage sister of the wife lived there during the academic year in order to attend a better school in a big city, and in the other the parents of both partners came to live in their children's house for most of the year.

Because it is seen as a legal imperative and a widely accepted social norm, all the marriages in this study group had been both officially registered and religiously recognized. Arranged marriage appears as another norm, and all of the interviewees reported that their marriages had been arranged by their families. With one exception, these couples had, however, seen each other in the presence of family members and had access to extensive information about each other through different channels before getting married. More importantly, these marriages were arranged with the compliance of the individuals concerned. The exception was a marriage perceived by both sides as a divinely arranged coincidence: family elders had tried to accustom the young couple to each other by providing information, and the couple saw their marriage as a blessing bestowed upon them by God.

In only three of these couples was there a kinship tie between the spouses. Some of them came from the same area or were neighbours. In other cases their families knew each other through social ties. Thus, in all cases, except for one, marriages were arranged between families who somehow knew each other. Most of the interviewees reported that the degree of religiosity did not necessarily play an important role in helping them decide on their marriage partners, but that it was of greater concern for them to believe that they had a similar world-view and lifestyle. In fact in some cases, although both members of the couple came from conservative families, one of them found the other more conservative and hoped somehow to influence their partner into a change of mind after their marriage. Before long, however, those who aimed at living an Islamic life were able to persuade the others to lead their lives according to Islamic rules. In other words, the partner with a more Islamic outlook and pious concerns persuaded the other to arrange both their family and personal life according to rules of Islamic conduct. Here again it can be said that compliance rather than resistance determined the nature of this persuasion.

The average age of the couples at marriage varied depending on sex. Women usually started married life in their early twenties. The average year of birth is 1955 for wives (the eldest was born in 1932 and the youngest in 1966), and 1951 for husbands (eldest 1928, youngest 1964). This may indicate that in the arrangement of these marriages an older husband was seen as preferable, although a generation gap between husband and wife was not viewed as socially appropriate. Hence generation-wise they were ranked within the same category.

The average length of time the couples had been married was fifteen years. Of the twenty-five couples, four of them had been married for fewer than ten years, thirteen for between ten and nineteen years, six for between twenty and twenty-nine years, and finally one for thirty years, and one for forty-one years. Except for two husbands for whom this was their second marriage, all were in their first and only marriage. Contrary to all assertions that in Islam polygyny is the norm, all these couples were monogamous and seemed to have no desire to engage in or consent to polygyny. This was also true for the three couples in this study group who could not have any children. If asked, they usually agreed that in Islam such a right is given to men, but it is not a religious obligation and must not be abused. Besides which, a woman may try to prevent her husband from marrying another wife or divorce him if she feels her husband's decision to make another marriage is inappropriate. Many of the women upheld this right of men if the present wife was 'ill' or 'unhealthy', if this prevented her from performing her marital (mostly sexual) duties. It was also apparent that they avoided thinking much about this subject as long as it did not affect them. As for divorce, they were neither categorically against it, nor did they find it desirable, but if conditions bring married couples to the point of divorce, they thought that both women and men have the right to initiate it. On the other hand, since in their view marriage was seen as a religious imperative for adults, in their own words 'to lead a normal, healthy life without transgressing the public norms', making an effort to find suitable partners for bachelor Muslims was seen as something which is also religiously approved. In this respect, older widows and widowers are encouraged to remarry, although it is not common to encourage women beyond middle age to do so in Turkish culture. In one interview I was told that it is good for women to be under a marriage contract when the Day of Judgement arrives because going to the other world as a married woman attests to her willingness to obey the rules of God. But this was the only case in which I was given such an explanation; otherwise I was told that being alone is a state peculiar to God, and since God created human beings as couples, it is appropriate to marry someone suitable at any age.

III.2.2. Education

Regarding the level of education, there is a big gulf between spouses. Women generally had received a much lower level of formal education than their husbands. Of the twenty-five women, only four had graduated from university and three from higher vocational training school; in contrast, four out of twenty-five men had obtained postgraduate education, ten of them were university

graduates, five of them had a college (institute of education) diploma and one was said to have received a *medrese* education. Four
men and four women had attended a lycée but of the women only
two had obtained their lycée diplomas. Of the three women who
had been educated to the middle level of secondary school, only
one had received her middle school diploma. Among the men,
there was only one who had not continued beyond the middle level
of secondary school education and this was the lowest level of
education of any man in this group. In contrast, there were eleven
women who had only attended primary school: nine of them had
completed it and two had left at different grades. Of these eleven,
six had also attended various needlework and dressmaking courses
at different ages and for different lengths of time, including the
two who had dropped out of primary school (see Appendix II,
Table 1).

There is a crucial point which should be underlined regarding
the education level of these women. At one time or another they
had all either attended Koran courses or received private education
in religion at home.[5] Although some women were continuing to
receive private lessons – for instance lessons in Arabic, lessons
in Koran recitation, or lessons simply to broaden their religious
knowledge – these were not regular efforts because of the highly
time-consuming nature of being a housewife. On the other hand,
there were three women in the study group who through their
personal efforts had attained certificates enabling them to teach at
Koran courses. Thus, despite their lower level of formal education,
all of these women had received either formal or informal religious
education of different length and degree.

It is difficult, however, to determine the level of religious education attained through Koran courses because of the disparate
nature of these. According to Scott (1971), Koran courses are
officially differentiated as *kadrolu* (those taught by teachers in
government payroll positions) and *fahri* (those taught by teachers
paid with locally solicited funds) under the joint control of the
Office of Religious Affairs of the Prime Ministry and the Ministry
of Education. The *fahri* courses are carried out at the local level by
müftülük (district branches of the Office of Religious Affairs) and
the Directorate of Education in each district (p. 240).There are
other types of Koran course which are not under government
observation and control, but they are also locally supported.[6] It is

also common for imams and *hocas* (Muslim teachers) to teach children in their homes or in classes attached to mosques throughout the summer season; these are also conceived as Koran courses by the local people. Attendance at such courses is most evident among young girls and small children, whom parents prefer to be educated by a female *hoca* (Scott 1965; 1971). In sum, as Scott observes:

> The official Qur'an courses are not found in all communities. Most are found in the larger settlements, towns, and cities, frequently attached to a mosque. But most, if not all, communities have a source of religious training: some more or less knowledgeable person teaching on a semi-organized basis, in situations with elements that would not meet the official minimum standards (1971, p. 254).

According to my interviewees' descriptions of their religious education in these unofficial courses, attendance was not compulsory and there was no regularity or formal and required acquisition of a fixed body of knowledge via structured classes. Primary expectation on the part of parents from Koran courses, whether officially organized or not, was said to be the ability to read the Koran in its original script, and the observation of religious obligations learned from the teaching of a 'religious man' rather than a secular school teacher. This echoes the findings of Scott (1965) when the parents in certain villages were asked to compare the quality of religious teaching at state-run public schools and that given in Koran courses. This is despite recent legislation regarding official Koran courses.[7]

Since these courses were usually taken by the women in their early teenage years on an irregular basis, unlike their formal education, many were unable to specify either the length or the full content of their religious education. They also seemed reluctant to discuss the extent to which they were qualified in their religious learning, except for the three who had obtained certificates. Seven of the eleven women who had only attended primary school had attended Koran courses for not less than one year either before or after marriage, in addition to attending summer courses in their early teens. Of these seven, one had reached a level where she could teach Koran recitation in summer Koran courses, three reported that their fathers were imams and that they had been taught by them at home and one had received private lessons on the Koran and *hadith* at home for four years prior to her marriage. There were another two women who also described their religious education: they were both Koran course teachers and had been educated beyond primary school level. One of them was a lycée graduate, and after school she had attended Koran courses for one year; subsequently she had started to assist her teacher and this enabled her to be licensed as a teacher of Koran courses. She gave private lessons at home as well as teaching at local Koran courses. The other woman had ended her formal education in the middle section of secondary school; she then attended Koran courses for two years, in addition to obtaining her diploma from the middle section of an Imam Hatip school, completing the extra courses and taking examinations externally. She had started to teach at Koran courses in her early twenties.

In the field of formal education, religion is the predominant area of study for women. All four of the women who were university graduates had graduated from the Faculty of Theology, so religion also appears as the only area of university education for the women interviewed in this study. The three women cited as higher vocational training school graduates, however, attended different sections of an institute of education – mathematics, English and literature. Among the four women who had attended lycée, two of them graduated from lycée level vocational schools, and the other two finished their lycée education at Imam Hatip schools. Of the three women who had only attended middle schools, one was the woman who obtained her diploma externally from the middle section of an Imam Hatip school and the other two dropped out because of headscarf disputes. The only woman with a middle school diploma had received it from one of the schools established to give a mixture of religious and secular education.[8]

In contrast to the fields the women were trained in, the range of the men's education is vast (see Appendix II, Table 1). The disciplines studied at higher level include economics, finance, accounting and business administration, engineering, mathematics, veterinary medicine, applied sciences, literature and finally religion. Of the seven men who received higher education in the field of religious education, four were at the Faculty of Theology, two at the Institute of Islam, and one at a *medrese*. As for those with lycée level education, two of them were Imam Hatip school graduates, one of them a military lycée graduate and one a public lycée graduate. The one who had only received middle level formal education had also attained a high standard of religious learning from private teachers. Men also attended Koran courses in their early teens for varying lengths of time, especially in summer schools, but attending mosque prayers and sermons and other kinds of men's religious gatherings with their fathers or with older male relatives also played an important role in their religious socialization.

III.2.3. Professions

The professional status and source of income was determined for fifteen of the twenty-five men by their professional affiliations with the state. Eight of them were employed in different state departments as higher level bureaucrats, three of them as university staff at public universities, three as teachers of religion at public schools, and one as a religious functionary. Of those working in the private sector, two were in the construction business, one had his own business, two were working in the media, two were employed as accountants at different firms, and one worked in a private university. The remaining two men were also dependent on the state in terms of their income and professional identities: one was retired from the military, and one was a retired member of parliament (see Appendix II, Table 2).

Eighteen out of the twenty-five women in this group were house-wives of whom only four could also be conceived as working part-time, occasionally tailoring and marketing clothing accessories at home. Seven women worked outside the home: two worked as preachers (which also included teaching public Koran courses in local mosques), two taught in various Koran courses, two worked as secondary level teachers (both at middle and lycée level schools, one in a private and the other in a public school), and one, who used to teach at a public school, gave private lessons at home in mathematics, physical sciences and Koran recitation (see Appendix II, Table 2). One other woman had worked occasionally as a Koran course teacher, but after having children she had left her job. In terms of their professional identities these working women, except for two, were all dependent on the state for their incomes. Others also generating an income relied upon their personally acquired skills, and their professions can be grouped in the informal sector.

In the light of this information it can be argued that when women receive a professional education, they are more likely to work outside the home. Nevertheless, as was evident in one case, they are only likely to carry on working as long as their jobs do not conflict with their religious identity and ideals. The woman who gave private lessons at home, for instance, had left her job as a teacher of mathematics in a public school because she was not allowed to cover her head there. The two who worked as teachers had to struggle to be allowed to teach with their heads covered. One of them solved this problem by transferring to a private school financed by Islamic circles. The other one was able to continue in the state school: she claimed that, as a teacher of religion, she had the right to dress according to the codes enjoined by her religion and to her surprise her demand was accepted by the school administration.

Thus, whether women worked outside the home depended on variable factors ranging from their level of education to problems of identity connected with the imperative of obeying Islamic rules of modesty. Men had much greater opportunity to work than women in terms of their ability to obtain higher education and to preserve their religious identity in the work environment. The experiences of both the men and women affected their understanding of education and work, and were reflected in the attitudes that they displayed towards the education of their children.

III.2.4. Children

The average number of children in the families studied was three (actual average number was 2.54) and numbers ranged from four children per family to one, with three of the twenty-five families having none. The parents of the families with a single child were fairly young couples and almost all of them wanted to have at least one more child. Women in these families had usually conceived their first child in the early years of the marriage. The number of children in the families was a result of a reconciliation reached between their understandings of family size and economic welfare. That is to say, the primary concern determining family-planning strategies was to have as many children as their economic and emotional situations would allow them to support. Having as many children as they could was not the norm, but to have a single child was not seen as desirable either. Therefore, mindful of economic constraints, they all supported the idea that any child should have a sibling if God permits. Following this 'rule', women usually preferred to have the births of their first two children as close together as possible but there was usually a gap before later children; the women maintained that they had their third or fourth children (as their last one) because of the happiness and new vigour another baby would bring to their family lives. Even when these later pregnancies were unplanned, they all tended to see their last children as a joy and blessing bestowed upon them by God. So, seen this way, although they had some idea of family-planning, the concept was intermingled with the belief that, in the final analysis, the determination of both the number and the sex of the children they could have was a divine decision.

Having a son, for the women as for the men, was especially desirable. When the first two children were female, the women usually had a third child in the hope that it would be a son, but if this third one was not a boy either, they tended to stop trying, accepting their lack of a son as God's will. But with the exception of one young woman, who hesitated to have children other than her only son due to her worries about her capability of raising more than one child properly, all the women in this group told me that they could not imagine themselves without a daughter. Consequently women with two sons but no daughter, for example, might become pregnant in order to try and have a daughter. In sum, their family-planning strategies concerning the sex of their children were based on an understanding of the desirability of having a family with children of both sexes.

As well as the number and the sex of the children, it seemed that name-giving was a vital concern for these people in their desire to follow Islamic rules and conduct. The importance that Muslims in general ascribe to proper names is helpful in understanding how these particular Muslims perceive both their purpose of existence in this life and the ways in which it becomes possible to construct a conscious Muslim identity. As Schimmel writes, 'Names can tell much about the likes and dislikes of people, about fashions and trends, about religious and political predilections, and thus a study of the nomenclature in any society is highly revealing' (1989, p. ix).

The names given to children in this study group were carefully thought about, first of all because of the religious responsibilities of the parents towards their children, since they believe that when the Day of Judgement arrives everyone will be called before God by their name. It was quite common to come across small boys with names such as Abdullah, Abdurrahman, Abdulkerim and Abdulekber, names many Muslims in Turkey see as outdated, especially those who lead their lives in urban modern contexts. However, again as Schimmel pointed out, two names, Abdullah and Abdurrahman, occurred very frequently in the Muslim world because of a *hadith* stating that 'the names which God loves best are Abdullah and Abdurrahman'. Other names beginning with the word '*Abd* (servant) were also popular because it can be connected with any of the ninety-nine names of God (1989, p. 26), but they went out of fashion in the republican Turkish context because of their overt association with Arabic. As for the girls, commonly preferred female names used in Turkey which were originally religious have almost lost their religious connotations and are thus used quite frequently and widely. These have also become fashionable again in the last two decades in the quest for authenticity, but they do not usually display a religious overtone at first sight. These are the names such as Ayşe, Zeynep and Fatma, the names of the wives of the Prophet and his daughter. However, in this study group, as well as these names and some names of saintly Muslim women, the nicknames (*lâkap*) of some of them said to have been given to them by the Prophet himself were highly thought of and given to girl children. Among them, for example, two are particularly favoured and their actual meanings were explained to me cheerfully with an affectionate tone. Although I was familiar with these names and knew that they were common in modern urban circles, I did not know that these were religious names, nor do I think that their actual meanings are known by many people. These were Betül (the nickname of Fatma, the daughter of the Prophet Muhammad who was the wife of the Caliph Ali and the mother of martyrs Hüseyin and Hasan), which means 'the virgin' or 'the weaned'; and Hümeyra (the nickname of the Prophet's favourite wife, Ayşe), which means 'little red one', and is said to have been given to her because of her characteristic of blushing easily. However, as well as names that either directly denote or indirectly connote religion, there were other names which did not fall into these categories but were ascribed different kinds of significance, for example, revealing a wish or sense of beauty or courage.

By chance, the sex distribution of children in this study group was equal in number: among the total of fifty-six, twenty-eight of them were female and twenty-eight male. Nine of the children did not live with their parents: five were married daughters, two were married sons and two were bachelor sons who had left their families and emigrated for work reasons. Thus, the actual number of children living in their parents' households was forty-seven, twenty-three girls and twenty-four boys. The average year of birth for daughters was 1977 (youngest 1989, oldest 1965), and for sons the average year of birth was 1979 (youngest 1987, oldest 1963). The oldest daughter was engaged and about to change her place of residence to the native town of her future husband. The oldest son was married and living with his pregnant wife in his parents' house.

Except for the eight children of pre-school age – though three of them attended nursery school in the *site* – all the children, depending on their age, had attended or were attending either primary or secondary schools, which at that time included both middle and lycée level secondary schools. A few of them had completed their lycée or university education. Among the twenty-three girls living with their families, most of them attended a school where religion constituted the core of the education. Although among the twenty-four boys living with their families there were some who were sent to religious schools, the schools that they attended at every level showed a higher variety than that of the girls (see Appendix II, Table 4).

The children not living with their families also had a good level of education. Of the five women, three had graduated from vocational lycée (and one of them had studied Arabic abroad), one of them was a trained economist who had earned her master's degree abroad, and the last was a graduate of the middle section of an Imam Hatip school. They were, however, all housewives. Their husbands were university graduates. All the male members of this group of children were university graduates (see Appendix II, Table 5). The wives of the two married sons were also housewives.

The overall information on the education level of children shows that parents are much more selective in their choice of schools for girls than they are for boys, sending their teenage daughters almost exclusively to 'religious' schools. The primary reason for this, as can easily be understood, is the tolerant attitude displayed by these schools after 1983 towards Islamic rules of modesty. In sum, girls are sent to schools where they will not be forced to bare their heads.

Concerning the educational preferences of the parents for their children, the choice of public or private schools is dependent on economic capacity. But parents seem more likely to anticipate a competitive future for their sons than for their daughters, and thus they plan and prepare accordingly. Thus, most of the mothers whose sons were in primary school expressed their wish to be able to send them to private lycées or to public lycées known as *Anadolu Liseleri* (in which science, mathematics and language classes constitute the most important part of the formal curriculum). However, for female primary school students, mothers seemed to be content with the idea of sending them to Imam Hatip schools, seeing pious education for girls as the most helpful in preparing them for their future role as mothers. When they wished to send their daughters to private 'religious' schools, in which courses of home management, needlework and dressmaking are taught to girls along with courses assigned by the formal secular curriculum, the mothers' primary aim was to be able to provide a good education, enhanced with religious learning, for their daughters. Nevertheless, like other urban parents who are cognizant of the demands of a rapidly changing world and wish their children to be trained according to its requirements, the overall aim of the parents in this study group was to provide their children with a better education than they, as new urban dwellers, had obtained. Here, it should be noted that, for these parents, the so-called requirements of a contemporary world primarily pertained to an Islamic one yet to be established. Whether or not this ideal could be realized, a religious education, at least to some extent, constituted the most important part of the 'cultural capital' that they envisaged for their children.

III.2.5. Place of Origin, Migration and Settlement

Most of these married couples were born in provincial cities, towns or villages, the exceptions being one who was from Istanbul, and four from Ankara. They came to Ankara at different ages – usually their late teens or their early twenties, after marriage. Including the four from Ankara, a total of nineteen women were originally from the various urban centres in Central Anatolia, three were from the East and South-East, two were from the eastern Black Sea Coast in the North, and one was from the Marmara region in the North-West (see Appendix II, Table 6). The men were also mostly from Central Anatolia. The East and South-East were also represented, and three were from the Marmara and five from the Black Sea regions. Thirty one out of fifty men and women came from Central Anatolia, with Eastern Anatolia and the Black Sea region the next best represented (see Appendix II, Table 6). It is interesting to note that Central and Eastern Anatolia are the regions in which the NSP gained its electoral strength and received the highest percentage of its votes in the 1973 national elections (the first time it participated in a national election). Some observers also maintain that in this election Eastern Anatolia stood out as an NSP stronghold.[9]

Most of the interviewees could not specify the exact date of their migration to Ankara (using rather vague terms such as 'in my childhood' or 'in my youth'). As most of the men had higher education, it is reasonable to say that they at least spent an important part of their youth in developed urban settlement areas, but the majority of the interviewees fully settled in Ankara only after marriage. Despite the fact that most of the men were employed by the state and thus dispatched from time to time to work in different parts of Turkey, most interviewees tended to see themselves as *Ankaralı* (resident in Ankara, but not necessarily born there) after living in the *site*. Thus, it can safely be assumed that among other things shaping the formation of their urban identity, living in this *site* perpetuated their attachment to urban metropolitan life. In addition, the fact that most of their children were born in Ankara reinforced their parents' perception of being *Ankaralı*. Forty-five of the fifty-six children were born in Ankara (see Appendix II, Table 6). The majority of the children born to these families are thus going to be first generation urban dwellers in a modern metropolis.

The construction of the *site* was accomplished gradually and lasted from 1970 to 1985. The first inhabitants settled there starting from 1973. The first of the twenty-five families in this study moved there in 1973 in order to supervise construction, and the last arrived in 1989. Eight families moved there between the years 1977 and 1979, and fifteen between 1980 and 1986. The most arrivals

occurred in 1980 with seven families. Fourteen out of the twenty-
five families were tenants, eight owned their apartments and three
had been allowed by their parents (either the wife's or the husband's
side) to live in apartments which originally belonged to them.

III.3. Faith and Taste: Bases of a Middle Class Ethos

Although most of the people in this study group can be grouped
under the classic category of 'white collar' salaried employees, in
the sense introduced by Mills (1951) to the literature of social
stratification, it was not possible to specify their income levels in
monetary terms since they avoided giving such information about
themselves. Rather, they tended to identify their economic situations through such concepts as 'good', 'ordinary-normal' and
'bad', a method to which many people resort in Turkey to identify
their place in the ranks of social stratification.[10] These terms, however, can provide us with knowledge about the way in which people
develop certain systems of self-reference in order to express their
socio-economic situation, both to themselves and to others. In this
group, except for four women who identified their socio-economic
status as 'good', and two who expressed their situation as 'neither
good nor bad, since nowadays we are on a tight budget' and 'not
that good', nineteen women preferred to use the terms *ortahalli*
(ordinary) and normal, which refer to the middle rank.

When socio-economic status indicators other than income are
taken into account (such as the ownership of consumer durables,
standards of eating, clothing, travelling and entertainment, children's education, home decoration, and the like), it is possible to
place these families among the middle ranks of social stratification.
In terms of their capacity to purchase goods such as home appliances, for example, they all had refrigerators, cookers, automatic
washing machines, vacuum cleaners, televisions and telephones,
which they saw as the basic equipment for the daily management of
domestic life in a modern Turkish house. Their 'taste of necessity'
(Bourdieu 1989) was expanding: many of them would not refuse a
dishwasher, for example, as soon as they could afford it and most
of them were planning to have one in the near future. It was as
important to spend money on the decoration of kitchens and
bathrooms as on the reception room (*salon* in vernacular Turkish),
the room where guests are received and the common living space

where the whole family comes together, especially at night. Larger and better equipped kitchens, fancier, marble bathrooms separate for parents and children, private rooms for each of their children and larger and separate living rooms were the standard dreams of the women. They tried to realize these dreams in their relatively small apartments, if they could find money after the expenditures on the pilgrimage to Mecca, their children's education and invest-ments for their children's marriages. The first luxury expenditure they made, as soon as it became possible, was generally expanding and increasing the kitchen cupboards and renewing the tiles. Since car prices only became affordable for fixed income groups in Turkey after the mid-1990s, car ownership was not very common, although it had a place in their understanding of necessity. Only five of the twenty-five families had a car.

Eating standards were quite high with food forming the largest item in the families' daily budgets. The mothers believed in the necessity of good nourishment for their children, and they were all fond of cooking and eating well. This included cooking fancy pastries at least every other day. Most of them also reported that they liked to go out for a meal with their families once or twice a month. Although thriftiness was part of their rhetoric, at least once in each season the women bought something new both for themselves and for their families, and the quality of their clothes also showed that they did not behave as modestly as one would expect. This was especially true at times of religious feasts, when buying new things for every member of the family was the norm, although some women made some of their own and their children's clothing at home.

The way they decorated their houses also showed that they had invested a fair amount of money in order to be able to fulfil the 'requirements' of having a presentable house. In the *salon*, the large piece of furniture which functions both as a buffet and a bookcase full of books on religious history, religious conduct and behaviour, as well as literary classics, constituted an indispensable part of this 'decoration', and was used as well to display fine tea sets, porcelain bibelots, and the like. Buying books and encyclopedias, including Islamic ones, by instalment was an important part of the family budget, and I noted more classic Islamic books than porcelain figurines and china on the bookshelves than would be the case with others from similar income groups. Wall plaques written in Arabic scripts, and souvenirs from the pilgrimage, which they had either bought themselves or received as gifts, took their place alongside the books and porcelain on the shelves of these large buffets. Other than the buffet, which is very common in ordinary middle and lower-middle class families in Turkey, in most of these apartments there was usually a separate bookcase, though of modest size. Other furniture in the *salon* usually included a round or rectangular dinner table with matching chairs designed for six or eight persons, usually placed in front of the buffet; a sofa and two or three matching armchairs with side tables round a coffee table (bearing crystal ashtrays placed on small lace mats and sometimes a vase of artificial flowers); and almost inevitably a nest of tables (*sikon*, from the Latin *ciconia*, stork), used while serving guests. There were plants and flowers around the room, but not necessarily in front of the windows. Machine-made imitations of the hand-made classical Turkish carpets, and, though rarely, original carpets, but almost never colourful Turkish *kilims*, completed the decoration of the *salon*.

A feature of their lifestyle was the inside/outside distinction they made between their home life and interior design and the world outside their homes. For example, the *salon* was designed to open on to a balcony, but the balconies were not used as a living space, and had no flower pots or tea tables, etc., a very common way of using space in Turkey, especially during the warm seasons. Another illustration of the inside/outside distinction they maintained is the long, thick draperies which were kept tightly closed at night and were another of the indispensable items of their home decoration. Although closing the curtains at night is quite common in ordinary Turkish home life, and not peculiar to these families, they adhered to this habit very strictly.

The inside/outside distinction was connected to their understanding of the maintenance of cleanliness and purity in the house. Here it is appropriate to mention the *alaturka* toilet rooms found in every apartment (after the French *à la turque*, pertaining to Turks and their taste and style). *Alaturka* toilets (which are built into the floor) are very common in ordinary Turkish houses, but not in modern, urban buildings. Although they did not object to the existence of a water closet in their bathrooms, an *alaturka* toilet room was seen as compulsory.[11] They also preferred to make their daily ablution there rather than in the bathroom. In addition to plastic water pots for *taharet* (canonical purification) they also put in these rooms a pair of plastic slippers, guest towels and sometimes a small bottle of lemon cologne.

Continuing this theme, not only family members but also guests were expected to take off their shoes and put on slippers when they came in from outside. In the lower drawers or shelves of the coat cupboard that was to be found in every entrance hall there were usually at least one or two pairs of slippers for guests. Women attending women's reception days, for example, usually brought a plastic bag with their chic new shoes which went with their clothes so that during these rather formal women's gatherings they wore their own fancy shoes rather than someone else's unstylish slippers. When they visited each other in the same apartment block, they brought their own slippers to their neighbours' houses. Such efforts to maintain indoor cleanliness were not, of course, by any means peculiar to these families. The custom of women taking their own shoes with them while visiting someone is old and widespread in small cities, provincial towns and also in the modest quarters of big cities in Turkey. Removal of shoes inside the house is very common amongst almost all Turkish people, regardless of social stratum, but expecting the same of guests is not. In the *site*, too, sometimes, though not frequently, not only guests but also residents left their shoes outside the entrance to the apartment. This practice was seen as inappropriate to urban life and was sometimes criticized quite severely by modern secular people who compared it with what takes place in front of mosques where people take their shoes off before entering, claiming that the whole apartment block was being turned into a mosque courtyard! Although the habit was not approved of by many of the people I met in the *site*, overt criticism of those who did leave their shoes outside was avoided.

Regarding their patterns of relationships outside the home, apart from making visits to relatives and friends who live in other parts of the city, people in the *site* also travel to other cities, mostly to see their relatives. It was clear that they were spending a considerable amount of money on travel to other cities and abroad. First, they were all in the habit of visiting their relatives and parents in other cities at least once a year, and could afford to accept guests as well. Second, eighteen out of the twenty-five couples could afford to make the pilgrimage at least once: all the men had visited Mecca for the pilgrimage, and eleven of the couples had done so more than once. It was also common to make trips to visit shrines, other holy places and famous mosques located in different parts of Turkey. Visits to the seaside were rare because it was not easy to find summer resorts and hotels designed to serve pious people. Only after the mid-1990s did such undertakings begun by Muslim entrepreneurs become widespread, mostly among upper and upper-middle class Islamic people. Teenage sons, but not daughters, were sent to summer camps where religious education was provided along with sports facilities. Also during holidays, some parents felt it was worth spending money on sending their sons to other cities to stay with relatives in order to attend the Koran courses of a famous *hoca*.

The families that I studied were not struggling to make ends meet or living at the edge of subsistence, but neither were they enjoying the comforts of upper-middle class life. In the standard terms of vertical mobilization, I would argue that defining them as 'social achievers' rather than 'social climbers' better suits their social position. This does not mean that they were not likely to climb the ladders of the social strata, but rather that for them 'making it' did not mean everything. Instead they tried not to fall behind the contemporary world, and at the same time tried to break the bondage of the image of backward, ignorant, narrow-minded religious fanatics, a burden which first of all restrained them as they tried to become 'true' Muslims, and also frightened them as much as it frightened 'non-Islamist' people. Thus they strove for a good education, to observe the rules of religion enjoined on them by God, and to make a living without falling into destitution, which they saw as one of the main causes of all sorts of corruption. They were people who wanted to build upon the 'fundamentals' and broaden their life space as much as they could without straying from Islamic precepts. If, following Bourdieu, our 'choices', which are actually the product of our 'tastes', constitute our lifestyles and 'taste is . . . the source of the system of distinctive features' (1989, p. 175), then what distinguishes this group of people from others who can also be placed in the middle ranks of society is the system of classification developed by them as a consequence of their taste, and hence the choices they made are embedded in this system of classification. Here, it should be noted that this system is not something which is static in its nature, nor can it be isolated from the societal conditions within which it has been created. In Bourdieu's own words:

> This classificatory system, which is the product of the internaliz-ation of the structure of the social space, in the form in which it impinges through the experience of a particular position in that space, is, within the limits of economic possibilities and impossi-bilities . . . the generator of practices adjusted to the regularities inherent in a condition. *It continuously transforms necessities into strategies, constraints into preferences, and, without any mechanical determination, it generates the set of 'choices' constituting life-styles, which derive their meaning, i.e., their value, from their position in a system of oppositions and correlations.* It is a virtue made of necessity which continuously transforms necessity into virtue by inducing 'choices' which correspond to the condition of which it is the product. As can be seen whenever a change in social position puts the *habitus* into new conditions, so that its specific efficacy can be isolated, it is taste – the taste of necessity or the taste of luxury – and not high or low income which commands the practices objectively adjusted to these recourses. Through taste, an agent has what he likes because he likes what he has, that is, the properties actually given to him in the distributions and legitimately assigned to him in the classification (1989, p. 145, emphasis mine).

Thus, in the specific context of this study, 'faith', intermingled with what Bourdieu defines here as 'taste', functions to generate such a system of classification for the Muslim people in question. Here, as a concluding point, I also argue that apart from certain demographic characteristics such as sex, age, birthplace, and family of origin, all the other cultural and socio-habitual characteristics delineated here can be regarded as reflections of a classificatory system realized by certain Muslims in which they have any say, i.e., 'make a choice', as either young or adult persons albeit in a given cultural framework. Therefore, I argue, too, that through the consequences of the 'choices' they made in order to build a social life, they not only occupied a place in the middle ranks of a given society, but they also aspired to constitute a 'model' for the middle classes of an imagined Islamic society, and hence tried to create an Islamic middle class ethos.

118   LIVING ISLAM

Notes

[1] The position of women as the main organizers of family life, in spite of their lower status vis-à-vis men in intra-familial relations in Turkish society, is discussed to some extent by a number of social scientists. They primarily aimed to show the way in which the role of women within the family displays certain continuities and discontinuities depending on the social roles that are attributed to them and that they attribute to themselves in patriarchally determined social structures. These structures are also subject to change in a social process within which transition from rural/traditional to urban/modern social structures constitutes the background of the social picture. In this respect, they all recognize the primary importance of women for the maintenance of family and kinship ties, not only in terms of keeping these ties alive and strong for the survival of the family, but also in terms of providing for the family's relationships with the community both inside and outside kinship ties. Thus they play a primary role in accommodating the family as a whole to changing social conditions. Kıray, for instance, argues that women play a central role in the family in terms of tension management in the presence of new role demands which have emerged as a consequence of social change for every member of the family (1976; 1982). Concerning the position of women in the family, with regard to changing urban social structures, Kandiyoti argues that, in spite of class and status differences, women continue to provide the basic comforts of the family and do not seem likely to disrupt expected norms of family functioning (1982; 1984; Kağıtçıbaşı 1984). In the case of women factory workers as the main breadwinners in their families in the largest metropolis of Turkey, Istanbul, for the central role women play in terms of organizing not only economic but also domestic and emotional relations within the family, see Bolak (1990). Sirman's study (1990) shows how the survival of community life, in the village context, as well as the lives of individual families, depends on the organizational efforts of women negotiating within pre-determined customary codes. To underline my argument once again, all these scholarly examples show that, without considering the central role played by women in family life, it is not possible to understand the parameters of domestic life, which in turn constitutes the basis of an expected life-order.

[2] Several studies on family in Turkish society show that the majority of families both in rural and urban areas in Turkey are nuclear. See Duben (1982), Kağıtçıbaşı (1981) and S. Timur (1972).

[3] For S. Timur, 'transient extended' family is a family in which the son or son-in-law rather than the aged father is the head of the family; it is formed when parents move into their children's house for care in old age (1972, p. 33).

THE CONSCIOUS MUSLIM: A SOCIOLOGICAL PROFILE 119

[4] S. Timur (1972) proposes using this term for families with no children.

[5] Certain Turkish social scientists concentrated particularly on exploring the education of women in rural and urban sections of society (Özbay 1979, Balamir 1983, Gök 1990), but have not paid much attention to the religious education of women whether in officially recognized Koran courses or at home. Özbay, however, mentions Koran courses in one sentence, referring to the education preferences of peasant mothers for their daughters: the data demonstrates that a low percentage of peasant women see the education in Koran courses as sufficient for girls (1979, p. 210).

[6] See Scott (1965; 1971). On the existence of unofficial religious schools in the 1950s see, for example, Reed (1956).

[7] According to relatively new government legislation, Article 10, published in 1991, official Koran courses aim to do the following: 1. to teach the student to read the Holy Koran in the Arabic alphabet; 2. to give knowledge and instill practices which will enable correct recitation of the Koran with the proper pronunciation (*tevcid* and *tashih-i huruf*); 3. to teach the meanings of the verses, suras and prayers and their proper memorization, all necessary for various forms of worship; 4. to train the *hafız* (a person who memorizes the Koran and can recite it by heart); and 5. to give correct information about the fundamental principles of Islamic belief, ethics and morals and about the life and moral conduct of the Prophet Muhammad (Bayraktar 1992, p. 106).

[8] Imam Hatip schools were established to train religious functionaries such as prayer-leaders (*imam*) and preachers (*hatip* or *vaiz*). Women can only become preachers if they graduate from these schools, since under normal circumstances a woman cannot become an imam in Islam. On the establishment and the development of Imam Hatip schools in the multi-party period of republican Turkey see, for example, Akşit (1991, pp.146–52).

[9] See Table 11 in Toprak (1981, p. 114), 'The Regional Strength of the NSP by the Number of Deputies Elected, 1973 Election'. Of the total 48 NSP deputies elected in the national elections of 1973, making the party the third biggest party in the parliament, 18 came from Eastern Anatolia and 16 from Central Anatolia. In addition, in the same election, the party received 28.7 per cent of the total votes in the region of Eastern Anatolia, thus appearing as one of the strongest parties in the region.

[10] For this point see, for instance, Akşit's study on social stratification and politico-cultural conflict carried out in a middle range Central Anatolian town. In this study, when the informants were asked to identify their socio-economic status, it was observed that 36.4 per cent of 571 informants utilized terms such as 'rich, poor, and ordinary (*ortahalli*)' instead of using the terms 'upper, middle, lower' usually referred to in

social scientific studies. Akşit argues that this may be an indication of the invention of an intermediary route between modern and traditional, which people developed in order to express themselves properly. Akşit also argues that the social conditions under which these conceptions acquired their cultural meanings and how they were disseminated among large sections of society is a topic which should be investigated by social scientists at large (1985, p. 187).

[11] In Turkish culture people believe that *alaturka* toilets are much cleaner and more healthy than *alafranga* (Western) water closets. This is because in *alaturka* toilets a person does not sit and therefore does not touch anywhere that others have touched. *Taharet* (washing oneself after using the toilet in conformity with canonical purity) is also much easier in an *alaturka* toilet.

CHAPTER IV

A New Storyline: Republican Secular Politics, Identity and the Islamic Challenge

IV.1. The Question of Gender Politics and the Transfer of Identity

Although the discourse of 'living Islam as conscious Muslims' has been developed as an extension of a recently implemented political idea, for the secular Republic of Turkey the question of how to reconcile Muslim identity with the new identity of Turkish citizenship has been a major social issue. The problem inherent in this question arises from a series of historical facts. With the establishment of the Republic of Turkey not only the entire political regime but also another important aspect of social reality, what I will call 'the subject constitution regime of the society', underwent a process of transformation. In the process of making a Turkish nation, which more or less historically coincided with the establishment of the Turkish nation-state, the very basis of the parameters of given forms of private life had to change, as well as the institutional organization of social life. To understand this process of transforming the subjects of an empire into the citizens of a nation-state, there is a series of special factors to be considered. This transformation required what I describe as the creation of 'rational individuals in a national society' out of the clay of 'pious members of an Islamic community'. This was obviously not an unproblematic or easy task. But contrary to many arguments concerning the republican state's radical attitude towards the gender issue affecting its ability to realize such a change, I argue that this transition occurred in a relatively smooth way precisely because of the constitution of the state's gender politics, and that these gender politics were the basis of national identity formation.

The extent to which, at both the discursive level and the level of behaviour-model constitution, the process occurred without transgressing the essential boundaries of Islamic patriarchal ethics was what enabled the republican modernization project to graft its ideas onto the prevailing patriarchal structures in the smoothest way possible. It also made the Turkish modernization project much more successful than similar projects in other Muslim countries. I believe that this was possible because the republican reformers were almost all men, who did not base their discourse on gender politics merely on women's issues, and nor did they address men through women. That is to say, when they built their discourse as a speech between 'I' and 'you', both the addresser and the addressee were men. More importantly, the object of this discourse was not generally women as such, but rather the creation of women Turkish citizens, the modernization of civil law, and the development of a whole nation. The identity transformation movement was realized, by and large, as something which took place as a struggle between men rather than manipulating women directly as women. This became possible by limiting the boundaries of social change to the acts of men; that is, by attributing to men the role of social mobilizer, the boundaries of this social mobilization were drawn within the framework of men's exemplary actions. Kandiyoti may argue that 'the decisive action of Kemalism with respect to women's emancipation was the evacuation of Islam from the legislative and broader institutional sphere, and the inclusion of women in a new notion of "citizenship" dictated by the transition from a monarchy to a populist republic' (1991a, p. 39). In this context, however, during the enactment of new reforms, it was not Islam which was to be condemned but backward-looking 'tradition,' which had to be separated from the new social life.

Similarly, the state's legislative actions designed to emancipate women have been portrayed as one of the methods by which it was aimed to establish a modern Turkish nation. Thus, even Mustafa Kemal Atatürk did not take any of his political decisions regarding women on the basis of women being under the tutelage of Muslim men. When he addressed women in his public speeches they were either 'half of the population' or the 'mothers of the nation'. He only referred to women as victims on rare occasions, as once happened in the presence of some peasant women when he mentioned their 'bizarre way of seclusion'.[1] If women had to change it was because they were also going to be citizens of the Republic and women's adjustment to the new social order was not seen as any different from that of men. In the modernization project, a new public space was to be established which required the transformation of men's social functions and identities as well so that they might become citizens of the new Turkish society. Consequently, in most of his public sermons Atatürk addressed people as 'Efendiler' (gentlemen). Thus, the target of the Turkish revolution was men more than anybody else. However, I do not agree with the point advocated by Kandiyoti and others, as exemplified here: 'the women question became one of the pawns in the Kemalist struggle to liquidate the theocratic remnants of the Ottoman state'. Kandiyoti was right, however, in pointing out that it was 'a struggle in which male protagonists engaged while women by and large remained surprisingly passive onlookers' (Kandiyoti 1991a, p. 38). I suggest that the fact that males were protagonists in debates on questions including the future position of women in the society should be seen in terms of the republican reformers being enabled to achieve modernization by maintaining the consent of men, thereby reducing possible resistance to their later actions. Since, first and foremost, political agreement was maintained amongst men, then the resistance which could come from men was also eliminated at the very beginning of the reformation movement. In fact, the exclusion of women's voices from the formation of men's discourse on gender politics served to assure men that women would still remain under their thumbs, and that men would be the main social actors in that the scope and actualization of social change would be dependent on their will. In the framework of this social change, then, men provided the example of how to become a citizen and women were to follow. Thus, the emancipation of women was brought about to provide the legal equality anticipated for all citizens of the Turkish Republic. It was not meant to underestimate men or to mobilize women to accept the cause of modernization which was imposed upon society from outside by westernizing forces; this would have resulted in the creation of a stratum that would break the cultural authority of indigenous patriarchs over the society, a model which was usually seen as appropriate in explaining the ways in which colonialist forces had tried to penetrate and transform political and cultural structures in the Muslim societies of North Africa. In republican Turkish society, however, women were not given such a role nor did the republican reformers, including Atatürk himself, dictate the ways in which women should behave in social life. Although Atatürk promoted the image that men and women should work side by side in public affairs by, for instance, bringing his wife, Latife Hanım, on his public tours and to official ceremonies, he did not attempt to remove even his own wife's headscarf.² Rather, he and his friends tried to set a model for society by recognizing a space for personal autonomy. He displayed the image of a modern and affectionate, but at the same time disciplinarian, father in his relations with his adoptive daughters. He behaved as a Western gentleman with women in public ceremonies and receptions. He did not intrude in the private lives of even his close friends.

The attitude and the method of Mustafa Kemal towards the emancipation of women differed sharply from that of other Middle Eastern leaders, for example, Reza Shah. Unlike the latter, he was sensitive to the autonomy of women and careful not to transgress the boundaries of Islamic rules of modesty, never issuing any decree concerning the veiling of women. Reza Shah, however, as Najmabadi (1991) reports in her elaborate study on the development of modernity and morality in Iran, subordinated everything, including his own beliefs, to state-building, in his attempt to initiate secular reforms. Thus he made unveiling of women compulsory, and, to demonstrate his personal rejection of polygamy, he divorced both his wives. More importantly for the point that I am trying to make here, on 8 January 1936, he took his wife for the first time unveiled to a public ceremony. Before the ceremony he said to her: 'It is easier for me to die than to take my wife unveiled amidst strangers, but I have no choice. The country's progress requires that women must be set free, and I must be the first person to do that', and he did not hesitate to do it (Najmabadi 1991, pp. 72–3, n. 24). From all the pictures taken of Atatürk and his wife, the enduring image in the Turkish public memory is that the head of Latife Hanım was covered with the elegant turban worn by fashionable upper class women of the day. This was a style called 'Russian head' which tightly covered the woman's forehead and was tied behind the neck so as to leave the whole face open, occasionally and stylishly showing a little hair.

It is possible that women felt a certain social pressure to uncover their heads in order to avoid being accused of opposing republican reforms, particularly those who started to belong to the newly forming state classes. It is also possible that many women from both urban and rural backgrounds were resistant to unveiling. What I am arguing here is that there was always a space of personal autonomy for women to choose whether or not to uncover their heads. There had been great controversy over the changes affecting men and convincing them to replace the fez with felt hats. But whether peacefully or forcefully, once men agreed to the change, this established a model for women. But a woman took more persuasion to uncover her head than the mere fact that her husband or father had started to wear a felt hat.

It is therefore hard to argue that Atatürk and his fellow reformers utilized women as symbolic pawns for the transformation of society. Instead, they fixed the boundaries of social change at both the personal and public levels while laying down a set of social directives and personal models first and foremost for men. So, I argue that inasmuch as women followed the model of their husbands, fathers, sons and, of course, most importantly, the 'father of all Turks', Atatürk,[3] no real challenge was posed to the power bases of Islamic patriarchy as such, but the process helped to create new modalities to which men as well as women had to adjust themselves. Therefore, in the identity formation of republican Turkish society, the state's gender politics not only necessitated a change in women's social identities but aimed at providing an identity framework which would contain both men and women, rendering them rational citizens of republican Turkish society. I do not disagree, however, with the point that any assessment of the place of women in the formation of the new Turkish society needs special attention and specific analytical tools to explore the ways in which patriarchal structures in Turkish society, as well as the identity of women, have changed. Nor do I propose to omit the peculiarities of the emergence of the women's question in Turkey. However, one of the most important underpinnings of my argument on Turkish identity formation is that the sociological celebration of republican gender politics known as the women's question is itself a consequence of the realization of these politics within boundaries set in terms of manhood whereby men constituted the primary public model for both men and women. Thus no problem was created for men in terms of the formation of their gender identities to the extent that men should resemble other men and not women. Women found themselves expected to resemble not other women but men and this created a problem for the public constitution of women's gender identities, and also made it legitimate, though in a rather tacit way, for the question inherent in republican gender politics to be named the 'women's question'. However, this question was not important from the point of view of the state's gender policies since these were introduced to create the citizen identity of the Turkish people. It was this specific perspective of the republican state which, later on, created its own shortcomings in giving answers to the problems of women in a much more complicated and modern, albeit underdeveloped, society. Nevertheless, I will build my argument on the question of identity formation from the perspective of the formation of citizenship identity. In spite of its gender blindness, this process did not violate the basic Islamic rules of patriarchal precedence over the formation of private relations, ethics and conscience. It did, however, determine the foundations of Turkish identity politics and offered a new subject constitution regime. The relegation of Islam to the private sphere in a secularized social life and its curtailment by legislative power, for example, the elimination of polygyny, the sole right of men to divorce and the delegitimization of religious marriage, were important ways of restraining the power of Islamic patriarchy and these have been seen especially by conservative Muslim men as obstacles which hinder Muslims in their desire 'to live Islam as conscious Muslims'.

In this chapter I focus on the assumptions which lie behind the demand to 'live Islam as conscious Muslims'. I will examine what kind of assertions form the characteristics of the study group in their endeavour to build a true Muslim identity in a secular order. I suggest that, to be able to do this, the way in which they perceive the social developments which have given rise to the emergence of their political identity should be examined. One of the most important tasks of Islamic circles in Turkey is the attempt to rewrite the history of the establishment of the Turkish Republic and deconstruct the stories produced through so-called 'official history', in which no place was given to the perspectives of Islamic groups.[4] This attempt, however, should be seen as one way in which Islamic circles provide a basis of legitimization for their socio-political demands: they do this by showing how the Turkish state has repressed their voices in the construction of the foundations of Turkish society. Here, my intention is not simply to convey the discursive components of that specific story of legitimization, but to try and analyse (through reading one specific part of Turkish history) at which point this story could have intersected the story of the building of a national Turkish society.

In order to be able to trace the parameters of the Turkish transformation I have pointed to above, I will build my argument on the level of identity formation. In so doing, I hope to show how the people in this study, as a kind of status group, narrate their place as social actors and where they base the origins of their oppositional position and political claims. Thus, I will first attempt to make a brief and stylized reading of that specific story from the point of view of the socio-cultural history of the formation of the republican Turkish society. Second, I will try to show what possible impacts this history could have had on the formation of recent Islamic activism, which has relied upon political demands to create a new moral and social order, and moreover, how those impacts could have worked within, and between, the intermediary social levels to which the process of building up a new Muslim identity is inevitably connected. The reading I suggest here will also enable me to develop an argument about the changing meanings of the discursive reality through which some Islamic activists construct and reconstruct their oppositional discourse in conjunction with the way of coding reality in modern, secular Turkish society. Moreover, this reading will also enable me to explore the ways in which they articulate the socio-political project of Islamization by juxtaposing them with and differentiating them from the dominant discursive domains of the secularization and nationalization projects of republican Turkey.

Much of what I have to say will not be new to those who have been working on the history of Turkish modernization. Yet, in what follows, I will try to unfold, highlight and then connect some parts of that discourse so as to provide a new storyline to follow both the present and future trends of one aspect of Islamic activism in Turkey. In so doing, I hope to elucidate the stories of opposition that Islamic activists combine with stories of injury and exclusion and which they constantly try to place in a specific framework of historical discourse while nourishing their sentiment of victimization. Here I will focus on the matter from the perspective of identity formation, something I believe cannot be separated from the endeavours to create an Islamic way of life, and indeed the latter makes the maintenance of the praxis of building up a 'true' Muslim identity in a secular order possible.

Up to recent times Turkish social scientific tradition, as well as common parlance, celebrated and studied the emergence of Turkey as an independent, sovereign nation-state as the result of institutional transformations launched by the revolutionary cadres of the Republic, the well known Atatürk reforms. These reforms constituted the foundations of the new, modern republican Turkish society, but very little attention was paid to their actual impact on social life or how they found their echoes in the process of cultural construction and the formation of everyday life. Social science and popular myth concentrated on the building of a national identity through new legislative, jurisdictional and executive institutions. However, what people did with this new identity and how they coped with it was left out of the picture. Instead, the advantages that these reforms provided for the entire nation were concentrated upon. Hence, all alternative readings and viewpoints were seen merely as attacks directed at the very basis of the Republic and were often evaluated as rude manifestations of a power struggle taking place between the progressives and the reactionaries, who were thought to wish to appropriate the power bases of the new state for their own purposes. Whether true or not, one important consequence of approaching the question in such a restricted way was the prevention of a better understanding of the nature of possible future social opposition as well as the alternative political proposals put forward by people who had problems adjusting themselves to this newly emerging social system.

IV.2. Formation of a National Identity and the Code of Honour

To begin with I shall look at the place of Turks in the Ottoman *millet* system. The Ottoman Empire was classified according to a system of ethnic and religious groups called *millets*, but it is also true that it was an empire where Islam reigned and Turks as an ethnic group constituted the majority and, at least in the view of external observers if not in that of the Ottoman élite, they were believed to be the sovereign *millet* of the Ottoman Empire. However, although the Greek, Armenian and Jewish *millets* were separately recognized, Muslims were construed altogether as one *millet*, without being differentiated, for instance, as Turks, Arabs or Kurds (Lewis 1968, p. 335). Towards the end of the empire, especially in the era following the defeat in the Balkan Wars, the distinction between Turks as Muslims and non-Turks as non-Muslims was removed. At the time the ideals of Ottomanism were seriously doubted due both to the struggle of Christian peoples for national independence – and thereby the creation in the Turks of 'a profound mistrust of their Christian compatriots' (Lewis 1968, p. 340) – and to the Albanian independence movement which, as the Albanians were Muslims, hurt more. The principle of Ottomanism, then, was no longer enough to unify the Ottoman polity. Nor could pan-Islamism, in the face of Albanian and Arab nationalisms, or pan-Turkism, with the impossibility of reaching Asian Turkic groups and the danger of undermining Russian military and cultural power, hold society together (cf. Inalcık 1978, p. 327; Keyder 1989, pp. 53–4). On the other hand, following Keyder, it should be also emphasized that during the Young Turk era (1908–1918), for the bureaucratic ruling cadres, Turks appeared as the largest and most loyal ethnic group and could be relied on in their attempt to save the state, a project on which the ruling class based their political mission and which formed one of the most important legitimizations of their hold on power. The Armenians and Greeks who comprised the largest and most powerful sections of the Ottoman bourgeoisie were seen by the Young Turks as a potential threat not only to the bureaucratic control of the state but also to maintaining sovereignty of the state due to their economic and politico-cultural cooperation with the imperialist powers. Therefore, this made it impossible to see them as entrepreneurs who could be subjected to the political control of the state bureaucracy. Keyder goes on to argue that it was this historical situation which shifted the focus of struggle between the bureaucratic state class and the bourgeoisie to the plane of religious and ethnic conflict (Keyder 1989, pp. 56–60). Departing from this argument, I maintain that if the parameters of what Mardin (1966) calls 'divisiveness anxiety', which were also characteristic of the later republican state, were originally constituted around the axes of religion and ethnicity, then it becomes possible to claim that the unionist Young

Turks also sought a religious and ethnic union in the constitution of Turkish society. It should also be pointed out that following the experiences of the First World War and the war of independence, the division between Muslims and non-Muslims became much more salient to the process of building a new society than it ever had been. Nevertheless, the Kurdish uprisings just after the establishment of the Republic in 1923, though grounded on religious worries mainly due to the abolition of the Caliphate (1924),[5] must have been perceived not only as an ethnic threat, but also as a lesson for the ruling group in the unreliability of religion to provide either social cohesion or a legitimizing and unifying factor. This must have given rise to the idea of a national society as one homogenized group undivided by religious and ethnic social pressures. So, as is known, that group was determined as 'the Turks', and 'Turkishness' became the code of the newly established republican sovereignty. Nevertheless, the majority of those 'Turks' were Muslims, and Islam in its various forms continued to be the major reference point in maintaining the boundaries of that imagined unity. Moreover, in the years following liberation from the occupying forces, during the population exchanges, religion became the major criterion for determining who would migrate from the former lands of the Ottoman Empire to Anatolia and vice versa. Therefore, in the formative years of the Turkish nation-state, before the enactment of various projects involved in creating a national identity based on the ideal of rational individuals in a national society, religion still constituted the basic tie between the members of the society. That is to say, concerning the problem of identity, people who remained within the boundaries of the *Misak-ı Milli* (National Pact) of 1920 were, by and large, part of the Islamic *umma*, rather than members of a national unity.

Mardin (1990a) analyses the process of identity transformation in a rather original way. The question he poses is from which (imaginative) sources did the Atatürk social reforms take their strength? To answer this question he introduces a concept called 'transformation of the code of honour', which, in my view, also determined the parameters of social belonging and identity formation among the members of that emerging society. According to Mardin, one of the most important social transformations Atatürk aimed at was the reshaping of the self-perceptions of the members of society in relation to this new and emerging republican social system. Underlying this new self-perception is the notion of 'a code of honour'. This code of honour, however, is quite different from the one previously seen within the patrimonial structures of the empire, as well as that aspired to from the Tanzimat period onwards. In making this new code of honour, however, the key term Atatürk constantly used was 'autonomy', and members of society were imagined as 'autonomous persons' with free minds and consciences in the sense of being free from patrimonial ties, traditional communal ethics and religious world-views. This, I argue, reflects the basis of the individualism developed within European Enlightenment thought, according to which, as Sennett and Cobb argue, persons should be assessed on the basis of natural ability and talent rather than on parental influence or hereditary right, thereby securing liberation from the bonds of culture and past history. The logic behind the celebration of natural talent leads to Enlightenment individualism insofar as 'natural ability means the individual ought to be the master, rather than the prisoner, of culture' (Sennett and Cobb 1973, p. 61).

On the other hand, one of Mardin's best-known theses is based on the idea that, especially during the periods prior to the Tanzimat reforms and the Two Constitutional Period, the social composition of Ottoman society had been shaped within the framework of patrimonial structures in which the subjects of the Sultan were seen as divided into *avam* and *havas* (the low and the high). Even the social attachments of the higher sections of that society were shaped within the parameters of a specific patron-client relationship set in the patrimonial bureaucratic structure of Ottoman society, whose basic characteristic was determined according to the rules of life-long apprenticeship and the notion of benevolence intrinsic to this somehow 'gerontocratic' system, through which younger generations rose to their social status and identity. The nature of this system also determined the social and personal attachments of its members to it, especially for those occupying significant positions in the higher reaches of the state bureaucracy. Long before the First Constitutional Period, however, with the emergence of proto-nationalist movements under the guise of patriotism, the notion of 'people' had been introduced by the Young Ottomans into the political vocabulary of Ottoman society. This notion included every member of society without making any distinction between the high and the low, and therefore between the rich and the poor. Nevertheless, again according to Mardin, before the establishment of the Republic and especially in the discourse of Ziya Gökalp (the pioneering theorist of Turkish society), the concept of 'people' was something which existed in an embryonic form (*rüşeym*) from which it was thought a sense of self-awareness and determination would develop (1990a, p. 202). In the newly established republican society, one of the most important tasks of the transformation movement was the obliteration of the repercussions of patrimonial bureaucratic structures from the Ottoman Empire.

The Ottoman understanding of the way in which a state should be structured, however, had already undergone a series of changes from the Tanzimat period onwards. According to the principles of the Tanzimat, priority was to be given to institutions rather than individual rulers. This was meant to replace the idea of dedication to the Sultan with the idea of serving the state, which consequently gave rise to the formation of a state based on a bureaucracy rather than a ruler, but at the same time the bureaucracy around which the state was structured stressed its legal, rather than its rational, dimension. In addition, particularly in the Young Turk era, another novelty gained prominence: the idea of impersonal concern for the welfare of people, which went hand in hand with the older motive of saving the state (Heper 1985, pp. 44–6). Nevertheless, the republican era witnessed the attempt to replace this somewhat modern understanding of the structural relationship between state and society with an understanding of a relationship between society and the egalitarian (functionally horizontal) social structures of the republican nation-state, in which the members of society would gain their social identity as equal citizens of the republic, i.e., as real, mature people holding ultimate sovereignty. This understanding of sovereignty, however, was quite different from the one that was expressed in terms of *shura* (*meşveret*), i.e., the Islamic notion of the necessity of consultation and mutual deliberation between Muslims for the governance of society. This was espoused by the Islamic reformers at the beginning of the Constitutional Periods as a way of limiting the political sovereignty of the ruler and would also constitute, together with the notion of *adala* (*adalet*, justice), the basis of administrative law in order to set the moral limits of that sovereignty (Tunaya 1991, pp. 43–4). This earlier understanding of sovereignty was also questioned by the Young Turks rallying around the Committee of Union and Progress, who were more inclined towards the materialistic and positivistic outlook of Western ideals, insofar as these ideals served to modernize the state machine and preserve its power basis, independence and strength in the face of the predations of powerful Western nations. However, it is quite well known that in the imagination of the Ottoman intelligentsia of the time, who were mostly from the military élite, the modernization of the army and the ways in which this was put into practice constituted the primary model for the modernization of state and society. What I want to argue here is that, as the overwhelming majority of that intelligentsia came from the military cadres of the state, their view of sovereignty must have been shaped around the idea of strengthening the state with a powerful army in a world in which the Ottoman Empire was fighting to preserve its shrinking dominions and getting progressively weaker relative to the imperialist forces. Thus, for that ruling élite, the need to get the full support of the entire population, and the desire to integrate with them in terms of finding a basis of legitimization for their cause of saving the state, must have given way to the formation of an ideal of sovereignty which, first and foremost, was to be backed by military strength. This view, intermingled with the fear of losing independence, would have limited the idea of people's sovereignty to an understanding of the necessity of collaboration between state, army and people to ensure the survival of the society in the face of impending imperialist interventions by European forces. Later on, this understanding of 'unity' between leading military groups and ordinary people was to be exemplified during the war of independence, inasmuch as the military were successful in rallying the civilian population to their cause, and in fact declared the episode a people's war. Therefore, the idea of sovereignty belonging to the people might have gained its legitimacy due to the collaboration of the people (formerly ordinary members of Ottoman society) with the soldiers to liberate at least the core lands of the country from the occupying forces. In other words, the 'people', in the embryonic state, passed the first stage of maturity by showing a determination for their own independence and liberty.

Yet this 'people' was almost entirely Muslim, and the fact that religious bonds played an important role in providing solidarity between different ethnic groups and the fact that the idea of saving the Caliphate from the infidel became one of the most important leitmotifs of the war of independence are well-known parts of Turkish history. The entire cultural history of the establishment of the republican society, however, has usually been construed in the tradition of heroic legend, such as the stories of martyrdom and *gazilik*.[6] Such celebration of heroism and its acceptance as a natural part of Turkish history, I think, though quite paradoxically, gave rise to a failure to understand what was transformed into what in the constitution of a new social identity. More importantly, there was a failure to inquire as to the previous life conditions of those who were once ordinary inhabitants of Ottoman society and who would later on find themselves the members of the new social order in the aftermath of that war of independence, rather than just seeing them as former heroes of that liberation war. This question is particularly important for the point that I am trying to make here, in that I maintain the 'transformation of the code of honour' should be taken as a guide in the unfolding of the historical process of transforming the pious Muslims in a multi-ethnic empire state into rational individuals in a national society.

Thus, when we look at the conditions under which ordinary citizens in Ottoman society lived and the possible sociological description of everyday life and the general structure of the society, I think Mardin's observations will be once more helpful in getting to the roots of the problem. I understand from Mardin's discourse on the basis of Ottoman society and culture that bureaucratic structures constituted one pillar of that somewhat patrimonial social system and the other important pillar of it was the *mahalle*. In other words, at the time when this bureaucratic structure consti-tuted the backbone of the patrimonial state and society, the *mahalle* type of social setting was the basis on which the everyday life of ordinary urban people was organized within the boundaries of the cultural norms of that specific type of social living, and hence bonded the minor structures of the society to the larger context of the social system. According to Mardin, *mahalle* was the 'smallest operative unit of the community in the Ottoman Empire' providing a cultural environment in which

> primary education was undertaken, births were celebrated, mar-riages were arranged, and the last rites were performed for the dying. It was here that the mosque operated as a social institution

bringing all inhabitants to hear what was expected of them. It was against the background of the *mahalle* that the authority of the paterfamilias was exercised and supported. And it was here that sometimes blood-money was paid; that the Islamic institution of morals-control wormed its way into drinking parties and gambling dens, and organized posses to surprise careless lovers; that the café – a communication centre – operated; that the firm stamp was affixed by the prayer leader on a petition that was to travel on to higher authorities; and that local saints' tombs could be visited and living holy men dispensed their own kind of influence and justice. ...The *mahalle* was more than an administrative unit with somewhat arbitrarily drawn boundaries; it was a compact *Gemeinschaft* with its boundaries protected by its own toughs and faithful dogs, and a setting within which much of the normal life of an average Ottoman citizen was shaped' (1981, p. 214).

Thus the *mahalle* ethos was an inseparable part of ordinary Ottoman social life, heavily coloured with its religious ideas of morality and conduct. This way of organizing the idiosyncratic characteristics of social life, however, again following Mardin, did not fit in with the ideal of creating a new 'code of honour' based on the notion of personal 'autonomy' gained primarily through breaking with religiously determined communal morals-control.[7] In fact this was the main reason for the distaste for Ottoman social life developed by the new intelligentsia and the civil and military bureaucratic élites, whose personal identity had already begun to be shaped within the framework of, and according to the rules of, positivist Western educational principles and school directives.[8] Here, in modern secular educational institutions, such as the Rüşdiye (lycée for the study of ethics) and the Mülkiye, Tıbbıye and Harbiye (colleges for government, medical and military studies), the pupils not only encountered the ideals of the European Enlightenment, modern sciences and the rules of positivist rationalism, but also a different kind of personality formation and social attachment. In this context, especially in the modern military college environment, the social attachments of the younger generations were not centred around the idea of loyalty to the Sultan but to the country. The notion of Islamic community began to be challenged by a more abstract concept of society. Moreover, the subjects of the Sultan had already begun to be conceived as citizens of the Ottoman society. This social change was not merely the result of new developments in the political and administrative spheres, but was also made possible by changes in the ideological context of society first evident among the new military-bureaucratic élite and élite-to-be, which are usually known as westernization.[9]

It should also be stressed that even for the highly westernized sections of the élite the roots of their cultural identity were to be found in an Islamic universe rather than in the Western world. In other words, it is hard to imagine that the social mobilizers who aspired to make the late Ottoman society part of the modern world civilization could envision any identity which was developed completely outside the parameters of Muslim identity. The importance of this point stems from the fact that this aspect of the identity formation problem of republican Turkish society has usually been omitted in discussions of the secularization movement. This omission usually leads to the perception that primordial ties of those social actors were shaped within a social context similar to the one shared by today's secular nationalists, liberals and leftists who struggle for the integration of Turkish society in today's 'modern world' without highlighting the Muslim aspect of their social identity or just by rejecting it. It is therefore helpful to keep in mind that, at the time when Mustafa Kemal and the Ottoman/Turkish military élite tried to reconstruct the ethical foundations of Turkish society, the idea of replacing religious ethics with science as a moral value was not a common one. In fact, it faced the strong opposition of the ulema and other religious sections of the society, particularly the Islamist thinkers from the Second Constitutional Period.[10] Similarly, the notion of being autonomous (*mustaqill*, *müstakil*) at the level of personality, as mentioned above, and the notion of independence (*istiqlal*, *istiklal*) at the national level – which in Mardin's terms constituted the key concepts of Atatürks's understanding of 'the code of honour'(1981, p. 212) – only came into being after both the attainment of a certain level of development and changes in the educational, political and moral systems, and experience obtained on the international platform during the struggle for independence.

Concerning systemic change at the ideological level, it is interesting to note Anderson's (1990) argument regarding the formation of the idea of nation as an imagined, limited community. He referred to the emergence of print-languages, which replaced the hegemony of holy languages, and hence paved the way for the secularization of the 'cosmos' which came into being with the spread of diverse printed material. Together with the advent of newspapers, this created the possibility of thinking of one's lived relations as connected to a framework of new forms of narrations. In short, this resulted in what he called 'print-capitalism' in his attempt to locate those new developments in their correct socio-economic place, especially in Europe from the eighteenth century onwards – a point easily traceable in even the early writings of Mardin and in his overall discourse on the origins of Turkish modernity in a much more critical way.

For Mardin, too, the spread of the 'book' as an intellectual vehicle is important. A 'world' shaped itself around the all-engrossing book, which could provide people with a point of reference for individual autonomy, a space for individual imagination, and the possibility of putting oneself at the centre of one's own ideas, to interpret the world 'as it is' and control one's own thinking, allowing people to make their own interpretations.[11] Although this change in perception was limited to a small group of educated people, its impacts on society were large. This was not because this group was in a ruling position in the society but because, in Chatterjee's (1993) terms, for instance, it led to the creation of a space for secularization, freedom, equality and cultural refinement. Nevertheless, to understand the emergence of national-ism and national societies as imagined communities in non-Western societies, one should not rely too much on the European experience, which was marked by the ascendancy of Enlightenment thought. On the contrary, as Chatterjee points out, we should also ask: 'if nationalisms in the rest of the world have to choose their imagined community from certain "modular" forms already made available to them by Europe and the Americas, what do they have left to imagine?' (Chaterjee 1993, p.5).

Similarly, although much of what the republican reformers of Turkish society imagined was parallel to what their European counterparts had assumed for the formation of a national society, the economic, political and cultural problems that they had to deal with were not of course the same, and nor were the solutions which were developed. In the formation of republican Turkish society, however, religion appeared as one of the most important problems to come to grips with. On the one hand, it posed a problem for the maintenance of state control over society, in the sense of sustaining the legal and the ethical legitimization; on the other hand, it constituted a problem in terms of building up a national identity to be shared by all sections of society, because of the extent to which religion formed the most powerful source of reference for the actualization of everyday life.

IV.3. The Secularization of Turkishness through Art and Science

In the project of building a new republican Turkish society, however, religion was no longer to perform the function of being the legitimate source for the regulation of social life. In other words, it was stripped of its power to regulate social life and people's personal and communal attachments. Before the establishment of the Republic of Turkey, again as Mardin indicates, 'despite the extensive secularization of the nineteenth century, birth, education, culture, marriage, death, inheritance had still required the services of Ulema' (1977, p. 287).[12] That is to say, the most elementary aspects of social life were mainly arranged according to religiously determined rules and presided over by religious officers. Thus, religion was evident in almost every area of public and private social affairs affecting people's ordinary daily lives and, moreover, it constituted the basic source of information for almost the entire society. Moreover, if not the religion itself, then cultural customs, habits and beliefs which were informed by Islamic ideologies and world-views played a great role in the shaping of people's ordinary social lives.

In the socio-political project of the Turkish nation-state, science was seen as the source of answers to people's existential questions, and religion was thus allocated no space whatever in the constitution of this new social order. The aim was to cleanse society of the backward-looking religious order while at the same time both transforming religion into an orthodoxy 'purified' of its superstitious elements which suffocated the masses and reducing it to a matter of individual conscience. In so doing it was hoped to orient society towards the rationalism and positivism that had produced modern industrial, developed, and thus civilized, nations in the West. Therefore, following one of the basic features of those modern Western nations, secularism, religion had to be placed under state control in the sense that 'religion and the world should be separated in matters relating to the state and the nation'.[13] Consequently, as well as the basic aspects of social regulation (birth, death, etc.), the society's entire institutional system, including education, commerce, the legislative and executive branches and the defence forces, were completely secularized. New secularized institutions (some of which had already been partly secularized from the Tanzimat period onwards, especially those pertaining to the areas of education and the military) were formed as the bases of the new republican state and society.

In this social project, as has been often pointed out, one of the most important efforts of the republican reformation movement was the banning in 1924 of major religious educational institutions by the Tevhid-i Tedrisat (Unification of Education Law), together with other traditional institutions and religious orders such as *tekke*s (dervish lodges), *zaviya*z (small mosques) and *tarikat*s (Sufi orders) in 1925, which performed various religious services and functions. These had been especially important in the sense of satisfying the needs of the popular and mystical faith of the Muslim majority. New republican educational and civil institutions attempted to fulfil their social functions, such as the maintenance of social information, communication, and thus to a certain extent, a 'coherent' world-view. Moreover, new civic rituals were gradually introduced to generate a new form of social collectivity, but these could not satisfy all sections of society as rapidly as was hoped. I argue that this did not stem from the unsuitability of republican reforms to create a modern, independent, sovereign, and centralized nation-state, but rather that the relative failure can be attributed to their contextual insufficiency in creating a democratic society in which both the free will and public participation of the people would be sustained to form the social, political and economic bases of the imagined modern social system. This was because, first and foremost, the Turkish republican system offered a corporatist society unified around the ideal of solidarist citizenship, instead of suggesting a liberal-pluralist social system in which cultural as well as moral pluralism be attained.[14] In this republican model, to provide the ideal of equality among its citizens in legal and judicial terms, the state had to stay the same distance from all its citizens. Therefore the state, at least in principle, had to homogenize all its citizens, in the sense of acknowledging no racial, ethnic, religious, sexual or class differences among them. It is no exaggeration to state that the only overt social differentiation recognized by the early republican Turkish state was age and pro-fession. One way of explaining the purpose of such corporatism may be to attribute it to the class characteristics of the revolutionary cadres, in addition to the developments taking place in world politics in general at the time.

According to Keyder (1989), for instance, these cadres were no different from the military-bureaucratic state class, nor was there a strong bourgeois class to challenge bureaucratic control. Although a Muslim bourgeoisie attempted to fill the space caused by the emigration of the Christian bourgeoisie, their political and cultural maturity was not yet enough to support a challenge to the strong ruling power of the bureaucratic élite. In this respect, they were not only totally subject to the state's legal and economic regulations, but were quite unable to propose social projects and models for the rest of society. They were under the control of the state élite and a handful of intellectuals, who were the strong supporters of that new state with Mustafa Kemal as its leader. However, most Turks tried to adjust to the new way of life, the general framework of which was drawn by Atatürk himself, and to set a model for new social behaviour and conduct. The most important reforms of all were those which occurred in the public sphere and aimed to provide models for the rearrangement of the private lives of Turkish people. These include the reformation of the Civil Law (1926); the enactment of the hat reform (1926); the invention of new civic rituals, such as memorial days; and the establishment of new cultural centres, such as Halk Evleri (People's Houses, 1932) which aimed to organize social activities and support and disseminate newly introduced republican reforms and provide the integration of people into the new space of nationalism.[15] Among these reforms, for example, the symbolic importance of the hat reform was usually seen merely as an expression of the desire to look Western.[16] But I suggest seeing this reform as another way of 'reshaping the heads' of Turkish men. Hence, as I have argued in the first section of this chapter, this reform also helped women to uncover their heads: once men accepted the change, this constituted a legitimate example for women to follow. Thus this reform was a brilliant way of persuading men to give consent to women's new 'open' way of dressing. Similarly, urging men and women to obliterate sexual segregation, at least in public life, by working side by side[17] and the participation of couples in public affairs[18] brought great differences to societal life. The adoption of the Roman Calendar (1925) and the European metric system (1928), along with the shift of the weekly holiday from Friday to Sunday (1934), changed the rhythm and the periodization of public and private life and the pace of work and production.[19] The abolition of traditional public titles such as Efendi, Paşa and Bey (1934) not only reshaped public representation of personal status, but also regulated the way in which people addressed one another. The adoption of the Latin alphabet (1928), as part of the language reform, was another watershed in the Turkish evolution.[20] The impact of these reforms is evident in the long run in terms of the formation of the contextual framework of self-perception and social identity of the Turkish people. However, it cannot be said that these social novelties met with the same enthusiasm from all sections of society, or that everybody adapted themselves at the same rate. Mostly depending on their distance from the social centre of power, some were eager and quick to adapt themselves, while others were not. In fact, considerable resistance was evident, especially among those who had lost their previous prestigious status and sources of income, as well as those who saw no use in changing the political regime and dropping Islamic legal and social precepts in favour of secularization and westernization. Yet, overall the desire for national sovereignty, equality and cultural refinement (at least at the discursive level) was stronger than the sentiment of loss and bewilderment, which generally stemmed from a belief that Islam was the only possible source of legitimization for the legal and civil affairs of society, and loyalty to Islamic roots and tradition.

Here, by tradition I refer not just to Islamic legislation, jurisdiction and the like, but rather to an entire patriarchal system regulating all sorts of relations between men and women in favour of men, and which cannot be confined either to familial relations or to the domestic space since it covers all aspects of life ranging from the regulation of legal and civil rights to self-actualization of people; that is, the whole of life itself. The extent to which transformation of the existing system of patriarchy, heavily coloured and regulated by so-called Islamic precepts, was seen as desirable affected the degree and the strength of popular opposition, as well as causing disagreement among the ruling group. The challenge which was posed to that transformation also differed according to the way in which Islam was interpreted by the reformers themselves. Although the main target of the reformers seemed to be the backward-looking 'little tradition' of Islam, they also aimed to relegate the 'great tradition' of Islam to a peripheral status, since it was associated with conservatism, and wished to control it by separating it from its power bases. On the other hand, this same 'great tradition' has also been presented as able to adapt itself to those new changes taking place in the order of life. This paradoxical situation, however, is not something that can be attributed to Islam as such. It is a consequence of both looking at Islam as something which can exist outside social interpretation and lived relations, and seeing it as an entity which can be disengaged from the ongoing power relations.[21] From this point on, then, I will maintain that in the history of the formation of national Turkish society the treatment visited on the religious sphere, whether great or little tradition, was not actually different from that in other social spheres such as politics, education and culture. To the extent that homogenization was a goal for all social spheres, religion underwent the same process. In the reformist understanding of the organization of society, as argued above, the only functional differentiation allowed was on the basis of occupation in order to justify economic diversity (although this was only actualized at the discursive level), and this was only possible if society was examined from the vantage point of centralist power: this is what I understand by the slogan 'modernization from above', which was frequently invoked to explain republican Turkish modernization. Therefore, in this process, as was constantly pronounced, religion was seen as a matter of individual conscience and the state was there to protect the freedom of that domain, i.e., the freedom of conscience, and to provide public religious services for its citizens. However, no version of religion was accepted and serviced other than that approved by the state. Furthermore, by confining religion to the private domain, its public visibility also decreased. More importantly, religion was not given a place in the attempts at cultural refinement, nor was there any considerable effort to refine the social condition of religion itself even by, for instance, making it a ceremonial component of the state.

In this imagined version of a modern Turkish society, the completion of homogenization in the sense of modernization of all society was seen only as a matter of time, and, through the enactment of correct policies and regulations, all sections of the society, including peasants of course, would be able to keep pace in the march of progress, and hence end up at the same level of development. The reactionaries, naturally, would be strongly repressed. In order to accomplish this national modernization project, however, Turks were to be proud, confident and hardworking and the power they needed was to be found in their pure blood. This power of the Turks, as with other positive characteristics, was in no way conceived as stemming from their Islamic faith. Thus, the association of Turks as Muslims and vice versa, which the Young Turks had made when they started to think in terms of a distinct and integrated social entity, lost its significance. Turkish people, then, regardless of their place in the pyramid of social stratification, had to be conscientious citizens, faithful parents, respectful and intelligent students, not because they were both Muslims and Turks but because they were merely Turks. In other words, Turkishness was completely secularized, and with this formula, which I will call the secularization of Turkishness, it also became possible to conceive of Armenian, Greek, Jewish, Circassian, Georgian and Kurdish members of society as Turks, regardless of religious and ethnic origin. In fact, it became somewhat shameful to address people publicly according to their ethnic or religious origins, since this was perceived as undermining their rights as equal Turkish citizens. This was also applicable in the case of the social inequalities between men and women as Turkish citizens. Since men and women were declared equal Turkish citizens, to talk about the social inequality between them was also viewed as impolite, and hence people pretended that they were social equals. The differences between Alevis and Sunnis were also rendered virtually meaningless by proclaiming them all as Muslims, despite the fact that religious institutions regulated by the state operated mainly according to Sunni precepts. This understanding of social equality, in the sense of an almost absolute sameness, went so far in the 1930s that even economic inequalities were seen as something to be suppressed, through the proclamation that Turkish society had neither class- nor privilege-based differentiation. If the authoritarian denial inherent in this endeavour is set aside, these unrealistic good intentions can be attributed to optimism regarding future realization of equality.

This was what Gellner (1983b) called 'forced homogenization'. But despite the expectation that people would become autonomous individuals, we should ask what they were left with for their private imagination. The paradoxical situation in which people were imagined as autonomous, free individuals on the one hand, and expected, on the other, to adjust to a given model of citizenship imposed upon them from above, also marked the republican regime's identity politics. Nevertheless, I will argue that for the republican reformers, and particularly for Atatürk, this situation was perceived as neither a paradox, nor as 'forced homogenization', but rather in terms of their belief in science and its universal and inherent moral value. For Atatürk, becoming a part of modern civilization was not a question of mere imitation of Western societies; rather it was a question of the adoption of science and the attribution to it of moral value, something which had made the development of Western society possible in the first place. Moreover, since science was universal, its intrinsic moral value could not belong to any one group of people, but was shared by the whole of humanity.[22] Similarly, the autonomous individuals of the national Turkish society could only emancipate themselves from patrimonial ties, traditional communal ethics and religious worldviews, i.e., from the traditional bonds of backwardness, and become civilized by adopting the moral principles of science, which were the combination of the principles of positivism, rationalism and secularism. In addition, the freedom of conscience which constituted the first condition of personal autonomy could only be gained by the materialization of these principles. The realization of the hypothetical sameness, which was understood as the core principle of social equality, would only come about when this belief was shared by every member of the society – as a consequence, then, of the free will of people. Therefore the motive for the westernization which took place in Atatürk's imaginaire was not imitation of the West as such and dependence on it, but the adoption of the universal values which flourished from the power of science, which he believed constituted the basic guidance for social life in the West. Similarly, secularization was also construed as one of the consequences of the application of science to the order of life. Since science was to be the guiding principle of life, then the moral value intrinsic to it should prevail. This 'truth' of modernity, i.e., the belief in the absolute power of science which also viewed rationalism as a value in itself, was a nebulous idea for most of the republican social mobilizers: they were unable to see it as the development of a well-equipped philosophical programme, having had no extensive experience of employing scientific principles in the course of social order.

Nevertheless, I think, all these discursive drafts formed the basis of the new 'code of honour' according to which it was hoped future generations of Turkish society would develop as rational and autonomous citizens/individuals. On the other hand, if science was seen as essential to the constitution of secular rational individuals, art with a capital 'A' occupied a similar status in the realization of cultural refinement in the making of a national identity. This was, I believe, because the generation of a distinct, modern, national type of culture, different from that developed within the boundaries of Ottoman élite culture, was another ambition of the republican modernization project. In this respect, Turkish Muslims, who had for so long been alienated from 'universal' art forms by Islamic conservatism, were to be familiarized with them, while at the same time preserving, discovering and flavouring their folk arts with a touch of universal (read Western) art styles, thereby forming the new basis for the Turkish people's spiritual refinement and thus their joy of living. Here, again, religion was given no role. Neither its cultural manifestations, such as hymns, narratives and symbolic objects, nor its spiritual essence were to be utilized. The encounter of the ordinary Turkish citizens with the high form of universal-yet-Western culture was rather dramatic, and was marked by a considerable sense of distaste, if not by strong protest.[23] As any Turkish citizen who has attended public school in Turkey can attest, school ceremonies have for a long time provided good examples of the effort to create a culturally refined environment for the new generations of Turkish youth, something which came into being as an extension of the combination of official and popular taste in 'art'.

Since the tastes of the Ottoman élite were associated with social corruption and blamed for the decline and degeneration of Turkish culture, the creation of new tastes in cultural conduct based on national or popular art forms was seen as necessary. In this respect, the modernization of Turkish women as the future mothers of the nation's younger generations appeared as a new necessity. The process was attempted through new educational institutions. Here young women would acquire new skills, which could be put to good use economically, and learn Western adab-ı muaşeret (rules of etiquette) combined with respect for Turkish family norms, and they would also create new, modern Turkish handicrafts and fashion lines. A type of cultural refinement and progress was also thought to be provided in these new vocational schools, mainly Kız Enstitüleri (Girls' Institutes), by the 'scientific' study of household management and child care.

The most effective way of creating a space for national culture was to tailor public space according to the needs of the new regime. This, together with the need to perform the administrative functions of the centralist nation-state, brought the development of new architectural forms, and the desire to consolidate the presence of the nation-state was evident in the new formal squares (hükümet meydanı), municipal parks (belediye parkı), stations, schools, and the like. These new public constructions connected provincial towns to the central authority and served a function in the dissemination of republican ideology,[24] and they also made people aware of the social context in which they were living. Mosques were also an inseparable part of the public space, but their presence was nationalized by the translation of the ezan (call to prayer) from Arabic into Turkish, thus replacing the sacred public voice of Islam with the profane voice of nationalism. This was the most dramatic intervention by the state in matters sacred. This overt transgression of the boundaries of the public sphere into the private sphere affecting people's right to worship was seen as a serious violation of the social contract between the state and the people, in that it intervened in matters of private conscience. Despite the justification that this action was part of the attempt to cleanse the national Turkish culture of elements reminiscent of Arabic culture,[25] it was seen as indicative of how far the republican state would go to eradicate the place of Islamic tradition in social life. The ban on the Arabic ezan was borne in mind in Islamic circles and affected the constitution of their discourse of opposition, even after it was lifted by the DP government in 1950 in the first month of its rule.[26]

IV.4. Shifting of Cultural Authenticity and Islamic Politics

The major tension prevailing in Turkish society during the single party regime of the Republican People's Party (RPP) from 1931, and also just after the establishment of the multi-party system in1946, has often been discussed under the heading of the duality between centre and periphery, following the analytical 'key' that Mardin (1973) suggested be used to explore the parameters of Turkish politics. The social cleavage that appeared in the form of cultural duality between the rural masses and the military-bureaucratic state class who, according to Mardin, successfully maintained the co-optation of a sizeable portion of the provincial notable class to the ranks of the RPP (1973, p. 184) stemmed mainly, I think, from the bureaucratic élite's failure to correctly assess the crisis of identity which emerged under the contradictory pressures of the old and the new, both at the individual and collective level. This created a sense of deprivation in the cultural dimension, in addition to a sense of distress which showed itself in various ways in the economic realm. In the view of the westernized, well educated modern élite, however, the masses in general, and peasants in particular, were not mature enough to know what was good and what was not good for themselves in terms of the requirements of the modern world. The ignorance of the peasantry made them prone to being easily deceived, and therefore, according to the RPP's élite, they had to be protected from the opponents of the regime (Güneş-Ayata 1992, p. 77). Instead of taking the demands of peripheral classes seriously, they tended to see their distress as signs of reaction and ignorance. If peasants were backward, small merchants and artisans were too conservative to ac-commodate themselves to the economic and social policies implemented by the state with the motto of 'For the people, despite the people.' These people, then, had to wait until they were mature enough to understand the rationale of the reforms. The ruling élite were also far from being able to see the class dimension of that distress due to their denial of class distinction. Similarly, they could not understand the changing relationship between local not-ables and peasants and thus could not see that, as Mardin argues, 'economic power rather than domination set the relation between notables and villagers' (1973, p. 185). It can also be argued that, despite the success in building the necessary infrastructure, the

republican reforms did not lead to a total change in people's living
conditions. On the contrary, as some observers maintained, the
early republican regime was marked by its exclusionary politics in
the sense that especially the rural masses were left to their own
traditional devices and they were politically untouched, ideologically deactivated and organizationally disjoined (Sunar and Toprak
1983, p. 427). Therefore when the DP was established in 1946 it
based its political propaganda on an oppositional line represented
as between the 'real populists' and 'bureaucrats' (Mardin 1973, p.
185), the former becoming the 'true' agents of social mobilization
and leading the participation of the masses in political and economic processes. It is interesting to note that the new order created
by the RPP, which was once appreciated by the Muslim land-
owners, merchants, traders and artisans because they saw commerce and industry in the Republic as possible avenues for their
advancement (and hence tolerated the social and political change),
was seen, at least by some of them, as an obstacle to both their
own advancement and that of society. At this point, following
McCarthy, I will argue that in the aftermath of both the First
World War and the war of independence, with a new psychological
awareness of the possibility of change caused by their own mortality
and by radical changes in their environment, the majority of the
Turkish population must have perceived 'change' as beneficial
(McCarthy 1983, p. 139) as must also have been the case after the
social impacts of the Second World War. Therefore, for most
Turkish people what was at stake here was not resisting change as
such but the problem of deciding on the correct direction and
social constituents of this change as well as on which bases of
legitimization it should be grounded. However, as Keyder (1988)
argues, in the early years of the Republic, in the single party regime,
state induced social change brought its own limits. It reached its
apex in the statist authoritarianism of the bureaucratic élite. A
single party ruling society in the name of nation, the RPP, which
assumed this responsibility in the 1931 party congress, not only
eliminated all kinds of societal autonomy but also attempted to
control the economic and ideological domains. In 1936, Ismet
Inönü, the prime minister and the general secretary of the RPP,
declared the full congruency between the state administration
and the party organization. Thus, all state officials in the administrative branch became loyal party officials. Nevertheless, the

previous alliance of the political élite and the 'nascent bourgeoisie', who joined forces 'to isolate a national economic space for themselves', started to collapse during the later years of the Second World War, especially with the enactment of the Wealth Levy in 1942. Under the conditions of wartime shortages, which saw the emergence of a profiteering stratum, bitter divisions among the bourgeoisie occurred. The increasing alienation between bureaucracy and the bourgeoisie revealed itself in a critique whereby 'statist policies were inferior to market liberalism', and the 'supremacy of pluralism [was] superior to corporatist solidarity' (Keyder 1989, pp. 205–6). In 1946, with the introduction of the multi-party system, the parliament became a platform for debate and, as Keyder puts it: 'The two pillars of the opposition platform were economic and religious freedom: these upheld the market against statist intervention, and traditions over the political oppression and ideological onslaught of the center' (Keyder 1988, p. 206).

In short, following Mardin (1973), it can be argued that until the establishment of the multi-party regime, the republican bureaucratic élite, in keeping with their Ottoman heritage, construed modernization as a social project to be implemented from top down with a fine sense of regulation. By ignoring the possibility of bottom-up mobilization, they could not utilize the integrative networks of modern society (pp. 183–4). It was this understanding which also entailed the relegation of religion to the periphery. This had a number of serious consequences. Firstly, the rural and urban lower classes, and also the provincial middle classes, experienced what amounted to a repression of religious expression and organization. As a result this large section of the population was, by and large, abandoned to their own devices in the structuring of their world. Secondly, the élite was no longer aware of the roles and meanings acquired by religion in the periphery. They tended to assess the role of religion in society by looking at the uprisings of certain religious groups in the early years of the Republic, the most brutal of which involved the beheading of a young reserve-officer, Kubilay.[27] Thirdly, the ability of peripheral groups to develop the means through which they could express their claims in ways that would be comprehensible at a national level was curtailed.

When the DP relegitimized Islam and traditional values, Islamic actors, released from their position of political powerlessness,

started to raise their voices through different channels. The establishment of the multi-party regime allowed people to rally round
the political parties and provided an appropriate forum for the
formulation of their various socio-economic demands, and for
transmitting them to the centre. At the same time it allowed people
to exercise a certain amount of political power. This became very
important in the process of identity formation since it provided a
space for the socio-political participation of people who sought
channels to transmit their socio-cultural and economic unrest.
Nevertheless, because the emergence of the multi-party regime in
general, and the DP in particular, was, first and foremost, experienced as an intra-group division in the ruling RPP, especially during
the years following the death of Atatürk, these new political tendencies were generally seen by the RPP as the political games of
opposition groups, who used religion as an instrument to build
their own power and hence exploited the religious feelings of the
ignorant masses (Mardin 1973, p.184; Ahmad 1977, pp. 367–9). For
example, in his public speeches, Adnan Menderes, the president of
the DP, even after he was elected prime minister, constantly claimed
that for the RPP there was only a 'handful of real human beings in
the country' and that these were the 'intellectuals and the reformers
who saw the rest of the people as being bigoted, enemies of reform
and the followers of reactionary principles'.[28] Whereas for him,
Turkish people 'were Muslims and would remain Muslims' and
they were 'true and sincere Muslims who, while united in their
own religious convictions and beliefs, also knew how to respect
the conscientious religious convictions and beliefs of others'. He
also proclaimed that 'just as dragging the army into politics is a
serious crime, so is trying to make a sacred institution like religion
the vehicle and instrument of various aims, interests and political
disputes'.[29] Thus, during DP rule, it became legitimate to publicly
label the founders of the Republic, as well as the strong supporters
of the reforms, as arrogant élitists who constantly despised the
pious people of Turkey as bigoted, ignorant and worthless.

This rather harsh propaganda deepened the rift between people
who saw secularization as the core principle of the modernization
of society and those who had problems with that process of secularization. Nevertheless, it can be said that this also made the
republican ruling classes much more aware of the problem of
reconciling the national identity with the Muslim character of

Turkish people than they had been just before the establishment of the multi-party regime. Later on, this point was salient in the political discourse of the National Unity Committee (NUC), which had brought about the military takeover of 27 May 1960 and overthrown the DP, proclaiming their aim of restoring unity and order to the country. The NUC tried to transform religion into a 'national instrument of the state' while giving it 'both a national and a progressive image in order to prevent its being used as an anti-reformist instrument' (Ahmad 1977, p. 374). This actually paved the way for stricter state control of religion, though the aim was 'to take it out of the exploitative hands of conservative interest groups', and to reform it to serve the modernization of society. For instance, by secularizing the curricula of religious educational institutions, for example, the Yüksek Islam Enstitüsü (Advanced Islamic Institute, established in 1959), by introducing subjects such as economics, astronomy, civil law and sociology, a new 'enlightened' generation of men of religion was envisioned. The Koran was translated into Turkish to make it available to Turkish readers. The Directorate of Religious Affairs became much more active in designing the Friday sermons and started to publish a new magazine *Hutbeler* (Sermons) (Ahmad 1977, p. 375) with several aims in view: to combat the possible superstitious tendencies of local imams and preachers, to provide a model, to limit the chances of religious opposition and to show which way was to be followed and was approved by the state. It was hoped that the awareness of the majority of Turkish people would be increased to the point that one day they themselves would ask for Turkish recitation of the *ezan*,[30] an idea that has yet to see the light of day. In the more democratic atmosphere provided by the 1961 Constitution, Islamic circles started to seek opportunities to find political expression in party politics in the re-established parliamentary political system of Turkey.

Throughout the 1950s, the Turks tried to come to grips with the question of democratization which went hand in hand with the questions of national identity and cultural authenticity. This was in a social context in which the ideal of developmentalism as associated with the ideal of modernization, i.e., catching up with the West, had already begun to set the boundaries of social imagination. The evaluation of the place of religion in the society has differed according to various vantage points, ranging from labelling it an obscurantist reaction to republican ideology to seeing it as an indispensable element of parliamentary politics. Yet, in any case, religion stood for cultural authenticity: the Islamic heritage of secular republican Turkish society was the definitive attribute of Turkey's exceptional national identity, both in the international arena and on the domestic plane, whether seen as a successful version of Muslim westernization or placed into the context of a constant struggle by Muslims to resist Western assimilation. Subsequently, during the 1960s and 1970s, in right-wing politics this attribute of the Turkish nation was to be preserved so as to carve out a national identity in the process of modernization whereby a non-imitative westernization would be realized. In social democratic politics it was to be softened as much as possible so that religion would not become an obstacle on the way to westernization and national democratization; in left-wing politics, it was to be totally eradicated as an element which kept the masses in a state of 'false consciousness', bonding them to their traditional exploitative cultural roots. Thus the theme of non-imitative westernization or modernization was widely embraced by various factions of the left and the right, and became one of the most important discursive elements in Third World politics, which developed especially against the emergence of United States hegemony in the cold war atmosphere of the post-war period (cf. Keyder 1993, pp. 25–7; Toprak 1981, pp. 99–104; Samim 1981). Yet, for none of them did Islam constitute as strong a source in searching for an alternative route to modernization as it did in the political line followed by the NOP/NSP/WP chain.

The century-old problem of pursuing modernization by adopting Western technology and enlightenment thought while remaining faithful to Ottoman/Islamic culture was taken very seriously by the NOP, which was established in 1969 but closed down after 1971 by the Constitutional Court for having used religion for political purposes. Concerning the need for national development in an industrial age, in the view of the NSP (established in 1972 by Professor Necmettin Erbakan, and basically in the same political line as the NOP), Western technology could be used for industrialization but, in the course of industrialization, Muslims should neither take Western work ethics as a model nor adopt the rules of the capitalist mode of production, particularly those concerning redistribution of wealth. Nor, furthermore, could European

Enlightenment thought be a guide for the advancement of Turkish people. As advocated by the NOP, what Turkish people needed for industrial development was a new spiritual awakening. The major goal of the NOP, as stated at its creation, was to 'revive the moral qualities and spiritual excellence dormant in the Turkish character so that Turkish society [could] regain peace, order and social justice' (Sayarı 1979, p. 174; quoted in Mardin 1983a, p. 145). As Toprak shows in full detail, the NSP saw no positive relationship between the West's technical superiority and its cultural heritage. On the contrary, according to Erbakan, Western countries developed their technology at the expense of the Muslim world. They had borrowed knowledge which Muslims had accumulated since the seventh century without, however, giving reference to Muslim sources. Thus, with the spread of Western cultural imperialism, it was thought that most modern technical innovations had originated in the West. What followed from this should be an ideal combination of a powerful Turkish nation with its Ottoman/Islamic heritage (Toprak 1981, pp. 100–1) since, in the NSP's understanding of culture, the reinterpretation of history was important in recreating a sense of cultural authenticity and emphasizing the contributions of Ottoman/Islamic culture to world civilization. According to Toprak:

> In contrast to secularist intellectuals who view the decline of the Ottoman Empire in terms of Islam's conservative role in the Ottoman society, the NSP interprets such decline as a consequence of the foreign cultural influences which penetrated Ottoman intellectual thought and gained prominence at the expense of Islamic philosophy and tradition . . . [T]he superiority of the latter . . . had been responsible for the Ottoman Empire's periods of greatness. Hence, in order to regain world prominence, the Turkish nation would have to regain its consciousness as a Muslim society with a distinguished historical mission (1981, pp. 100–1).

Thus, in the discourse of cultural authenticity, the meaning of science, previously explained by Atatürk in universalistic terms and viewed as a common asset of all humanity (and hence placed at the core of modern civilizations and emptied of any nationalistic claim) was challenged by the NSP, in that the science which led to

Western technical innovations was proclaimed as originating in Muslim civilization and as having been carried onto the world stage by the Ottoman Empire of Turkish Muslims. The NSP therefore sought to redefine the project of gaining an independent, sovereign national identity constituted by rational, autonomous individuals in a modern society; it stressed the idea of scientific compatibility with other modern, namely Western, countries and, at the same time, emphasized the Islamic nature of Muslim Turkish society. More importantly, the discursive attempt at the transformation of the 'code of honour', which underscored the project of building up a Turkish national identity, occurred without setting aside nationalistic elements, in the sense that the NSP valued the attainment of an independent national character, a scientifically oriented inquisitive mind, and the willpower to make Turkish society prominent among other nations, including Muslim nations. It was totally differentiated from non-Muslim nations, however, by its replacement of the secular rationalist claim to 'truth' with the Islamic claim.

More importantly, the most difficult part of the republican identity formation project was the combination of particularistic nationalist assertions, i.e., the creation of Turkishness as a distinct, integrated and potent identity among other nationalities, with universal-yet-Western identity ideals. It was especially difficult in view of the fact that Turkey was an underdeveloped country where the rural population exceeded the urban and where, later on, the migration from rural to urban areas made the still unresolved problems of urban areas much more complicated than ever before. Here, I am not only concerned with the technical problems of urbanization, but also with its cultural meaning. To the extent that civilization and urbanization have been linked, as Gilsenan (1982) argues for instance, intellectuals emerge as a particularly urban species, and in the Turkish context they form a well-educated, westernized élite. But the city, particularly the big city which pulls migration, is not exclusively the domain of the intellectuals or the upper class urban dwellers who enjoy the possibility of high consumption and have access to the ways of attaining cultural refinement. The shanty-towns and other deprived districts are as much part of the urban landscape as the universities, business and shopping centres, concert halls, bookstores, stadia and so on. The inhabitants of such areas, often first or second generation urban dwellers, have not only had to adjust to new economic conditions, but also have had to shape their social and cultural perceptions to cope with and make sense of their new environment. This process of reconstitution of reality and identity is a difficult struggle which requires considerable effort and creates serious disruptions. It brings new types of insecurities to people's living conditions and creates a sense of ambivalence about the future, while still preserving the hope of better living conditions. Insofar as Western lifestyles, behaviour and conduct set the dominant model for these better living conditions, for the people far from attaining them, a sense of exclusion from the higher levels of a socially appropriated state of being, and thus a sense of oppression, becomes evident. That is to say, the sense of cultural inferiority experienced by those who feel thwarted in attaining better, mostly coded as Western, lifestyles, has not been primarily bestowed upon them from outside, but rather from within their own society. Migration to urban areas is not the only way to encounter Western lifestyles; for instance, officials and teachers without local ties (i.e., who are appointed to the area from the big cities) in small towns can, to a certain extent, perform the same function, as can television. In other words, the paradox inherent to being both national (Turkish) and Western (modern) has brought its own modalities of social contradiction in an underdeveloped country which had a long glorious past. The modalities of the sense of oppression, which emerge as a consequence of those contradictions, take various forms and are of course closely connected with the class, income, education and gender positions of the people. But, for my purpose, what is important here is through which channels, and how, people recognize oppression. If becoming modern means behaving like a Westerner, which is a difficult task for most of the traditional Turkish population, the social cost of modernity increases. But if the model for modernity can be set within the boundaries of local cultural norms, so as not to exclude the Muslim character of the Turkish people and its standard of morals or conduct (as the NSP movement aimed to do), the sense of oppression caused by modernization in general, and secularization in particular, can be decreased. The NSP tried to act upon the common sentiment of discontent shared by those who had to pay for modernization at a cost to both their identities and self-confidence.

Although they evaluated secularism as the code of Western

oppression imposed upon Muslims, the NSP did not directly attack secularism and modernization as such in its political propaganda. Nor did it frequently pronounce the name of Islam, but instead addressed Turkish people as Turkish Muslims and called Turkey a Muslim country. In addition to the label of nationality in their party name, they named their ideological world-view 'Milli Görüş' (National Vision). Here, the older term *milli* (national) was evocative of the Ottoman *millet* system, under which Turks were part of the Muslim *millets*. This usage, rather than the modern *ulusal* (national), was not peculiar to the discourse of the NSP, but was adopted by almost all the factions of right-wing politics. The term *ulusal* was a neologism invented during the Kemalist language reform; thus the NSP was faithful to its Muslim origins in its language too.

But the path the NSP saw as necessary for the implementation of its politics was not so different from that of the republican reformers, in that they saw education as one of the most important agents of social transformation. This understanding was not confined to the opening of the new Imam Hatip schools, or to the provision of better religious education for high school students, but rather the whole educational system was to be renewed, and the curricula changed from mere imitations of Western culture and technology. Moreover, young people should be guaranteed universal higher education, instead of mere dance halls and stadia (Toprak 1981, p. 103). Similarly, the NSP appeared, like the RPP, to have an explicit programme for the reshaping of family and social life. Here again, the 'other' was the West and, as Toprak points out, it was claimed that the moral corruption endemic in Turkish society was the result of Turkey's opening to the West (1981, p. 101). Finally, what the NSP advocated, in Toprak's terms, was 'the reaffirmation of a Moslem way of life' (1984, p. 125). However, I will argue that the socio-political project of the NSP was wider than this and should also be seen as designed to invent a new Islamic moral and social order, a completely new project of civilization which could be attained, first and foremost, by following an Islamic way of life. Only after actualizing this model could Turkish Muslims develop a true Muslim identity in the prevailing secular order and live Islam as conscious Muslims. The possibility of realizing this ideal seemed increasingly plausible as the NSP's ongoing electoral success made it an indispensable partner in various coalition governments established between 1973 and 1978.

I suggest that the social project of the NOP/NSP/WP movement should be evaluated as the second attempt to offer a coherent civilization project after that offered by the founders of the Republic, especially when it is considered that it has also managed to accomplish an effective political party organization, and networks of close ties with a number of youth, women's and professional groups, including labour unions. It has organized migrant Turkish workers in Germany, France and Holland, and thus also acquired experience at surviving in the diaspora. With respect to its explicit, but informal, ties with religious orders, it has mobilized deep-rooted traditional religious resources (at least to a certain extent) in support of its cause (see, for example, Toprak 1984). It has also managed to offer an ideological outlook: according to Mardin (1989b) an ideology must operate in a framework of social mobilization, use modern mass communication and be promoted by an intelligentsia – conditions met by the NSP. Furthermore, it has put forward an alternative way of life, forming a counter-culture through its educational institutions, economic organizations and pious foundations and, most importantly, through the participation of people in these processes. The movement has also built its own economic and political ties at the international level, but is still short of making its own intelligentsia influential in Muslim world politics. This last point does not constitute a disadvantage relative to other ideological currents in Turkey, since the same is also true for other groups such as Marxists, liberals and conservatives. Consequently, I maintain that due to the political achievements of the NOP/NSP/WP line, the project of building a 'true' Muslim identity in a secular order – once seen as threatened – is now seen much more positively in Islamic circles. In fact, it has become possible to pose a real political challenge to what Göle (1991) calls the civilization project of Kemalism. Yet, at the same time, the movement itself is also completely a product of republican Turkish society – not because it is bound by legal limits but because it follows the institutional framework sustained by republican society. In spite of its universal assertions, however, this understanding of civilization is quite different from that of the secularists, who saw modern civilization as the common property of humanity. Here, civilization originally belonged to Muslims and must be defined in Islamic terms. This project of civilization has not yet been accomplished and probably will never be. Even the formation of its conceptual framework and its set of social directives was only gradually developed, requiring a constant effort to revitalize the beliefs and hopes of Muslims.

Notes

[1] See his speeches delivered in İnebolu and Kastamonu in 1925, cited in Taşkıran (1976, pp. 61–2).

[2] For example, from the many stories relating details of Atatürk's private life and his attitude towards women, the only example that can be found, even by the Islamic circles, of his removal of a headscarf is when he gently removed the untied headscarf of a respectable old lady (who was an admirer of his) at the end of a chic wedding ceremony held in Dolmabahçe Palace. He kissed her white hair, asking, 'Why should this beautiful hair be covered?' In return, in tears she kissed his hands and promised him that she would never cover her head again. Quoted from Iclal Işık in Dilipak (1988, pp. 169–70).

[3] For the impact of their 'father' on the formation of identities of early republican women see, for example, Durakbaşa (1988).

[4] An extensive critique of the emergence of official historiography in the Turkish Republic is found in a recent study examining the politico-ideological context in which the First Turkish History Congress (1932) was convened. This determined the theoretical and ideological boundaries of Turkish history and became very influential in Turkish education. With the establishment of the Turkish History Society (1930), new research was carried out in support of the new regime's vision of Turkish nationalism. See Behar (1992). For a deconstructionist attempt at writing republican Turkish history with the aim of rearticulating the Islamic circles' perspectives on it, Dilipak's journalistic study, which comprises five separate but related books devoted to examining different periods of the political life of the Turkish Republic, constitutes a very appropriate recent example (Dilipak 1988; 1989a; 1989b; 1990; 1991). Here, however, I do not base my argument on either of these studies.

[5] See Toprak (1981, pp. 68–70). Toprak argues that although the Şeyh Said rebellion started in the name of religion the larger goal behind it was the establishment of an independent Kurdish state. See also Lewis (1968, p. 266).

[6] Mardin shows the ways in which Islamic idioms of *gazilik* (becoming a ghazi, a Muslim fighter) and martyrdom worked as the main legitimizers of the war of independence, mobilizing support for it as well as making it

meaningful and worthwhile in the sight of lay Muslims. Mustafa Kemal was known and celebrated as 'Gazi Mustafa Kemal Paşa' by large sections of the population, reflecting his heroic image in terms of Islamic values, especially because he was regarded as having saved the Muslims of Anatolia from conquest by the infidel. The Islamic concept of *cihad* (*jihad*), 'the struggle for internal as well as external mastery' by Muslims to preserve Islamic faith, constitutes an inseparable part of this *gazi* culture, i.e., the culture of the fighters for the faith whose *cihad* was called *gaza*. 'The *gazi-gaza* cluster is a root-metaphor providing lines of force which shape social relations and at the same time enable these to be transformed' and the culture is still quite active in contemporary Turkey (Mardin 1989a, pp. 3–5). For the transformation of religious symbols in Turkey, see Mardin (1984).

[7] For the differentiation of communal *mahalle* ethics due to the emergence of new prestige settlements in nineteenth-century Ottoman society, see, for instance, Ortaylı (1987, pp. 198–9).

[8] For the distress felt by the Ottoman intelligenstia over the patriarchal customs concerning the relationships between men and women, see Kandiyoti (1986) and Mardin (1974).

[9] The heading of westernization or Westernism marked one of the most remarkable characteristics of the ideological changes which became influential in Ottoman society and gave rise to the emergence of the progressive/reactionary divide among the Ottoman intelligentsia. See, for example, Berkes (1978, pp. 375–80), Mardin (1974; 1983b, pp. 245–50). See also 'Batılılaşma' in *Tanzimat'tan Cumhuriyet'e Türkiye Ansiklopedisi*, vol.1, pp. 133–52. İstanbul: İletişim Yayinan.

[10] See Berkes (1978, pp. 419–42) and Tunaya (1991).

[11] I do not mean to imply that the impact of the dissemination of 'book culture' on the formation of intellectuals who fostered the emergence of democratic ideals, a major aspect in the development of modern societies, was an idea which was first studied by Mardin. But it is Mardin who has constantly pursued the importance of the theme and employed it in his analyses of the ideological background of Turkish modernization in general, and in his study of ideology in particular, and also made his own contributions at the theoretical level. See Mardin (1992, pp.141–69).

[12] For a more detailed analysis of how religion played a controlling role over the culture-mediated link between local social forces and the political structure, see Mardin (1971, pp. 202–7). Mardin argues that in Ottoman society there was a split between 'official' and 'popular' religion: one established 'much of the upper class politico-ideological basis', the other 'functioned more as a community-reinforcing and identity forming process among the lower classes', but both provided 'a single road to integration in Ottoman society' (p. 206). The two 'shared many aspects of

Islam, but also differed significantly from one another', since, 'for the population at large religion was a moral prop, something to lean on, a source of consolation, a patterning of life; for the ruling élite it was in addition, and probably much more, a matter related to the legitimacy of the state' (p. 206).

[13] The principle of secularism was first debated in parliament in 1928 as 'the separation of religion from worldly concerns'. It became part of the Turkish Constitution in 1937. For the understanding of secularism in the early Republic under the single party rule of the RPP see, for example, Karpat (1991, pp. 51–5).

[14] See Parla (1989, pp. 67–79 and 81–101).

[15] Öztürkmen cites the activities of People's Houses as divided into nine categories: 1. language; history and literature; 2. fine arts; 3. theatre; 4. sports; 5. social assistance; 6. public classes and courses; 7. library and publishing; 8. village development; and 9. museums and exhibitions. By 1939 there were 373 People's Houses. In 1940 Halk Odaları (People's Rooms) were introduced as smaller local extensions and village branches of People's Houses; their number reached 4,371 by the end of 1949. See Öztürkmen (1994, pp. 163–4) and Karpat (1963).

[16] As an example of an argument seeing 'hat reform' as an extension of the civilization project of Kemalism to induce westernization, see Göle (1991, p. 52).

[17] See, for instance, selections by Taşkıran from Atatürk's speeches delivered in Izmir and Konya in 1923 and in Inebolu and Kastamonu in 1925. In all these speeches Atatürk advocated the importance of women's participation in public life, and criticized women's seclusion and ignorance as uncivilized, and pointed to them as enlightened mothers to whom the younger generations of the society would be entrusted (Taşkıran 1976, pp. 55–63). In the same volume, see also 'Civil Law and Public Life' and 'Women at Work Under the Republic' (pp. 67–79 and 79–91). For a similar attempt at compiling Atatürk's speeches on women, see Doğramacı (1992, pp. 129–39).

[18] Among limited evidence of how important the public visibility of women's encounters with men was as an indicator of asrilik (being civilized), there is a particular photograph published in Aylık Mecmua in 1927. This shows ordinary Turkish couples, that is, not necessarily the kind of people who attended Atatürk's receptions, dancing cheerfully in a dancing hall. For me this is a striking representation of the pride felt in such affairs both by the people seen in the picture and the publishers. This is the caption under the picture: 'Dans iptilası memleketimizde de salgın halindedir. Her akşam sabahlara kadar bir çok çiftler mütemadiyen dans etmektedirler' (Addiction to dance is epidemic in our country as well. Each night, several

couples dance until morning) (*Cumhuriyet Dönemi Türkiye Ansiklopedisi*, vol. 1, p. 242). İstanbul: İletişim Yayinan.

[19] For the conception of time in the organization of social life see Mardin (1989a, pp. 196–8). For the Friday holiday see Toprak (1981, p. 147, note 47).

[20] Language reform was assessed by Western observers as one of the most important parts of the social and cultural transformation which the country underwent. See, for example, Heyd (1954) cited in Toprak (1981, p.145, note 18). Toprak gives an extensive survey of literature on the subject (1981, p.145, notes 18, 19, 20 and 21). See also other classics on the subject: Lewis (1968, pp. 273–81), Tachau (1964). For a comparative study on language reform in Turkey and Iran, see Perry (1985).

[21] I am not arguing against the point made by Mardin to show that the principle of laicism was first and foremost applied by Atatürk 'to erase the possibilities of legitimation offered by the framework [supplied by official/institutional Islam]'.According to Mardin, that was why Atatürk struck at the foundations of official religion, at the same time trying to break the local alliance between religious notables and non-religious notables and eliminate the former's power bases by controlling their candidacy for political office, i.e., 'by controlling elections to Parliament through a laicized People's Party' (Mardin 1971, p. 208). See also note 12 above. Rather, my contention is related to the usual assumption that the thorough secularization of 'institutional Islam' could be made possible by placing it in the secular educational institutions – as if the new members of those institutions would not have any cultural engagement informed by pre-republican official and/or popular Islam and, more importantly, by their former power bases.

[22] For a similar argument about how in Atatürk's thought science (ilim) worked as a means of reaching the level of universal civilization, but not imitating the West as such, see Timur, 'Atatürk ve Pozitivizm', *Cumhuriyet Dönemi Türkiye Ansiklopedisi*, vol.1, p. 95. The point that westernization did not mean the imitation of Western civilization is based on the argument according to which the roots of westernization were thought to extend back to the Central Asian history of Turkish civilization. This idea was backed by the so-called Sun-Language Theory which advocated that 'historically, human civilization had originated with the migration of the ancient Turks from Central Asia into various parts of the world and consequently Turkish was the basis of all subsequent languages' (Toprak 1981, pp. 42–3). Heper also argues that in order to liberate society from its backward Islamic past, Turks based their origin not on their Islamic past but on their ancient civilization (1981, pp. 350–1). For Göle, insofar as the westernized Kemalist élite dedicated themselves to educating the

people and dealt with their problems, they thought that through the populism they advocated they were not imitating the West but utilizing its principles for the development of the people itself (1991, pp. 55–6). Although each of these arguments explains various facets of this problem, my argument is more concerned with the philosophical essentials of the principle of universalism, which I believe was an important component of Atatürk's agenda for westernization.

23 I think it can be said that the consequences of this encounter, i.e., with Western art forms, were visible most rapidly in the area of music, since this was more accessible to large sections of society than other art forms. For a very articulate discussion see, for instance, Boğaziçi Üniversitesi Türk Müziği Klübü (1980).

24 Bozdoğan (1994, p. 39).

25 See, for example, Toprak (1981, pp. 41–2 and note 19 in chapter 3).

26 As Feroz Ahmad writes, as soon as they came to power, 'the Democrats' first measure was to amend Article 526 of the Penal Code, which forbade the *ezan* (the call to prayer) in any language other than Turkish. The Assembly simply lifted the prohibition, giving the *müezzin* the choice of singing the *ezan* in Turkish or Arabic, and most chose Arabic'. He adds that 'the decision to introduce this amendment . . . was taken over cocktails!' Ahmad (1977, p. 365). See also Toprak (1981, p. 79).

27 The Kubilay affair occurred in 1930 in Menemen, in the Aegean region of Turkey. In the republican order, the first explicitly religious rebellion was a protest against the wearing of hats by a Nakşibendi group in November 1925 in Rize (in the Eastern Black Sea region) and this was followed by demonstrations in other cities. In the same year in Erzurum (in Eastern Turkey) a crowd led by a group of *hocas* marched against secularism. Later on, during the subsequent trials, it was learned that two associations, *Muhafaza-i Mukaddesat Cemiyeti* (Association for the Protection of Religion) and *Islam Teali Cemiyeti* (Association for Advancing Islam), had played major roles in organizing the demonstrations. The Kubilay affair was followed by the Bursa rebellion in 1933, led by a Nakşibendi group protesting against the recital of the *ezan* in Turkish (Toprak 1981, p. 69; Tunaya 1991, note 51). In 1949, a group from the Ticani order recited the *ezan* in Arabic in the visitor's gallery of the National Assembly in defiance of the law. Members of the same order also became famous during the DP period by frequently attacking Atatürk statues. This led to the passing of the Atatürk Kanunu (Atatürk law) in 1951 which was designed to protect his memory (Toprak 1981, p. 83).

28 Quoted in Ahmad (1977, p. 369).

29 Ibid.

30 Vice-President Cemal Gürsel delivered a speech in 1961 in which he proclaimed that the path the DP had followed was 'such that the day will

come when, for the enlightenment of our people, the demand for the recitation of Qur'an in Turkish will come from below, from the people themselves. . . . We are preparing the relevant organizations and training the necessary elements in such a way as to ensure that our people are trained and prepared in this way'; quoted in Ahmad (1977, p. 375).

CHAPTER V

Imagining an Islamic Community

V.1. Actualizing the Ideal Past

When the adherents of the Zahid Kotku branch of the Nakşibendi
order and the founders of the NSP movement came together and
decided to establish a building cooperative in Ankara, their aim
was not only to have houses of their own but also to create an
urban space where they could 'live Islam' as 'conscious' (şuurlu)
Muslims. Being a conscious Muslim, however, meant more than
having been born into a Muslim family or acceptance and following
of the five pillars of Islam. To be a conscious Muslim, one's entire
life should be led in accordance with Islamic precepts. Although
these must be guided by Islamic law and tradition, in our specific
case by the Hanafi school of law and Nakşibendi tradition, the
determination of these Islamic precepts is a duty which falls to
the Muslims of any specific time and society while following the
example of the Prophet Muhammad. In other words, as in the case
of the Muslims of contemporary secular Turkey, they must create
their own Islamic patterns of living concerning the requirements
of the society in which they have to live.

According to the would-be 'conscious' Muslims, however, the
society in which they had to live was not an Islamic society in the
sense that the source of its ruler's authority did not emanate
from God's law, and nor were the guiding principles of social life
determined according to Islamic rules. In fact, it was thought that
people in the Republic of Turkey had been forced to forget the
essence of their religion and had been deprived of learning the true
meaning and cause of their Islamic faith. However, as Esposito
explains, the Muslim mission to become servants of God and
spread God's rule, i.e., to learn and actualize the true faith in Islam,
is not only an individual obligation but also an obligation for the

community: 'Guided by the word of God and the Prophet, the Muslim community has a mission to create a moral social order.' This point is, of course, based on Koranic verses, such as, 'You are the best community evolved for mankind, enjoining what is right and forbidding what is wrong' (al Quran 3:110, Esposito 1991, p. 30). Muslims could fulfil this mission by following God's guidance, the shari'a (şeriat, path or way), for humanity:

> Once committed to Islam, the believer's overriding concern and question is 'What do I do, what is God's will/law?' Law is essentially religious, the concrete expression of God's guidance. . . . Throughout history, Islamic law has remained central to Muslim identity and practice, for it constitutes the ideal social blueprint for the 'good society'. The Sharia . . . has been a source of law and moral guidance, the basis for both law and ethics (Esposito 1991, p. 75).

If the primary source of God's revelation and law is the Koran, the sourcebook of Islamic principles and values, in Esposito's terms, the second and complementary source of law is the sunna (sünnet) of the Prophet, the normative model of Muhammad's behaviour. Sunna includes what the Prophet said and did and those actions that he permitted or allowed, and the records of Prophetic deeds known as hadiths (Esposito 1991, pp. 79–81; Rahman 1984).

The primary mission of Muslims is to actualize an Islamic moral social order, following the example of the Prophet and taking the asr al-sa'ada as a model, but it should not be seen merely as a manifestation of contemporary Muslims' utopian concerns, as Göle, for instance, claims (1991, p. 100). It should also be seen as an extension of one element of Islamic faith, since, as many observers of Islam and Islamic law argue, faith in Islam is 'something that people do rather than something that people have . . . it pertains to something that people are or become' (Smith 1981, p. 122). Similarly, faith does not simply mean to profess belief in God but 'to realize God's will – to spread the message and law of Islam' (Esposito 1991, p. 70). Thus, taking the Prophet's thoughts and deeds as an example, setting the boundaries of correct actions in a modern secularized world becomes the most appropriate way to create morally justifiable ways of living and to make what Giddens calls 'life politics' (1991, p. 215). In addition, following the example of the Prophet also enables Muslims to gain time and space to develop new strategies, to create a space for action and to achieve the mission of establishing an Islamic moral social order.

If the Prophet is seen as a model and his life and 'career' as setting an example, it becomes possible, according to Lewis (1985) to follow either of his two patterns of political action, described as 'activist' and 'quietist'. According to Lewis there are two stages in the career of the Prophet, but one of them is better known and more frequently cited, that is, the Prophet as the sovereign of Medina, as judge, general and statesman. However, before the *hijra* (*hicret*), the migration of the Prophet from Mecca to Medina, he was the leader of an opposition movement, a critic and an opponent of the pagan regime in Mecca and, although his opposition took the form of political action, it was primarily religious and moral in purpose: this stance was quite different from the one he took in Medina, which was a real revolutionary challenge, forming a new regime and waging war against Mecca until victory and conquest were achieved (p.15). Because in the Muslim view the sole source of sovereignty is God, if a ruler does not draw power from God, disobedience becomes a religious obligation and the faithful must wage war against the infidel – *jihad* in its 'activist' form. But *jihad* can also assume a 'quietist' form, manifesting itself as a struggle, that of Muslims for internal mastery on the way to becoming true Muslims.

The group that I am concerned with here were waging this internal form of *jihad* when they rallied around Zahid Kotku and accepted his spiritual guidance when he was the imam of the Iskender Paşa mosque in Istanbul. This allowed them to develop new ideas about the ways in which a Muslim should live as well as new economic and political strategies that would be effective at the national level. The latter is particularly important as the Nakşibendi order was always highly politicized, starting from the fifteenth century when they virtually dominated Central Asia following the spiritual guidance of Bahaeddin Nakshband (d.1390) (Schimmel 1986, p. 365). Its influence was widened in the sixteenth and seventeenth centuries by Ahmad Faruqi al-Sirhindi (1563–1624), who became known in Indian religious and political life as a religious *mujaddid* (*mujeddidi*, innovator) (Friedmann 1971; Schimmel 1986, p. 367). A similar process was also seen in the Ottoman Empire, especially with the increasing influence of the Halidi branch of the Nakşibendi order in government circles in Istanbul in the nineteenth century (Mardin 1991b, pp. 129–32). In sum, 'the Nakşibendi order has always been on the alert for opportunities to use power for what it considered the higher interests of Muslims' (Mardin 1991b, p. 135).[1]

Although it is not new for Sufi orders in general and for the Nakşibendi order in particular to be in conflict with the ruling power, the ways in which they have protected themselves from oppressive governmental intrusion and the worldly contamination of political avarice have always displayed, I think, this 'quietist' aspect of Sufi orders. When Zahid Kotku started to be influential and began to establish a growing circle of disciples from 1958 onwards in Istanbul, Islam had been given more freedom to organize by the political parties as a consequence of the establishment of the multi-party regime in Turkey. It is therefore not surprising that Kotku used his chance to proselytize and to channel the influence of the Nakşibendi order into both state and party politics. Both Kotku, and his son-in-law, Esat Coşan, who succeeded him upon his death in 1980, were operating from inside state institutions. The former was the official imam of the Directorate of Religious Affairs, and the professional career of the latter has been completely shaped in the public universities of the Republic, the Faculty of Arts and Sciences at Istanbul and the Faculty of Theology at Ankara. They were also both from families in the inner circles of the Gümüşhanevi branch of the Nakşibendi order.[2]

The relationship between Zahid Kotku and his disciples and his guidance of them form a good paradigm against which the aspect of social mobilization of religious orders in the socio-political development of Turkey may be understood. In a social context in which many people had been raised traditionally but educated in secular universal educational institutions, many experienced a cultural void. In their search to reconcile these two modes in a socially meaningful order, the religious orders, especially a lodge like that of Zahid Kotku, based in Istanbul, the largest city in Turkey, fulfilled the function of providing ethical answers which would help in the creation of morally justifiable ways of living. At the same time they helped to lessen the identity conflicts arising from the contradictory nature of being neither fully modern nor suitably traditional, i.e., what Piscatori calls 'being not belonging' (1986, p. 29). The tension between the old and the new, which overlaps with the tensions between the traditional and the modern, the Islamic and the Western, was not unknown in Turkish social life. In this case, these tensions were nurtured by the need to impart meaning to a rather blind, meaningless and shallow world characterized by the perceived injustice of the social system. In addition, the age-old tension which predominated in Ottoman society between those who saw themselves as adhering to the values of justice and equality which stemmed from the *shari'a* and those who constantly violated its rules in favour of *qanun* (*kanun*, secular law), was also evident for these people. Mardin defined the representatives of these tensions as the teams of the 'just' and the 'unjust' (1991a; 1991b, pp. 137–8). This was another conceptual key used to explore the ways in which the formation of social cleavages as well as the discourse of the just, which in fact might link the 'upper' and 'lower' classes, had now entered the realm of a Marxist approach to social justice and equality. This evolved around such notions as class consciousness, appropriation of the means of production and surplus value and emancipation of the labour force being used to shape a discourse usually articulated by means of an Islamic vocabulary.

It is also true to say that in the political discourse of modern Turkey religious idioms of justice and equality have always been harnessed by factions of both the right wing and the radical left, though the latter heavily relied on Alevi religious idioms.[3] The first and most outstanding example of the rather crude use of religious idioms for political propaganda was the emblem of the centre-right Adalet Partisi (Justice Party, JP, the successor of the DP).[4] By its symbolic evocation of the names of God and the Prophet, the emblem gave the impression that this was God's own party. The emblem was an open book with the letter 'A' on one side and 'P' on the other; the book symbolized the Koran and the letters stood for *Allah* and *Peygamber* (God and the Prophet) (Ahmad 1977, p. 377) or even 'Allah'ın Partisi' (the party of God).[5] The NSP, by contrast, shaped its political demands using the idiom of Islamic liberation, *selamet* (salvation, or freedom from evil), in its party name, and basing its political discourse on the aim of establishing an Islamic moral social order which would entail creating an Islamic way of life according to the example of the Prophet.

I shall argue that the attempts by some Muslims to lead a life modelled on the period of the *asr al-sa'ada*, and their efforts to emulate its supposed patterns of social and personal relations, stem from the longing to live in the kind of social milieu in which Muslims could have a close and actual relationship with their Prophet and could ask for his advice about almost all their problems, ranging from the most private to major public issues. That is why the people that I encountered during my fieldwork repeatedly used terms such as 'light', 'warmth', 'enthusiasm' and 'pride' when they spoke of how they imagined life at that time. 'Pride' here refers to their feeling at the thought of being able to witness the revelation of the Koran and its dissemination throughout 'infidel' lands. Another theme was the oppression to which the early Muslims were subject, but in this case too the term 'pride' overrode other possible expressions they might have used to explain their feelings about it.

I am quite aware of the fact that for anyone who is familiar with Muslim faith the veneration of the Prophet, the messenger of God, is not an original starting point for the exploration of the constitution of Muslim subjectivity and imagination. But it is impossible to avoid the subject in any attempt to examine the ways in which this fundamental element of Islamic faith works to give directives to the imagination of Muslims in their attempts to actualize the *asr al-sa'ada* in a highly modernized secular age. It is particularly important for my purpose in assessing a social movement in which the political incentives are mainly shaped around the maxims of a Sufi order whose religious doctrine has been based on the idea of devotion to a 'path' which will lead to the perfection of prophethood. To follow the path entails reliance upon orthodox religious duties rather than what Schimmel terms 'supererogatory works and intoxicated experiences', which in Nakşibendi thought lead only to sainthood (Schimmel 1986, p. 366).

The Nakşibendi way is said to be very effective as a defence against the kind of syncretism which took place in India and various parts of Central Asia through the intermingling of Sufi practices and the symbols of other religions. The same is true in Ottoman society of the heterodox movement which prevailed in Anatolia. In spite of some of its latitudinarian characteristics, what distinguished the Nakşibendi order from other Sufi orders was its sobriety. This emerges from the critiques by Sirhindi of certain forms of Sufism that were prevalent in his time. Mardin gives a well integrated summary of this attitude:

> For Sirhindi, dissolving one's earthly moorings through the quest for union with God is an incomplete, and therefore harmful, exercise. The true believer has to return to earth and come to grips with the realities of the world – and this world is one where one's task is to establish the reign of Sunni morality (1991b, p. 126).

What should follow from this is the development of a better understanding of religious law and orthodox practice since, if I am correct in comprehending Schimmel, for Sirhindi and later on for the Nakşibendi tradition influenced by him, to reach the 'unity of Being' should not be an aim in itself. The stage of 'intoxicated love' 'in which an enraptured mystic sees only the divine unity', should be seen as the 'infidelity of the path' since it did not comply with the words of the divine law which may lead a person to the sober state in which he becomes aware of the subjectivity of his own experience. This 'intoxication' therefore can only denote the station of sainthood, whereas, says Schimmel, according to Sirhindi's thinking, 'the prophet excels by his sobriety, which permits him to turn back, after the unitizing experience, into the world in order to preach God's word there: prophecy is the way down, is the aspect of reality turned toward creation' (Schimmel 1986, pp. 368–9). Thus 'way down' is connected with prophetic activities and qualities. After his ascent to heaven, the Prophet was blessed with the vision of God. As he entered into intimate proximity with the beloved (God), a blessing received by only the Prophet Muhammad among all the other messengers of God, he was not lost in the vision of God but turned back to his people to teach them that it is the will of God that they should be forever united with the divine. Even at this point, the Prophet could not neglect his duties. Faced with such an example, how could any conscious Muslim avoid performing their religious duties?

The Nakşibendi order has developed as a sober order in regard to its teaching and its teaching methods. It is said that the Nakşibendi order was built on the following eight principles laid down by 'Abd al-Khaliq Ghijduwani (d.1220): awareness in breathing; watching over one's steps; internal mystical journey; solitude in the crowd; recollection; restraining one's thoughts; watching one's thought; and concentration upon God (Schimmel 1986, p. 364). As many observers of the order point out, as opposed to vocalized *dhikr* (*zikr*), 'recollection', repetitions of divine names or religious formulae, often with musical accompaniment, the silent *dhikr* constitutes the centre of Nakşibendi education (Algar 1990b; Schimmel 1986). The other important characteristics of the Nakşibendi order have been described by Schimmel as follows:

> The second noteworthy characteristic is *suhbat*, the intimate conversation between master and disciple conducted on a very highly spiritual level . . . . The close relation between the master and disciple reveals itself in *tawajjuh*, the concentration of the two partners upon each other that results in experiences of spiritual unity, faith healing, and many other phenomena. . . . It has been said that Naqshibandiyya begin their spiritual journey where other orders end it – the 'inclusion of the end in the beginning' is an important part of their teaching, though it is an idea that goes back to early Sufi education. It is not the long periods of mortification but the spiritual purification, the education of the heart, instead of the training of the lower soul, that are characteristic of Naqshibandiyya method (Schimmel 1986, p. 366).

This close relationship between the master and the disciple maintained through warm, but respectfully conducted, conversations is a very important aspect of Zahid Kotku's influence over his disciples (Gürdoğan 1991, pp.19–77), though it is not peculiar to the Nakşibendi order. *Subhat* provides a medium for anyone who wants to participate in gatherings of the order without entering into the path, in its strict sense of Sufi religious practice.[6] This specific interpersonal relationship can be channelled into a kind of political activism. Mardin explains this process with reference to the Gümüşhanevi branch of the Nakşibendi order,[7] though, considering its distinctive impact on successive branches of the order, it may well shed light on the formation of the structural characteristics of other paratexts:

> The substance of religious teachings of Gümüşhanevi provides a frame for an Islamic hermeneutic which is both a matter of

textual interpretation proper but also one of reading proscribed Sufi interpersonal relations as a paratext. The way in which this frame led to a structuration of social action among his followers can only be understood if we take the religious inner drive of his disciples as a 'legitimate datum' in our analysis. It is only in a setting where the structuring force of this inner drive is taken as a 'social fact' that we can understand his influence and that of later, contemporary, Nakşibendi şeyhs. At this point we have to remember some of the elements which enter into the acquisition of knowledge in the Nakşibendi mode. In this method both the items of book knowledge, the use of memory in propagating these themes and one's positioning with regard to a mentor are considered to be part of the substance of knowledge. Knowledge is defined as the pursuit of self-purification and this is to be achieved both by keeping closely to the central orthodox line but also by the intimate link established between mentor and pupil. Partly libidinal and partly authoritarian, this link, once established, is only the first bond in what operates as a chain of linkages producing a network of Nakşibendi influences. The fear of God and the love of God provides an example for the bonding power of the first human link: that of master and disciple. These parameters made up the operational setting of Gümüşhanevi's influence. To this basic frame we have to add innovation, namely the increased use of the traditions of the Prophet, the examples taken from his life, as a source of ethical guidance. This new element thereafter functioned as a template for the interpretive action of the mentor. What we have here is an attempt to bring back the 'original' meaning of Islam into the nineteenth century but by the use of the frame which allows considerable flexibility for interpretation. It should be emphasized that this develop-ment is not one associated only with the Nakşibendi but a characteristic which one sees throughout the Islamic world in the nineteenth century. This set of inner-structuring constraints and human linkages are still today one of the strengths of the Nakşibendi organizational strategy. Together with the social mobilization of the urban Muslim population they make up a type of populism the religious and the liturgical propellants of which have never been taken seriously by mainline Turkish sociology. A third kind of Nakşibendi social behavior inherited by Gümüşhanevi was activism which, in his case, took the spe-

cific form of an appeal to citizens to harken to the mobilization
of Ottoman defense during the Russo-Turkish war of 1877–78.
But Gümüşhanevi also reacted to Ottoman modernist
reformism. At the time when the first banks were established in
Turkey he created his own 'Loan Fund' for his disciples. He
established four libraries in Istanbul, Rize, Bayburt and Of (Gündüz, 1984, 51). A pedagogic innovation he used was to 'stream'
his students according to their qualifications. This ability to
respond to a kind of modernization seems to have been a quality
found among Nakşibendis of the later nineteenth century (Mardin 1990b, pp. 26–8).

In sum, in the 'renewalist' Nakşibendi tradition, the ultimate aim
of all Muslims is to reach a 'unity with God', and to achieve it both
the 'quietist' and the 'activist' characteristics of the Prophet's life
and example can be followed. Thus it becomes much easier to
understand how Zahid Kotku could motivate Necmettin Erbakan,
a professor of mechanical engineering and the leader of the NOP/
NSP/WP line of Islamic politics, to establish in the 1960s an irri-
gation pump factory called Gümüş Motor, to which he himself
made financial contributions. This factory was to be a model for
other Islamic industrial plants. Over the years similar enterprises
followed, ranging from financial institutions to media establish-
ments, on the way to constituting the institutional basis of an
Islamic society.[8] But the most important project of all was the
formation of a model for an Islamic way of life that would help
Muslims in the daily conduct of their lives. This was the aim of the
group who came together to establish a site in Ankara. Its timing
coincided with the establishment of the NOP whose pioneering
figures needed to move from Istanbul to the capital, Ankara.
Zahid's son-in-law, Esat Coşan, had already begun to teach at
Ankara University in the Faculty of Theology in the second half
of the 1960s. Thus it was that the idea of creating a social milieu in
emulation of the community life of the Muslims who lived in the
age of the Prophet took root and grew in Ankara, the political heart
of the Republic of Turkey.

V. 2. Politics of Resentment

The Muslims who lived in the *site* had obviously tried to lead their lives in accordance with Islamic precepts before its establishment. However, much of their accounts of those days reflects a sense of resentment at the way in which they were treated by their fellow citizens. This was more so for those who had lived in Ankara and Istanbul than for those from provincial cities or towns. But the sense of contentment of all of them at being able to live in this particular *site* was expressed through phrases such as, 'Here we feel confident, knowing that no one will harass us because we are Muslims'; 'Life is easier for a Muslim here'; 'Nobody criticizes you here for living like a Muslim'; and 'Here you can be sure that behind every door there lives a Muslim family.' These kinds of utterances reflect what Esposito (1991) calls the Muslim mission, which views service to God as a community as well as an individual obligation, 'enjoining what is right and forbidding what is wrong'. Yet, I think, they also reflect in a broader sense what Sennett (1992) calls the politics of *ressentiment*.

For Sennett, what marks the twentieth century is the disappearance of public space, in the sense that the psychological space of the personality wiped out the space of impersonality, that is, the public space. This entailed the end of public culture. Instead of talking about the dominance of public space over the private, as is usual, Sennett describes the definitive feature of today's secular society as the 'tyranny of intimacy'. In his attempt to develop a perspective on the beliefs, aspirations and myths of modern life Sennett claims:

> The reigning belief today is that closeness between persons is a good moral. The reigning aspiration is today to develop individual personality through experiences of closeness and warmth with others. The reigning myth today is that the evils of society can all be understood as evils of impersonality, alienation, and coldness. The sum of these three is an ideology of intimacy: social relationships of all kinds are real, believable, and authentic the closer they approach the inner psychological concerns of each person (1992, p. 259).

This ideology of intimacy defines the 'humanitarian spirit of a society without gods', and through 'warmth' it becomes 'our god'. More importantly, this ideology of intimacy 'transmutes political categories into psychological categories' (p. 259). Thus, 'the myth-ology built up around impersonality as an evil' also served to define 'a landscape of human loss', in which a total absence of human relationships is said to be experienced. For Sennett, the equation of impersonality with emptiness should be seen as the reason for this loss. Therefore, in our context, as a response to this fear of emptiness, people tend to conceive of the political realm as a realm in which personality will be strongly declared (pp. 260–1). Taking the risk of oversimplifying Sennett's argument, I will say that the secular 'charisma' of today's politicians is organized around the principles of forceful personality, according to which what the politician feels, rather than what he does, is focused upon. This charisma is no longer a religious type of charisma relying upon impersonality, in the sense of depending on the gift of God's grace and proclaiming the supremacy of religious truth. Instead it depends on the person's feelings displayed through a 'psychic striptease'. The politician's sentiments are directly felt. This becomes valuable and important in a culture ruled by belief in the immediate, the immanent, the empirical, and which rejects everything which cannot be directly experienced, the hypothetical, the mystical or the 'pre-modern'. In such a culture, then, it becomes easy to lose the ability to make assessments about the future consequences of a politician's policies. This is the consequence of measuring rationality by the empirical truth of what is seen and felt, instead of disengaging from the immediate moment and asking whether things have really changed significantly. For Sennett this situation constitutes the very basis of the politics of *ressentiment*, which is often led by politicians of 'humble origins, who found a career in whipping up the public by attacks against the Establish-ment, the Entrenched Powers, the Old Order'. This politics is pure resentment felt against the existing order, rather than a commit-ment to some new order. The politics of resentment, then, is a way of playing on the anger of people who feel excluded from the circles of the privileged (without, however, aiming to destroy the privilege itself), and on the envy and shame arising from status injuries. The protagonists of this politics hope personally to escape from this state of suffering through some lucky break, some accident of mobility, and therefore have no egalitarian concern (pp. 269, 276–7). Sennett is quite aware of the fact that resentment of status inferiority may be a universal human trait, but the resentment he talks about has two peculiarly modern features which apply only to advanced industrial society. The first comes as a consequence of the bureaucratization of power, according to which one's social place in the structures of power ought to be determined by merit. Hence he states, 'the notion of careers open to talent voiced in the late eighteenth century is here brought to its greatest point'. However, since it is believed that people at the top have no talent, and they survive by banding together and keeping the people of talent out, this comes to mean that they keep out the world below through unfair means. Thus the term 'unfair' becomes the key to the myth invented by people of lower status in order to explain what is happening in the face of the increasing invisibility of actual power in advanced capitalist societies: 'If you are down below it is not your own fault, they took what is your right away from you' (p. 278).

The second modern characteristic of this resentment is its anti-urban bias. At this point we must deal with the notion of community found in Sennett's discourse. In modern society community is thought to be, and is presented by the representatives of this politics of resentment as, a 'healthier place' for 'decent people' – so says Sennett at one point in his argument (p. 278). Briefly, community is a place where the class of arrivals mobilized through the politics of resentment can supposedly exercise an 'emotional withdrawal from the society' and build a 'territorial barricade within the city'. Although this new territorial shield was to provide a place to exercise 'fraternity' and also order, in the sense that individuals know each other and their respective terri-torial places, it also entails an exercise in 'fratricide'. This aspect of community, for Sennett, is what creates a discourse which main-tains the rhythm of disclosure, disappointment and isolation, since the major contradiction in community life is its function of surveil-lance which makes 'brothers' turn on each other. The mentality of fratricide is also turned towards the world: a distinction is made between the community as 'inside' and real, and the world out there, the 'outside', something which does not respond to 'us' in terms of 'who we are', hence something which fails 'us'. Therefore in the modern world what Sennett calls the 'logic of Gemeinschaft community' becomes more and more local in its terms and becomes an emotional withdrawal from society:

This warfare between psyche and society has acquired a real geographical focus, one replacing the older, behavioural balance between public and private. This new geography is communal versus urban; the territory of warm feeling versus the territory of impersonal blankness' (pp. 301, 300).

According to Sennett it is mainly this anti-urban bias, the fear of 'strangers' and developing skills to cope with impersonality, which leads contemporary societies to a state of incivility, in which social actors are deprived of their 'art' of acting and become passive audiences, instead of interacting with what is happening on the 'stage'. This is what Sennett calls 'the fall of public man'.

How can the elements of this politics of resentment, the target of which is basically defined as the petite bourgeoisie of advanced capitalist societies, be combined with a politics whose target is basically a religious group? Here I will not base my argument on class similarities between the group I studied and the one used by Sennett. Nor will I highlight the point that what Sennett defined as the class of arrivals, that is, the middle classes, which replaces the notion of petite bourgeoisie in today's societies, actually constitutes the class basis of religious politics in Turkey. I will argue instead that there is a specific political enterprise here in the process of defining the boundaries of the politics of resentment. According to this, Muslims constitute an underprivileged or disenfranchised group, excluded from the circles of the privileged, and hence an object of status inferiority due to their religious political affiliations. In this respect all the conditions of the politics of resentment are fulfilled in the case I have studied, though with a single exception which at the very first glance seems to be an important one. That is the lack of commitment to create an actual change in the existing order. However, if we consider that here the emphasis was on the lack of commitment to changing the inegalitarian power structures of the existing capitalist social order, it can be said that it fits well with the specific politics of resentment raised by Muslim activists in Turkey, who are rallied round right-wing political parties whose prevailing discourse is an attempt to displace the secular discourse of justice and equality with a discourse emanating from a Sunni Islamic morality.

However, the most interesting aspect of the comparison I am trying to make here can be based on the operations of the ideology of intimacy. It is important to note that the inhabitants of this urban *site* gave me the impression that, in spite of their search for an intimate collectivity through personal closeness and warmth and a sense of 'fraternity' developed on the axis of religious affinity, they also acknowledged the virtue of impersonality insofar as a kind of personal sobriety and mutual restraint were seen as necessary in human relations. I will cover this important point in the following chapter. This can be also attributed to their specific search for a kind of 'humanitarian spirit of a society' which is not 'without God', but occurs within a frame of mind in which the omnipresence of an Islamic God prevails to make Muslims constantly aware of their religious duties and responsibilities for both here and the hereafter. In this case, the value of Sennett's analysis lies in its penetrating perception of modern society where the 'tyranny of intimacy' prevails to set the boundaries of social imagination. It does not make an exception for Turkish society in general, but it becomes important in understanding attempts to actualize an Islamic way of life within similar boundary conditions, in this case the effort to sustain the balance between the 'territory of warm feeling', the communal, and the 'territory of impersonal blankness', the urban.[9]

The imagining of a specifically Islamic community is connected with the meaning of community in Islam; this does not entail a small-scale refuge but the *umma* (*ümmet*), the single universal Islamic community embracing all the lands in which Muslim rule is established and where Islamic law prevails (Lewis 1991, p. 32).[10] This is just the representation of an image, *umma*, but we also have to understand, as de Certeau (1984) asks, how the representation of an image is used by the people who are not the actual makers of it. This brings us to the concept of 'ways of operating', tactical extensions of the strategies of everyday life, with which I will also deal in the following chapter.

However, the strategies which provide direction in actualizing the model for an Islamic way of life which supposedly flourished in the *asr al-sa'ada* are not merely based on an image of isolated community. They are also able to render Islam a living social practice in a secular order, in which the secular nation-state controls the public and, to a certain extent, the private space by regulating phenomena in the public sphere to which private lives are linked for the maintenance of social life and the determination of civil rights. This situation is not of course peculiar to Turkish society. As Sivan puts it: 'In the Middle East and North Africa, the 1950s and 1960s witnessed the high-water mark of the mass-mobilizing state, all-pervasive bureaucracy, mass production factory system, and official culture' (Sivan 1992, p. 96). It was in this context that the presence of the state was assured in all walks of life, assuming the role of setting a model for the construction of social life. The boundaries between the state and civil society, then, shifted in favour of the state, but this same economic, social and cultural dynamism also entailed the integration of the masses in the political and economic processes, which prepared the conditions for the expansion of civil society and, particularly due to the 'state's failures in certain domains to modify the core values of its people in relation to the ultimate meaning of life' (Sivan 1992, p. 100), caused the state to lose its cultural hegemony over society. I have tried in the previous chapter to delineate the specific conditions which caused these failures of the state or the mobilization of civil society in Turkey. Here, I want to show that one response to new economic and political developments in the Middle East and North Africa has been Islamic activism, often taking the form of fundamentalism, and hence one of the efforts of Islamic activists to detach themselves from the cultural hegemony of the state was the establishment of what Sivan (1985) called 'counter-society'.

V.3. Counter-Society, Private Space and Islamic Community

Sivan argues that in the effort to bring Islam back into the political arena there was no monolithic political attitude among what he calls new radicals. Despite the decentralization and factionalism, however, there is a common denominator: this has been the sense of urgency felt concerning the 'malady of Islam' and if it has not necessarily led to violence, it has led to a divorce between the present Muslim society and polity. This attitude can be discerned in the theories of two highly influential Islamic leaders, Mawdudi and Qutb. Sivan argues that according to Mawdudi, as Islam has reverted to a state of *jahiliyya* (*cahiliye*, ignorance), true Muslims should fight against the apostates, and that *jihad* is but a defensive response to the 'war of annihilation' the apostates conduct against Islam. For Qutb, the true Muslim, as vanguard, must live apart from infidel society in a sort of 'counter-society' (Sivan 1992, pp. 84–5). 'Dissociation', which is said to be one of Qutb's seminal ideas for Islamic radical circles, can be epitomized in his own words: 'the summoners to God must be distinct and a community unto themselves' (Choueiri 1990, pp. 146, 136).

This notion of counter-society, which was first employed by Sivan to define this Islamic socio-political effort, has been subsumed in the Turkish case, too – without, however, any elaboration upon the concept itself. It was originally developed by a political ethnographer, Kriegel (1971). His definition of counter-society, which is quoted by Sivan, goes as follows:

> [a counter-society is] a microsociety which constitutes a closed society while maintaining some ties with society as a whole. The counter-society must be capable of being self-closed in order to avoid fragmentation or abdication. It must prevent alien influences from penetrating it, yet must remain sufficiently open and aggressive to draw from the outside whatever it cannot itself produce. It must pursue a dream of ultimately becoming a majority. It struggles to demolish old society while at the same time hoping to become heir to that society; radical destruction on the one hand, preservation for the sake of new order on the other.

Sivan adds that joined to these two functions is a third one: the counter-society is a model for the society of the future (Sivan 1985, p. 85).

There is no doubt that the theoretical framework of Islamic activism in Turkey has also been sustained to a large extent by the works of Mawdudi and Qutb. The high circulation of Turkish translations of books by these two Islamic ideologues is sufficient evidence in itself. However, their influence in the formation of Turkish Islamic oppositional thought, attitude and behaviour has differed somewhat from their influence elsewhere due to the peculiarities of the development of the Turkish Islamic movement. First and foremost there are important structural dissimilarities. The Islamic movement in Turkey did not develop in a social context in which the appropriation of nationalism emerged as a challenge to European colonialism and became a battlefield between secular and religious nationalisms (cf. Al-Azmeh 1993; Arjomand 1984; Choueiri 1990; Juergensmeyer 1993; Lawrence 1989). Islam was not the official religion of state as was the case in almost all Middle Eastern countries (cf. Ayubi 1991; Choueiri 1990; Dessouki 1987), nor was it referred to as a source of legislation in society. The political regime in Turkey was therefore not apologetic towards Islam but was completely secular: the diagnosis of the 'malady of Islam' (Mernissi 1975) did not produce a compelling urge to mobilize the Muslim people.

Another dissimilarity, not necessarily related to the influence of the thoughts of 'foreign' Islamic ideologues, is that in Turkey the Islamic political appeal has always been able to find its way through the channel of legal party politics, albeit restricted by constitutional law. Therefore, the radical tenor which has marked Islamic discourse in the Middle East due to its proponents' relegation 'underground' and also sometimes their execution, has not been a major issue in Turkey. Here, I do not underestimate the oppressive impacts of military interventions, all three of which (1960, 1971, 1980) were legitimized as saving secularism in Turkey as well as securing peace and order. Maintaining order meant, among other things, keeping religion under state control and within the limits of the secular republican state's constitutional legitimacy (cf. Dodd 1990; Heper 1985). Religious political activities and their cultural counterparts (such as intellectual publications, youth and women's associations, Koran courses, student hostels), as well as the domestic and foreign economic enterprises which rapidly proliferated especially after the 1980s under the permissive political attitude towards Sunni religious affiliations of the ANAP (1983–90), all penetrated Turkish social life legally, though sometimes they were prosecuted and sometimes tolerated.[11] Generally, as long as it remained within the boundaries of the private sphere, religion has always been permitted to exercise its power.

The question of religion for Islamic activists in Turkey, therefore, has not been a question of retreat or withdrawal from a society where the 'maladies of Islam' are evident in all walks of social life. Nor has it been a question of 'dissociation' as such. It has been, rather, a question of making Islam visible everywhere and making public the grievances of people with religious affiliations. It has also required great concentration on their part to be able to see how far they can go in actualizing an Islamic way of life, and realizing their private emergence as conscious or true Muslims. Until 1991, before the abolition of Article 163 of the Penal Code which proscribed any political organization committed to forming a religious social order, the safest bastion of religion in Turkish social life was the private sphere. It was especially so in the 1960s and 1970s when, in spite of its success in parliamentary political life, the political and social organization of Islam at the national level was still assailable in the sense that its discourse and space of socio-political manoeuvre was kept under state control, and moreover under the watchful eye of the military forces. Thus, first and foremost, the private sphere provided religion with a fertile ground to prosper.[12]

Parallel with this, it is not surprising to find the expansion and empowerment of civil society in general, in line with the enlarging political and economic autonomy of the middle classes, as the most blessed actors in consumerist capitalist society the world over. Even if we set aside the impact of grass roots politics (as in other parts of the world) and of the revolutionary spirit of student movements on Turkish social life, I would argue that the impact of rapid developments in communications pushed private life into the political space. The politics which emerged took its legitimacy from a kind of politics shaped within the boundaries of what Giddens calls emancipatory politics, that is 'the politics of freedom from exploitation, inequality, and oppression', something appropriated by all types of modern political trends such as radicalism, liberalism and conservatism (Giddens 1991, pp. 242, 210). More importantly, the idea that 'personal is political', a prominent discovery of the women's movement (cf. Sichtermann 1986), and parts of the student movement in Western societies, not only came out as an extension of that emancipatory politics, but also reinforced the politicization of the private sphere, in other words politicization of culture. I think that even at the highly intellectual urban level, this has appeared as an unavoidable social phenomenon affecting the idiosyncratic boundaries of the formation of several types of 'life politics'. Insofar as life politics is a response to the ethical question 'How should we live?' in a modern context, it no doubt also develops in conjunction with the politicization of the private, i.e., the culture of everyday. And similarly, as far as emancipatory politics primarily concerns itself with the conditions liberating us to make choices which prepare the formation of life politics, life politics is itself the 'politics of choice' (Giddens 1991, p. 214). Thus, I argue that the politics of resentment is an insepar-able part of life politics in that it maintains one of its most important discursive components.

Hence, when a group of people banded together to establish an urban space to live Islam as conscious Muslims, the question of redrawing the boundaries between state and civil society was slowly entering into the political imagination of Turkish society. For the Islamic circles to have a role in this new development, the first step was to detach themselves from the cultural hegemony of the state in many areas of social life, but without totally abandoning either the discursive or institutional aspects of secular emancipatory poli-tics which could allow them to exercise considerable power in both the public and private realms. More importantly, the ability of the NSP, and its successor the WP, to appropriate secular nationalist discourse allowed them to make themselves politically visible at the national level and also enabled them to respond to the need of Islamic circles to grasp the opportunities of modern society.

The overall significance of this argument for my present dis-cussion comes from its congruity with my general effort to explain the parameters of creating an Islamic way of life in urban Turkey. If we are to explain this creation as an extension of a political struggle largely dedicated to the establishment of a counter-society, we should be able to place it in a context where the development of the religious movement occurs in a secular order like that of Turkey where religion has primarily been placed in society as a legitimate component of private life.[13] In this way we can also make an analytical distinction between the motive behind the effort to create an Islamic way of life and the social conditions which led to this effort, before attaching the concept of counter-society to the specific Turkish case. We should also consider the differences between the emergence of the counter-society in Turkey and else-where in the Middle East, though the Turkish example also verifies structural characteristics of the definition of the concept.

The role played by the confinement of religion to the private sphere in the development of Islamic movements in Turkey is seen by Mardin, however, as an unexpected result of the republican reforms:

Atatürk wanted to make religion a private concern, but unantici-
pated social consequences soon caught up with him. As the
boundaries of the private have become enlarged in Turkey an
unforeseen development has occurred. As private everyday life
has increasingly been given a new richness and variety, religion
has become a central focus of life and acquired a new power.
Religion has received a new uplift from the privatizing wave
(1989a, p. 229).

This was one aspect of the impact of expanding the meaning of the
private on the development of Islamic revitalization in Turkish
society, but Islamic circles in Turkey, particularly the group I
studied, also attempted to develop new strategies of containment
and resistance vis-à-vis the secular ethics of modernity in their
efforts to build an Islamic way of life and respond to the question
of how they should live. Seen from this perspective, then, we can
place the effort to create an Islamic way of life in the larger context
of the effort to establish a counter-society. Here, the task of imagining an Islamic community flourished from within the discourse of
the *asr al-sa'ada* in the sense that the creation of a society following
the path of the Prophet Muhammad appeared as an ultimate task
of conscious Muslims. But, to the extent to which this task could be
realized, it has also turned out to be a way of becoming consciously
Muslim. In this context, I will also bring into discussion the point
I tried to make while introducing Sennett's concept of the politics
of *ressentiment*. I argued that this can provide a perspective from
which to understand the development of Islamic oppositional discourse. Moreover, by using this politics of resentment, people
who call themselves conscious Muslims in Turkey can express an
important aspect of their feeling of being 'the other': that is, having
been injured due to their exclusion from the circles of the privileged
as a perceived threat to the prevailing order. But another part of
this sense of 'otherness', the pride born out of a sense of being on
the true path, is not directly related to the politics of resentment.
Nevertheless, the general characteristics of what Wallace (1956)
calls 'revitalization movements' can also be applied to this politics
of resentment if we consider the basic departure point of Wallace's
argument. According to this, revitalization movements occur when
individuals feel themselves to be under severe stress and are dissat-
isfied with the prevailing social order and identity. Consequently,

as Piscatori argues, it also becomes possible to see revival as a 'sum of individual unhappiness'. However, I agree with Piscatori that to an even larger extent revival can be seen as 'the sum of individual contentment' (1986, p. 36). In his experience, the many Egyptian, Indonesian and Malaysian people who had become more devout than previously did not always explain their new situation as a consequence of social, economic or political dislocation, nor did they formulate it in terms of emotional and psychological distress. This was the case with the people I studied. Their situation is closely related to the faith dimension of Islamic revitalization, and this should be seen as part of the self-narrations of these people who call themselves conscious Muslims and whose sobriety is determined within the dialogical boundaries of Nakşibendi ethics. But it should also be remembered that this only came about as the result of the attainment of a sense of self-confidence and belonging, that is, trust in being powerful enough to create an Islamic way of life. This sense of self-confidence comes from the sense of being on the 'true' path, and is reinforced by the sense of empowerment which concomitantly arises out of being able to live Islam as conscious Muslims and the recognition of the Islamic movement as an alternative social force in the society of which they form part.

To conclude this chapter, I note that analysing the formation of this *site* as an extension of a project to actualize a counter-society, rather than a closed, isolated local community, enables us to see its place in the wider sociological processes. It should not cause us, however, to omit the discursive image of community which operates in shaping these people's further discourses and imagination. By this I mean we should also be able to see that the image of Islamic community as vested with prophetic qualities and Sunni Muslim morality will continue to matter as a problem of organization and disorganization with all its intimate connotations insofar as the Islamic community is seen by and large as an overarching entity which unites all Muslims. In this sense of the term, then, the endurance of the image of an Islamic community will continue to set the boundaries of a broader ideological perspective of Islamic activism, creating what Elias (1991) calls the 'we-identity of I's', but how the actualization of this ideal takes its specific sociological forms will, of course, continue to be contingent on the conditions in which this construction takes place.

Here, I have tried to maintain a general theoretical perspective to trace this ideal's conditions of emergence and its way of development in a modern context, preserving its authority within the discourse of sociology without, however, tracing the development of the sociological concept of community and its typologies from eighteenth century European thought onwards. If the meaning of the word community, as Nispet maintains, goes beyond mere local community in that it 'encompasses all forms of relationship which are characterized by a high degree of intimacy, emotional depth, moral commitment, social cohesion, and continuity in time' (1973, p. 47), then it seems that it may also encompass the broader definitions of the specific imagination of Islamic community which gave way to the establishment of this *site*. Yet, although these definitions can maintain the fundamentals of a specific imagination, they do not tell much about the ways in which what I call the 'action-based orientations' of such an imagination can be traced. Nispet studied how the concept of community was employed in the theoretical projects of the founding fathers of sociology and how it worked as a template for building their critical stands towards the existing social systems and for the establishment of their own projects of moral community. One particular point he makes inspired me in my thinking about the 'counter-society projects' of the Turkish Muslims I studied. Nispet argues that in Marx's utopian 'moral community' we can say that his project of socialism can be seen simply as capitalism minus private property, and similarly Comte's project of Positivist society can be seen as medievalism minus Christianity (p. 58). By the same token, for the action-based orientations of the project of Islamic counter-society in Turkey, I think, we can also ask whether it is a modern-capitalist-republican Turkish society minus secular ethics and morality.

Thus, I use the term 'counter-society' when I refer to that broader socio-political project, but when I use the term 'community' in the course of the text I mainly refer to the urban place where I conducted this study. I also use the term to denote Muslim congregations or assemblies such as those in mosques, convents, charity meetings, seminars or just in neighbourhoods and districts, as in *cemaat* or *topluluk* in vernacular Turkish,[14] without necessarily referring to its Islamic political connotations, but also without necessarily rejecting its religious dimension. Finally, I also use 'community' to denote the imaginary aspect of making an Islamic way of life. Thus I do not abandon the pursuit of the discursive parameters of imagining an Islamic community while analysing it at the sociological level as part of the process of formation of a counter-society.

Notes

[1] Mardin develops this point in detail in a paper (1990b) which attempts to compare the past and the present of Egyptian and Turkish fundamentalism. This runs contrary to other assertions about the Nakşibendi order, namely by Algar (1985), who argues that Nakşibendi do not have a bent for power.

[2] For the Gümüşhanevi order, whose first lodge was established in the nineteenth century in the Black Sea region of Turkey, and its founder, Ahmed Ziyaeddin Gümüşhanevi (d. 1893), and his methods of proselytizing, see Gündüz (1984).

[3] The first religiously oriented party was the Birlik Partisi (Party of Union), established in 1966 by the Alevis in the atmosphere of tolerance for the Alevis after the 1960 coup. Mardin argues that although the party was unsuccessful at the polls, 'the energy that went into its formation was diverted to the support of other minority groups, among whom the Turkish left hold a prominent place. Conversely, there was a barefaced attempt by Turkish Marxists to exploit some Alevi themes as general themes of rebellion and revolt. Alevi religious dissent . . . thus became an ambiguous mixture of radicalism and support for minority rights' (1983a, pp. 144–5).

[4] For the establishment of the JP and its political structure see Ahmad (1977, pp.191, 232–6) and Levi (1991).

[5] This information came to my knowledge during a discussion of similar issues in a sociology class of mine in METU. One of my students from Eastern Anatolia told us that in his village there was a long-lasting quarrel between elders about whether the emblem meant the party of God or not, though they were sure that these letters stood for *Allah* and *Peygamber*. Similarly, and I think much more interestingly, another long dispute took place between his grandfathers about the name of the RPP (Cumhuriyet Halk Partisi), with one who was a fervent supporter of the RPP arguing that it is not *Halk* (People) in the name but *Hak* (Truth), one of the names attributed to *Allah* as opposed to vanity or falsehood (*batıl*).

[6] For instance, in another branch of the Nakşibendi order in Istanbul, the Ismail Ağa Community, led by Mahmut Hoca, the leader-disciple relationship was rigidly defined. It is said that in this lodge the encounters of the disciples with the shaykh take the form of a lecture (*ders*) based on the principles of edification, listening and obedience instead of conversation (*sohbet*) through which a medium for discussion and collective search for

answers to problems might be created. This order relies for its teaching upon *fikh* (*fıkıh*, canonical jurisprudence) rather than the principles of *hadith* or *sunna*. See R. Çakır (1991, pp. 61–2). The reason for such differences within the same order is that in the Nakşibendi order there is no need to obtain the consent of the *pir* (leader) in establishing a branch. This organizational aspect of the order was seen by Mardin as one of the reasons for its long-term success in the twentieth century (1991b, p. 135).

[7] Ahmed Ziyaeddin Gümüşhanevi's (d. 1893) order originated on the Black Sea Coast of Anatolia. He completed his religious studies in Istanbul and became the most important nineteenth-century Halidi leader in Turkey.

[8] For the individual, commercial and intellectual activities initiated by circles close to Zahid Kotku and Esat Coşan, see R. Çakır (1991, pp. 22, 40–4). For Zahid Kotku's understanding of technological transformation, see Gürdoğan (1991, pp. 87–98).

[9] To what extent a city like Ankara can be compared with the cities of developed Western societies in terms of 'impersonal blankness' is questionable. However, if we keep in mind that Ankara had been originally established as a city of bureaucrats, and its urban landscape is mainly dominated by official state buildings designed to symbolize the central power of the nation-state (Aslanoğlu 1984, pp. 275–88), we can understand how, both for the new 'class of arrivals' who settled in the low-prestige districts of Ankara and for the lower-class immigrants who inhabit *gece-kondu* areas, Ankara might also present an official type of impersonal blankness.

[10] The concept of Islamic community, *umma*, has been extensively studied. Several attempts have been made to understand Muslim political inclinations and Muslim societies through exploring the characteristics of *umma* in general; among these, two distinguished examples are Gibb (1963) and Watt (1960). Hodgson, an exceptional anti-orientalist historian of Islam, defines *umma* as follows: 'Muslims share their experience in a total society, comprehending (in principle) the whole of human life, the Ummah, built upon standards derived from the prophetic vision; comprising a homogeneous brotherhood, bearing a common witness brought to mind daily in the *salat* worship and impressively reaffirmed *en masse* each year in Mecca' (1974, vol. 2, p. 338)

[11] During the years of ANAP rule, the integration of Turkey with the world economic system was supposedly the driving force of the nation. These years saw the launch of export-oriented liberal economic policies, which were also said to be accompanied by freedom of thought and speech, and thus conscience, as well as freedom of enterprise. This can be described as Turkey's second mobilizational phase, the first taking place throughout the 1950s. Because of the atmosphere of political and economic 'libera-

tion', and because the ANAP leader, Özal, was personally affiliated with the Nakşibendi, the religious forces in Turkey had the opportunity to legitimize their cause at the national level, mostly articulating it as an outcome of basic human rights. This did not lead to a totally peaceful political expression, but gave rise as well to the development of Islamic militancy, which served to aggravate the cleavages between the secular and religious forces, culminating in the assassinations of a number of prominent secular figures of Turkish intellectual life.

[12] The mosque, where Muslims were to perform their public religious duties, was also construed as a kind of 'private sphere' for religion, to be used only for collective religious worship; religion would thus remain within the confines of its walls. Moreover, it was also thought that religion could be kept out of politics by regulating the sermons delivered in the mosques according to directives issued by the Directorate of Religious Affairs. Compulsory prayer in the sermons, particularly those during major religious events, for the founders of the Republic, the national military forces, and so forth, would reinforce the pre-eminence of the national ideology.

[13] This was the belief held by many social scientists who interpreted secularization in the modern world as the development of religion as primarily an individual concern which thus lost much of its public relevance. Peter Berger (1967), Thomas Luckmann (1967) and Robert Bellah (1970) are among many who based their argument concerning the impact of modernity on religion on this specific perspective. On this subject, especially on the analysis of Luhmann's argument on the privatization of religion, see Beyer (1991).

[14] In modern Turkish the term *topluluk*, community, bears no religious connotation, whereas *cemaat*, from the Arabic *jama'a*, usually refers to a religious community. It is interesting to note that here again the Turkish language reform also involved the cleansing of religion from language.

CHAPTER VI

Inventing the Islamic Way of Life

VI.1. Otherness: Setting the Boundaries of an Islamic Way of Life

The Islamic way of life is most clearly distinguished from the ordinary secular urban lifestyles prevalent in Turkey by its understanding of Islamic faith, *iman*, which entails ' *ibada* (*ibadet*, service to God). According to some observers, notably Smith, the notion of belief in Islamic faith is different from the notion of belief in other contexts. A person can believe in the correctness of something according to the knowledge or information he has about it; depending on the information he has, he can change his mind if he wishes. But in Islam, 'the believer is one who accepts, who says "yes" to God ... recognizes the situation as it is and commits himself to acting accordingly' (1981, pp. 124–6). Esposito points out that 'for Christianity the appropriate question is, 'What do Christians believe?' In contrast, for Islam (as for Judaism) the correct question is, 'What do Muslims do?' (1991, p. 69).

This understanding of faith in Islam gives rise to a struggle between the secular and Islamic forces in society over the question of what Islamic law is, and to what extent it can be contained in the politico-societal projects of the social order. This struggle concerns the formation of the society's basis of legitimization; the Islamic revivalist movement takes strength from its claim to form this basis of legitimacy on the structural characteristics of Islamic faith. The discourse of 'living Islam as conscious Muslims' is closely connected to this claim which sustains the sense of being on the 'true' path. Thus, answering the question 'How should we live?' becomes a matter of how to fill the structure of Islamic faith in a modern, globalizing context. For Islamic forces this question should first and foremost be answered in the daily articulation of Islamic ideologies in the course of challenging the secular ethics of modernity. This entails redescribing and reshaping what de Certeau calls ' "ways of operating" – ways of walking, reading, producing, speaking, etc.' (1984, p. 30), i.e., rendering Islam a living social practice. The organization of the 'domestic' space, raising children as 'true' Muslims, and making efforts to expand the meaning of the 'private' become the most strategic aspects of this, and women are the main actors in this area.

In the *site* I studied, the political ideals of the WP were predominant among its inhabitants, who mostly comprised either followers of the Esat Coşan branch of the Nakşibendi order[1] or of the Ramazanoğlu branch of the same order, as well as other Sunni Muslims who were not necessarily adherents of either. However, if I attempt to collect them under one single ideological category, its major elements would be derived from an Islamic fundamentalist metanarrative, in which the main authority for any Islamic move is in the written scripture rather than in tradition, except for the social practices which took place in the *asr al-sa'ada*, the age of the Prophet Muhammad. These traditional sources, however, are open to *ijtihad* (*ictihad*, reinterpretation) in order to rebuild Islam as a 'distinct and integrated' system. The idea of progress is thus contained, but in such a way that it is dissociated from Western-oriented modernization and it is the anti-imperialist voice of Third Worldism that carries the narrative.[2]

The studied families are easily placed in the middle and lower-middle ranks of society through conventional sociological indicators such as family type, level of education, income and professional status. Most earned their livings as civil servants, self-employed professionals, politicians and journalists, while others engaged in commerce. Regarding such aspects as home decoration, cooking, women's indoor clothing and ways of receiving guests,[3] their basic lifestyle differed little from that of others in their class. The forms of voluntary associations they established and their patterns of intellectual activity duplicated the intellectual life of the modern urban élite in terms of charity meetings, seminars and conferences. The private schools they established to provide primary and secondary education in line with their religious ideals followed similar patterns to other schools, offering a participatory learning process in a materially and intellectually well-equipped environment.

Nevertheless, the code they followed made them distinct: women could not go out without a headscarf and loose fitting overcoat; they could not meet strange men without covering themselves; the use of interest as a financial instrument was prohibited, as was drinking alcohol, dancing and gambling, etc. Most importantly, they emphatically rejected modern cultural rituals and celebrations borrowed from the Western-Christian world which have become hallmarks of modern life, such as the celebration of Mother's Day and Father's Day. They replaced them with celebrations such as *kandil* to show respect and affection for their parents and children. Celebration of New Year's Day was a particular target because of its association with the Christian rather than the Muslim calendar. Their cultural rituals are worthy of more careful consideration in order to understand the maxims for the way of life that they wished to establish. They aimed to perpetuate a sense of cultural authenticity in that their rituals were the signifying practices of a given culture, through which not only the rhythm and periodicity of cultural life are organized according to certain meaning systems, but also culturally identified personal relations are regulated within certain types of mannerism.[4]

In constructing an Islamic way of life, the women especially paid considerable attention to avoiding the creation of a cultural gap which could cause particularly the young to be lured by modern urban life. They were, however, quite careful not to be labelled as backward, narrow-minded or obscurantist. They tried to revise socio-cultural patterns which register modernity in a way which would not violate basic Islamic rules.

They watched television but tried to be selective. They went to the movies but watched only religious films. They attended theatrical performances but only those given by Muslim artists. Some went to the seaside for vacation but chose secluded places. They visited historical sites but preferred Ottoman Islamic ones. They let their brides wear long white wedding dresses but with their heads covered. Important life rituals, such as weddings, circumcisions and women's henna evenings, were rarely accompanied by dancing. Although they celebrated anniversaries and their children's birthdays, they were careful to use the occasion to express thanks to God, rather than using it as an excuse for enjoyment. Meeting places were set up for the young but these were of course segregated by sex; here teenagers could improve their religious learning while enjoying the company of their peers and good food. Young women met to recite holy verses, to write and perform small parodies of Western, non-Islamic lifestyles and to sing hymns. Since men were mostly away from home, they did not always have the opportunity to tutor their sons, and this duty fell to older brothers who socialized younger boys by organizing small group discussions and quizzes on religious subjects, as well as history, literature and science. Mothers prepared the food and provided the encouragement and approval necessary for the warm and loving atmosphere in which such education could be imparted. When men came home they engaged in evening visits which had usually been arranged by their wives earlier in the day, or they perhaps went to the tea-house annexed to their mosque. During evening visits men would help their wives look after the guests. When visits were between close relations, men and women did not necessarily sit in separate rooms. At the weekends especially, women would expect their husbands to take the whole family out for lunch or, depending on the season, on a picnic. One of the favourite shared activities of the married couples I observed was to read books of religious literature or history in the evenings, and to discuss details of Islamic history and other matters. This cultivated their sense of sharing an intellectual milieu and of having similar emotional ties in their life together.

In all these activities, Islamic faith worked together with what Bourdieu (1989) calls taste. This, as we have seen, is the distinguishing feature of our lifestyles and emerges from the choices we make, which consequently differentiate us from others in similar categories of social stratification. Here, the discursiveness, the rhythm and the strategy-generating principles of the given quotidian, which set the dialogical boundaries of an Islamic way of life, were arranged around the legitimizing power of faith and within its ambient emotional context. Similarly, whether culturally given or newly implemented, the social activities these people participated in defined the matrix of an Islamic way of life and instituted an Islamic solidarity, as did those activities they deliberately avoided. This sense of solidarity was also perpetuated by a specific emotional bonding, namely trust, which rested here on ethical foundations rather than cognitive techniques and provided the idiosyncratic attachments of its members to this living space, as well as cultivating a sense of security in carrying out their daily lives according to Islamic precepts.

VI.2. 'We women can even go out here at nights': Trust, Hope and Life Politics

To understand the development of a call to an Islamic way of life in order to revitalize Islam in Turkey, in which imagining an Islamic community becomes the most strategic aspect of it, one place to start is by exploring the meanings and functions of major institutional sites of Islam around which the organization of an Islamic community is seen as possible. These are the mosque, the school and home. However, it is also my belief that the body, as the site of the 'micro-physics of power' (Foucault 1979, p. 28), also constitutes one of the most important sites of Islam in that it is the 'initial' site of inscription of the principles of Islamic faith. It can also be argued that the body can be taken as an institutional site, considering the worshipping practices of Islam which start, in a Foucauldian sense, from disciplining the body through a series of personal and communal disciplinary techniques.

In the course of making an Islamic way of life, however, I maintain, with Campo, that it becomes very important to understand how in Islam people develop attachments to the places in which they reside, and in which they imagine themselves to reside (1991, p. 3). Therefore, although the mosque and the school are thought to be indispensable components of an Islamic social environment, the question of 'domestic space' in Islam appears as a major issue in Islamic imagination in which self-placements of people as Muslim persons can also become possible. As Campo says, in Islamic imagination the house constitutes one of the key metaphors helping Muslims to place themselves on earth, as well as in the hereafter, and it links major components of belief and practice (1991, p. 7).

As I have shown in detail in Chapter I, in the Islamic imagination house is understood as being no different from home. The description by the inhabitants and the founders of this *site* of how they imagined themselves, where they resided and where they wanted to reside, matched the broader notion of house in the imagination of Islam, in the sense of any living place which functions as a home for the survival of community while providing an Islamic solidarity.

They believed that the survival of the Muslim family could only be maintained by the establishment of such an Islamic community. In this context, in addition to the political concern to build an Islamic way of life, another basic need behind the establishment of a *site* enabling these people to live close to one another was that of creating an environment in which they would have the security to carry out daily life according to Islamic principles and the strength to protect themselves from any 'dangers' of the outside, i.e., non-Islamic, world. Here, my basic argument is that, for the kind of trust involved in the attachment of members of an Islamic community to their living space, the protection of women and children from the outside world is a central issue.

Mardin shows how an Islamic idiom created by a spiritual leader such as Said Nursi works in a modern differentiated society as a means of communication: it functions as a social cement to sustain the productive order, i.e., 'the belief in the way things will work themselves out in our lives', in other words the trust in society which is said to be required to change its basis from a reliance on a normative system to a system based on cognitive skills in modern society.[5] The sense of trust that I observed in this specific case of building an Islamic way of life works here as an ethical template for social legitimization and, as Mardin indicates, rests on ethical foundations rather than cognitive techniques (1989a, pp. 218, 220).

This sense of trust differs from the sense of ontological security central to the notion of trust suggested by Giddens (1990). Giddens sees a clear-cut distinction between the ways of replacing trust and risk in pre-modern and modern social environments, conceiving of 'kinship relations', 'local community' and 'religious cosmologies as belief systems' as the characteristics of pre-modern conditions.[6] However, he also holds that faced by many options in the course of monitoring our lives according to the information flowing from abstract and expert systems,[7] 'the trust may be suspended in some or many of the systems which routinely or sporadically impinge on the individual's life' (1991, p. 142). Living in the modern context of high-consequence risk may cause some people to take lifestyle decisions which propel them in the direction of more 'traditional authorities'. Religious fundamentalism for Giddens is thus one of the recourses providing 'clear-cut answers as to what to do in an era which has abandoned final authorities: those final authorities can be conjured up again by an appeal to the age-old formulae of religion. The more "enclosing" a given religious order is, the more it "resolves" the problem of how to live in a world of multiple options' (1991, p. 142).

To be sure, to live in an environment where daily life is organized by and large according to religious precepts entails taking certain lifestyle decisions and thus making selections among all the available options. But this is not the unproblematic process presented by Giddens; here it is not the case that the making of life choices becomes any easier as the religious order gets more enclosing. This is because the inhabitants of this *site* were not likely to abandon their trust in expert systems or abstract systems in modern life as a whole. They tended rather to integrate an Islamic perspective in their process of monitoring social life. That is not to say that the boundaries of individual behaviour and its social criteria were not basically set by religion. On the contrary, they were all arranged around the legitimizing power of Islamic Sunni morality and faith. Moreover, as their trust in the social environment in which they lived intensified, the multiplicity of options also increased, without, however, the boundaries of Islam being transgressed or the aim of protecting the Muslim family from the seductions of urban modern life being abandoned. But for the inhabitants of this *site* who are not adherents of certain religious orders, but just lay sympathizers with Islamic political ideals, the behaviour patterns developed within an Islamic matrix as a guide by which they may lead their lives in the most appropriate way, i.e., according to Islamic precepts, become much more important than for those who adhered to a spiritual guide.

Combining trust in abstract and expert systems with spiritual guidance is also one of the consequences of the importance of immanence in modern life, in the sense that Sennett uses the term, that of the need to experience everything here and now. That sense is here intermingled with the religious connotations of the word, in the process of what Giddens calls the monitoring of social life, a basic characteristic of modern 'men'. This helps to explain why a spiritual guide like Professor Coşan was so eager to disseminate his 'sermons' through Islamic journals and magazines at the risk of losing the impact of face to face conversation with his disciples. Besides providing him, and those like him who use such modern vehicles, with the advantage of reaching a larger audience (who cannot have personal contact with spiritual leaders), these publications offered models of 'living Islam as conscious Muslims', which were as important as those that could be directly observed, particularly for those whose religious affiliations were not maintained through a specific bonding with a religious guide. I observed that many people read journals such as *Islam* and *Altınoluk* (following the line of Professor Coşan and the Ramazanoğlu branch respectively), without making too much distinction between them; all such publications approve the general framework of Nakşibendi Sunni tradition and hence all are treated as valuable Islamic sources. But at times when political tension forces people living according to Islamic precepts to take precise decisions regarding political support of particular groups, the guidance of immediate relationships in an Islamic social milieu becomes much more important for the sense of immanence.

I think the following quotation will be helpful in several aspects of the point I am trying to make here. It is taken from an in-depth interview with one of the inhabitants of this *site*. She had graduated from the Faculty of Theology in Ankara and worked both as a preacher and Imam Hatip school teacher. She was married to a journalist and was the mother of three children:

At the beginning, we were not sure about how to dress, what to read and watch, which school to send our children to, where to go or not to go and sometimes even how to address people. I mean, we were not confident of whether we were on the right track or not in the sense of keeping ourselves away from non-Islamic intrusions. For instance, some ten years ago we didn't have a TV set in our house since we refused to watch it. We thought that it might be harmful to training ourselves as true Muslims in that we would spend too much time watching non-Islamic programmes, which might also hinder us in performing our religious duties by taking most of our time. We also did not send our elder daughter to secondary school for a year after she had finished the primary school since we thought that we should not send her even to an Imam Hatip school, because even there girls were not allowed to cover their heads. We hired a private teacher to teach her the Koran, Arabic and other subjects suitable to her school level, thinking that she could obtain her secondary school diploma externally. Though I am not myself attached to

any religious order, I went to X Efendi and asked him whether
we should send her to school or not. I requested another *hoca*
to lie down for *istihare*[8] for me to be able to decide whether to
send our daughter to school. Both of them gave us positive
answers. They all told us not to be afraid of taking our own
decisions on the way to becoming true Muslims as long as we
were dedicated to leading our lives according to Islamic rules
and did not stray away from God's path. Now, when I look at
the past, I can see how perplexed we were by those social matters.
Though our worries were not groundless, since I had many
unpleasant experiences related to the headscarf issue when I was
attending university. So, I wondered if I, as a mature enough
young person, had felt so humiliated, how a little girl could cope
with such an insult. In the meantime, her present school was
opened (an Imam Hatip school) in the district of X and it was
said to be directed by conscious educators. I did not hesitate to
send her to that school. However, later on, I decided not to worry
too much about the school environment since I started to see
that if you raise your children in a Muslim family and are able
as parents to set a good example for them, the outer environment
does not matter too much in the formation of their personalities.
For instance, when my second daughter wanted to attend a
vocational girl's school where girls do not necessarily cover their
heads, and where she could not receive a full religious education,
I did not hesitate to send her there, both because I was sure of the
moral appropriateness of the school environment and because I
trusted the positive impact of our family life on our children.
Besides, now I also believe that we, Muslims, should not with-
draw ourselves from social life in general. On the contrary, we
must make our presence felt in all walks of life. We should not
of course go to places and social gatherings, such as those modern
weddings, where alcoholic beverages are offered and men and
women behave in an immodest way. But we should be able to
display an alternative social behaviour so as to show that we are
not mere obscurantists.

Similarly, when we had just started to live in this *site*, I and a
group of my friends were trying to find our own style of dress
as proper Muslim women.[9] We usually made ourselves long-
sleeved, shabby looking loose clothes in pale colours and wore
quite simple, low-heeled shoes. It is funny to remember now,

how a friend of ours, an older sister, a very learned Muslim teacher from a well-off Muslim family who lived in another neighbourhood in a well-positioned detached house with a nice garden,[10] used to make fun of the way we dressed when we visited her. She would call us the 'X Muslim société' [X standing for the name of the *site*], and liked to make comments such as 'Aha! The X Muslim société has finally arrived!' That is, we were timid in expressing ourselves even in our indoor clothes. Now, look at our young girls: they even wear jeans when they are at home and some of them go out with them under their long coats. Actually, the latter is not too much approved of yet. Anyway, the important thing is that, now, we feel confident in what we choose to wear and how to adapt many new things to an Islamic way of life, and how to behave in public. As long as we remain within the boundaries of Islam, every sober minded Muslim can decide by him or herself what to do and how to behave. Of course, we are aware of the fact that in our behaviour we set examples for each other. But for most of our behaviour patterns we do not just sit and decide. For instance, as you have observed, in this *site* men and women do not get into elevators together. If there are both men and women waiting for the elevator, no matter how young those women are and what their number is, men wait to get into the elevator when there are no women left waiting. I am not saying that we do not elaborate upon such issues in both our formal and informal meetings so we can invent appropriate behaviour patterns and make them common in order to provide a peaceful social milieu in which no one will be disturbed by the others. This is what we understand from living in a Muslim community. There are of course some differences between us to a certain extent, especially in terms of child raising. Unfortunately you can find here children, especially boys, who swear while they play and are quite aggressive towards their friends. Or sometimes, when girls under the age of puberty go out to play without a headscarf and play with their male peers, this is criticized by some of us. Actually, there is nothing wrong with it from a Muslim point of view but if some families do not want to send their small daughters out without a headscarf it is their problem, and we usually do not interfere with each other over such matters, but most of us do not approve of such unnecessary rigidity either. Nevertheless, we mothers can always warn each other politely about the wrongdoings of our children, as well as about our own faults. It is one of the most unpleasant and even sinful things for a Muslim to speak loosely about another Muslim. Since we all believe that, as was said in a *hadith*, for a Muslim to gossip about other Muslims is like chewing the flesh of a dead Muslim. No one would dare to commit such a sin. Thus, I can be sure that my neighbours will not speak about me and my family. In addition to that, neither mothers nor fathers worry about their children when they leave them alone at home. Likewise, our men feel quite confident when they leave their wives here at home. They know that in this environment nothing wrong can happen to them. We women can even go out here at nights.

These kinds of uncertainties about lifestyle decisions can be revealing in the context of understanding that there was a need to form an Islamic middle class ethos, as well as understanding how a sense of security, confidence and hence trust was essential to develop its quotidian. The following quotation will demonstrate the existence of the sense of trust necessary to build an Islamic way of life for those who were already quite familiar with middle class lifestyles. This young woman came from a large, affluent Islamic family from the largest city of the Marmara region of Turkey and in every respect the living standards in the *site* were very modest for her. She was a relatively newly married woman and she, her husband and her small daughter had moved to this complex after her husband started his PhD studies. She was well aware of the shortcomings and rigidities of the social life offered in the *site*. She did, however, greatly value the sense of solidarity provided by *site* life, as well as the variety of social activities offered by an intellectually lively Islamic milieu.

Our apartment here looks like a small *gecekondu* compared to my parents' house in my native town. And the size of this apartment is not the only small thing here. Wherever you turn you can find an eye watching you, though everybody is respectful to each other. In spite of the respect shown for privacy, everybody knows what everybody else does. But here you can also feel how an Islamic way of life can look. Especially after all those people moved from the complex, this environment seemed to

me much more relaxed than before.[11] Before starting to live here,
I was also quite socially active in my native town, but it was
not easy to find people with whom I could act to materialize
my projects. After living here, I felt much more conscious
and tactful as a Muslim person than I was before. I regularly
participate in the activities of the Hanımların Sesi Derneği
[Association of Ladies' Voices], organize discussion groups, seminars and panels, and have the opportunity to improve my
religious knowledge while participating in *tefsir* studies and the
studies of other prayer groups. More importantly, during both
these intellectual and charity activities I have learned the importance of solidarity between Muslims and become grateful to
God for He blessed me with a Muslim heart. When I saw the
difficult conditions under which Muslims did not stray from
their faith, it gave me a sense of strength to pursue an Islamic
way of life. My husband also participates in some of the activities
of X Ilim, Hayır ve Güzelleştirme Derneği [Association of
Science, Prosperity and Environmental Enrichment]. On all
these occasions what makes me confident is the sense of trust I
feel for the moral superiority of the way of life we lead. Insofar
as I know that we share the same ethical values with those people,
it does not matter whether they sometimes criticize me for being
a little bit outspoken and extrovert, or a little bit impulsive in
political matters such as women's rights in Islam and so forth.[12]
I have learned a lot in this *site* and more importantly I have
learned to trust myself and other pious Muslims in our endeavour to become true Muslim persons. However, in all our deeds
and thoughts, first of all, of course, we should strive for the
mercy of God.

Confidence in relations with neighbours, the knowledge that
anyone in the community would unconditionally help anyone else
because they were all pious Muslims, the knowledge that no one
would disturb the peace of the Muslim environment and harass
women and children and the certainty that no one would mis-
lead the children were all positive factors constantly referred to
by the inhabitants of this *site* when describing how their emotional attachments to it were sustained. The most important aspect
of living in this *site* was the possibility of self-actualization as a
conscious Muslim, without the fear of being harassed. Here a

fundamental aspect of trust relations, what Giddens called civil inattention, comes into play.

Civil inattention is the opposite of the 'hate stare'[13] and 'the most basic type of facework commitment involved in encounters with strangers in circumstances of modernity' (Giddens 1990, pp. 81–2). It involves

> not just the use of face itself, but the subtle employment of bodily posture and positioning which gives off the messages 'you may trust me to be without hostile intent'– in the street, public buildings, trains or buses, or at ceremonial gatherings, parties or other assemblies. Civil inattention is trust as 'background noise'– not as a random collection of sounds, but as carefully restrained and controlled social rhythms. It is characteristic of what Goffman calls 'unfocused interaction'. . . . Encounters with strangers and acquaintances – people whom an individual met before but does not know well – balance trust, tact, and power. Tact and rituals of politeness are mutual protective devices, which strangers or acquaintances knowingly use (most on the level of practical consciousness) as a kind of implicit social contact (pp. 82–3).

Civil inattention was evident in the *site* in the observance of the Islamic rules of modesty and seclusion, and also Muslim tact and ritual politeness, that is, what is usually understood as Islamic *adab* (*adap*, regular customs and norms) observed by cultivated, in this case conscious, Muslims.

Men and women in public places avoid eye contact, do not turn fully towards each other, do not speak loudly and do not address each other without using titles such as *Bey* (Mr) and *Hanım* (Mrs) or *Kardeşim* (my brother/sister). In addition, in necessary social encounters, men and women never shake hands and never kiss the hands of elders of the opposite sex (this is a custom observed in Turkish culture to show respect to 'elders' by the young regardless of the actual age of the older persons). Similar 'rituals' are also valid for same-sex encounters. For instance, when women shake hands it usually takes the form of an Islamic kind of greeting: one holds the other's hands between their hands and says a little prayer of salutation, wishing peace upon the other. Women bend forward slightly when they walk and usually lower their heads or look straight ahead, while avoiding any eye contact with passers-by, though they are very self-conscious and give the impression that they carry their bodies as a fragile thing. This is a good illustration of how, in every patriarchal society, differences between masculine and feminine body postures are developed to restrict women's body space and movement. Bartky contends that 'feminine movement, gesture, and posture must exhibit not only constriction but grace as well, and a certain eroticism restrained by modesty' (1990 pp. 63–82, especially p. 68). In the Islamic type of modesty, any eroticism in public places is eliminated by the bodily seclusion achieved through the use of veils, headscarves, long loose overcoats, etc., as well as through the avoidance of eye contact and the suppression of voice. This does not altogether, however, prevent women from being sensual, if not erotic.

Men, on the other hand, walk upright and look straight ahead, avoiding gazing at any women. In places where women may not immediately be aware of them, they make their presence felt by clearing their throats.[14] Due to these 'rituals of civility' designed to protect the privacy of men and women, that is, Islamic seclusion, the women felt very comfortable, for instance, when they were shopping in the complex's supermarket. This was not just because there were also women salespersons there, but also because the shopkeeper behaved as if women customers were not there and vice versa. When the shopkeeper and the women customers had to speak to each other, they did not usually look each other straight in the face and they kept a reasonable distance between them, the shopkeeper keeping his body half-turned from his customers. Likewise, when women went out at nights either to visit each other just for fun – quite a frequent activity – or to perform religious duties, such as *tarawa* (*teravih*, rest)[15] in the month of Ramadan, in somebody's apartment or in the *site* mosque, they felt secure in the knowledge that no men would bother them: on the contrary, when men and women passed each other on the street, the men acted as if there were no women around, but also managed to convey the impression that they would protect the women if something untoward were to happen. Thus it seemed that the men felt obliged to be in charge of the security of their immediate environment and to perform the role of collective protector.

As far as I can see, these behaviour patterns perpetuated these women's sense of freedom in living in an Islamic environment;

they could imagine themselves to be living like the Muslims of the
asr al-sa'ada when the female members of the Muslim community
in Medina were said to be able to move around freely at nights,
wearing their veils to protect themselves especially from the hypo-
crites (those who pretended to be Muslims). Although this subject
was usually broached in a humorous tone, the analogy was made
joyfully and was often followed by long but light-hearted discussions of the living conditions of Muslim women in the Prophet's
time, the types of tact and politeness introduced by him into the
lives of Muslims, and so on. They were all, not just the religious
professionals among them, inclined to tell stories, anecdotes and
hadiths thought to pertain to the periods of the *asr al-sa'ada* and
taken from the lives of the *ashab* (*sahabe*, the companions of the
Prophet Muhammad). They stressed the points of preservation of
human rights, dignity and politeness inherent in the *sunna* of the
Prophet. By the same token, the behaviour patterns of the Prophet's
family members were frequently mentioned to set examples for
their own, although they were well aware of the differences between
their own life conditions and those of the early Muslim community.[16] Being able to base the legitimacy of their deeds and
thoughts on the authority of the Prophet made them feel stronger
in their endeavours; it also enhanced the sense of trust which relied
upon Islamic ethical foundations and the sense of security which
stemmed from living in a Muslim environment.

The inhabitants of this *site* complained that in most parts of the
city they did not experience this 'background noise' of trust.
Instead they encountered what Giddens (1990), after Goffman
(1963), calls the 'hate stare'; they were perceived as fervent opponents of the existing social system, as opportunist obscurantists who
benefit from the system but in return attempt to destroy it, as
ignorant people who spoil the social order, and so on. They also
maintained that they, especially the women, were sometimes
treated respectfully on buses, in shopping centres and other places
because of their Islamic modesty, but this was said to be uncommon. Almost all the women I encountered had an unpleasant
story, for the most part with regard to treatment at the hands of
disrespectful doctors, even while giving birth (at a time when
private hospitals catering to Muslim people could not be found in
the medical sector). The impoliteness with which they were usually
treated cultivated a sense of bitterness, disaffection and, to a certain

extent, aggression among the inhabitants of this *site* towards 'out-siders', something which has particularly affected the younger generation in certain ways. For example, I was warned in summer that 'open' women like me who wear no stockings in summer are likely to have stones thrown at their legs by 'naughty' little boys who live in this complex. This sort of aggression does not neces-sarily emerge as the result of the maltreatment of so-called Islamist people in Turkey, since justification of aggression on the grounds of bringing about justice through the use of force is not an uncommon cultural characteristic of Turkish society, nor is it something alien to the Islamic imagination and memory. Moreover, imagining the ability to commit violence against others in order to gain strength and confidence, even though it may be justified as self-defence, is neither a new nor a receding phenomenon in Turkish culture.[17] It is regarded as an obvious expedient and people who try to sustain a secluded life in terms of being able to save themselves from non-Islamic intrusions are no strangers to its use. Thus the dis-course which maintains the rhythm of disclosure, disappointment and isolation and which may entail fratricide in communal relations (Sennett 1992), can also maintain a certain amount of hostility towards the behaviour of 'outsiders'.

This community, however, is not closed to the outside world and its effects. Kinship and other types of relationship provide links with that world. Differences in political affiliations, as well as differences in religious attachments in terms of following different *velis* (saints, friends of God), give rise to controversy and discontent in this *site*, even if they do not cause fratricide. But ethically justified Islamic fraternity and trust were used in attempts to contain per-sonal or group discontents.

I will now give an example of something rare in this environment: a person who was ambivalent about adjusting to life in the *site*. I interviewed this particular young woman as a result of 'snowball sampling'. It was not easy to balance this informant's some-what pretentious narration after listening to the stories of all the women who were 'conscious Muslims' *par excellence*. I neverthe-less appreciated her candour, in spite of her long-winded effort to express herself from within a cultivated Islamic discourse throughout a quite long afternoon, since her main interest was to tell me in minute detail the things that had gone wrong at her wedding ceremony. It was very interesting to observe how she was striving to develop trust in an Islamic way of life by living in this *site*.

She was quite young and newly married. She had graduated from a vocational girl's school training needlework teachers and had taught in village courses as assistant teacher for a while before marriage. Her husband was a research assistant in a university and they had a small child.[18] The couple had known each other since their teenage years in their native town in Central Anatolia, and though both their fathers were active politicians they came from families with completely different political allegiances. However, her family did not prevent her from marrying him, despite knowing that her husband would expect her to cover herself. After a series of dramatic family disputes, when they finally managed to marry she did not immediately cover her head but changed her way of dress gradually. When I interviewed her she had lived in the *site* for just a few years, but her sister-in-law and other members of her husband's family had been there longer. She was the kind of young person likely to be called *cahil* (ignorant) by elders in Turkish culture, in the sense that she was inexperienced in life and hence should be tolerated and supported by the elders. I deliberately mention this to underline the difference between this woman and other interviewees who displayed no ambivalence about living an Islamic life as covered women. In spite of the difficulties she had in living like a 'conscious' Muslim, she seemed to have put great effort into developing a sincere but also intellectually intricate discourse concerning the superiority of Islamic morality in regard to her experiences when working as a village teacher. Beyond the peculiarities of her life experience, I believe this case is important in that it demonstrates how the way of life in this complex can function to provide a sense of trust even for those who had difficulties in adapting to an Islamic way of life.

> When we moved here I was too timid to enter into relations with the others because I did not find myself particularly knowledgeable about Islam. I was not raised like them, though I had been always curious about religious matters and had learned how to perform my ritual prayers from my grandmother when I was a child and occasionally had attended the Koran courses in our neighbourhood in summer with other daughters of secular families. I know that a woman should not live according to Islam

just because her husband wants it, but on the contrary she should
do it for the mercy of God. I really want to become a conscious
woman like all those dignified Muslim women who live here.
But at the beginning I was a little bit scared of being criticized
since I could not spontaneously behave like them. I mean, it
took time for me to say 'hayırlı sabahlar' instead of 'günaydın',[19]
for example, or I could not automatically repeat religious formulae like 'sallalahu aleyhi ve sellem'[20] each time I mentioned the
name of the Prophet Muhammad. Likewise, even my genuflexions during namaz[21] were not as smooth as the others'.
Besides, I was not used to covering my head. I must admit that I
feel quite uneasy when I go out and walk on the streets as a
covered woman because of the way in which people stare at me.
It is a really unbearable thing. At those times I don't know where
to put my hands and which direction to look. Once or twice
when I went to the parties of colleagues of my husband, I noticed
that people treated me differently, and especially women could
not decide how to approach me. This really embarrassed me.
So, I gave up going to such gatherings with him and similarly I
did not pay visits to those who had come to visit us when we first
moved here to say welcome to us. Thank God my sister-in-law is
a very tolerant and knowledgeable Muslim woman. Although
she is also quite young, she was very affectionate to me. In order
to familiarize me with the environment she introduced me to
some girl students who live together in some of the apartments
of this site. I wish I could be like them. They are joyful as well as
responsible girls. She also took me with her to irşad [guidance]
meetings as well as women's reception days, and so on. Regardless of their age these women were all very nice and friendly,
though they also behave in a discreet way and preserve their
distance from you as long as you do not show any inclination to
become friends with them. I mean, nobody imposes anything on
you. This is what I like most here. Now, I really feel sorry for
the time I lost in becoming friends with such women. From the
very beginning I had that feeling of trust in the superiority of the
way of life here, but I could not trust myself since I thought I
was not as conscious a Muslim as they were. Here, each day I am
learning to develop myself. In our school, they taught us a lot
about child-rearing but you cannot imagine how much knowledge the women I have met here have about this subject and

how modern they are in these matters. I am sure that here I can raise my daughter both as a literate person and a true Muslim – unlike the way I was raised. Have you noticed how gentlemanly the men of this *site* are? They always respect you and never attempt to treat you in a different way. At the beginning I thought that people would belittle me since I came from an 'open', irreligious environment. No, never. Though sometimes I could not interpret their solemnity and thus thought that they were looking at me as if I had done something wrong. Nevertheless what I like here is that neither men nor women stare at you. I believe one day I can also be just like them.

However, my sister looks down on these Muslim people. She deliberately smokes and wears tight jeans when she comes to visit us. She asks my husband whether he will marry three more women, what chastity has got to do with a bit of woman's hair, and why God does not prevent all the poverty and injustice and the like. She accuses us of being members of an interest group which exploits innocent people. I cannot think of any other sister so thoughtless and rude toward her sister's marriage and way of life. She does not have any fear of God. Had she ever read the Koran, she would not behave like this but she never listens to me. I really don't understand her. Why doesn't she want to see how decent these people are who live here? She behaves as if they had done something very bad to her, whereas they are very respectable persons who want to live in peace and harmony while fulfilling God's commands. Even my father did not criticize me when I covered my head although he was known as an earnest Atatürkist politician in our native town. When he first saw me like this he looked at me and said: 'This also suits my daughter. May God bless you and your family, my dear.' Anyway, when I look at my sister's and my old friends' lifestyles instilled with no fear of God but just gossip and backbiting I appreciate my life here much more.

It can be said that the 'other' for this young woman was her sister who showed no tolerance to her older sister's new way of life. However, together with the affection shown to her by her fellow women neighbours and her father's approval of her life choice and marriage, this only served to increase her trust in the Islamic way of life. Unlike many other men and women I met during this study, who put great effort into creating an Islamic environment to render Islam a living social practice, since she was a 'newcomer' she took for granted the facilities offered in this *site* and did not have much idea of how these people had struggled to create an Islamic *site* together with its own school, mosque and *awqaf*. These facilities provided an Islamic social environment and served to cultivate a sense of Islamic solidarity which perpetuated a special emotional bonding and trust that helped her to develop a sense of security and maintain her personal attachment to this particular living place.

A relatively small building, which was to be a Koran course school, had initially been built in the *site* but it was later closed down because of legal obstacles. As there were other schools available in the district, as well as other public and private Koran courses, not much resentment over its closure was shown. I do not think this would have been the case if there had been no mosque in the complex. A reading room and a tea-house annexed to the mosque also functioned as a school, especially for the young males. The construction of a minaret was seen as pointless by some of the older male members of the *site*, who argued that their funds could be used for much more urgent needs: the inhabitants of this *site* would need no call to prayer. If a call to prayer were needed, it could be made through a public address system, which could also broadcast the various sermons given in the mosque to each apartment. Others, however, saw the minaret as the most important symbol of Islam and thus indispensable. Its detractors pointed out that there had been no minarets in the Prophet Muhammad's time, but that the early Muslims had been much more 'conscious' than today's Muslims. As far as I could see, with or without a minaret, a mosque of their own was a great source of pride for the inhabitants of the *site*. As I observed several times, when Professor Coşan came to give sermons in this mosque, a kind of 'pious tracking' with buses carrying many people from different cities and towns located in the hinterland of Ankara turned the *site* into a religious centre. Instead of creating a sense of unease among the members of other religious orders or political opponents of Professor Coşan, this was not only perceived as a welcome opportunity to increase the prestige of the *site* but it also enhanced the inhabitants' endeavours by giving them the opportunity to disseminate Islam to larger groups. I was interested to note in connection with the women's enthusiasm for their evening visits that even at times when the *site* was virtually invaded by 'strangers', these were not interrupted; if anything, they increased.

The parameters of trust in the Islamic way of life that I have discussed so far can be seen as basically arranged around the axes of emotional bonding sustained by the ethical foundations of Islam and the ontological security necessary to lead life according to chosen moral ideals. In this specific process of imagining an Islamic community and the ways in which it was rendered a living social practice by the implementation of a particular 'life politics', the self-perceptions which its Muslim actors developed contingent to their life experiences played the most significant role. For instance, apart from those occasions when the *site* is open to other Muslims and it is linked to the outside world, its inhabitants' attitudes towards it were said to have changed as their confidence in becoming true Muslims increased. In addition, concomitant with the empowerment of the Islamic movement in Turkey, social life in this *site* became much more open than previously, when Muslims had felt politically less powerful both at the personal and national level. Towards the end of my study, one of the 'mental architects' of the *site*, who did not live there but maintained relations with its prominent figures and was known as a strong supporter of the NOP/NSP/WP movement as well as being one of the best known Turkish Muslim intellectuals, 'theorized' the past, present, and the future of this complex as follows:

> In the very establishment of this *site* the aim was to defend ourselves. It was an act of seeking a shelter, a need for seclusion. It was a requirement to turn inward to see the light coming from our Muslim essence. To be able to own a house without using interest money should also be seen as part of such an effort since it is part of leading one's life as a true Muslim. A true Muslim always stands before God torn between hope and despair. At the beginning there was this despair, a strong feeling of fear that this entailed the need for seclusion, which basically stems from this subconscious drive. Therefore we can say that the idea of establishing an Islamic living place was not the product of an intellectual effort, it was rather the product of a biological drive, an instinctive sense of defence. There was a utopian primitiveness in that idea of building up an Islamic way of life within the

boundaries of a *site*. Later on, it transcended the utopian ideal of collectivity and became real when, as for all Muslims in Turkey, fear started to be replaced by hope for the inhabitants of this *site*. Political developments in the world and also in Turkish society, and especially the Iranian Revolution, helped Muslims to nurture their hopes about the future. Muslims started to actualize their own identities and began to stand on their own feet. This *site* also helped its inhabitants to develop a trust in themselves. If hope and trust can control fear, this engenders progress. Now, in the 1990s, the basic motive behind the effort to make an Islamic way of life depends on hope. This is not a subconscious drive any more. After the 1980s Muslims embraced hope, which enabled them to see their responsibilities as Muslims and helped them to become conscious Muslims. In this respect it should be said that morality constitutes the legitimate basis of consciousness. Consciousness transforms knowledge into comprehension and comprehension brings responsibility. Thus the formation of consciousness is based on a fourfold system: Action (*fiil*), comprehension (*idrak*), knowledge (*bilgi*) and politics (*siyaset*). At present this *site* stands between the second and the third level of this hierarchical structure and forges ahead to its final fourth stage that brings us to a completely Islamic society.

Another person, a notable male figure living in the *site*, a well-known teacher of religion who had also worked in the Ministry of Education for several years on the development of national religious curricula, explained the situation in a more concrete way:

Twenty years ago, we Muslims could only govern a small town. Now, when we come to the 1990s, we have reached a stage of knowledge and experience that could allow us to govern a province (*vilayet*) properly. The number of our statesmen and professionals such as lawyers, physicians, engineers, university teachers, journalists, soldiers and policemen is not sufficient to govern a whole country yet. But our achievement in raising our own intellectuals has been great. Before that, our youth could hardly contest with those Marxist intellectuals. Now, the latter cannot grasp the scope of knowledge that our youth has. Bülent Ecevit was the first Turkish political leader who deigned to have an intellectual dialogue with us. We viewed him with a kind of 'noble hatred'. Now, our intellectuals are likely to be on the same level as many Turkish academics, politicians and statesman. What makes our youth superior to others is their ability to see matters also with their hearts' eyes. Likewise, our young girls are so successful and well-bred that they were constantly bothered by that headscarf ban. My wife must have told you how the administrators of one school did not give our daughter her first prize certificate since she refused to uncover her head. What happened? Nothing! She is going to take her master's degree in England. Our other daughter is attending university in Saudi Arabia. How far can they hinder these intellectual minds? You have observed what kind of harmonious family lives our housewives have brought into this Muslim environment and I am sure you have also envied it. You leave your children to come over here to carry out this study. Do you feel comfortable? Are you sure that they are under the surveillance of trustworthy people? Whereas our Islamic way of life is the guarantee of our younger generations.[22] We elders dedicated ourselves to building them an Islamic life but I am sure they will build a better Islamic life than we could for them.

It is usually men rather than women who can, based on their own life experiences, freely produce 'abstract' theories or make comments that could be generalized to include the whole of life and society (cf. Bartky 1990, pp. 91f). But in this case, the female preacher quoted earlier had very realistic observations about the communal solidarity and its basis as it was maintained in this specific environment:

The political inclinations of the inhabitants of this *site* have always changed according to which group was in power. At the very beginning, in the 1970s, Nurcus were prominent. After the 1980s, people largely supported the ANAP, then the religious orders such as Ramazanoğlu and to a certain extent Esat Efendi Hazretleri [Esat Coşan] became quite active. Among both the former and the latter there were always some people who never withdrew their support from the WP. But what I mean is that people are likely to be close to power. Nevertheless, insofar as the religious political ideals of the WP fulfil the function of an umbrella of faith for Muslims in Turkey, no one can fail to pay attention to its political instructions. Besides, we people who support the WP have always tried to keep different Muslims in touch and diminish the tension between them. After all what keeps us strong is our trust in Islam and the Islamic way of life. If our determination to lead our lives as conscious Muslims were taken out of our hands, nothing could hold us together. Therefore what bonds us to each other is the Islamic way of life that we try to follow, create and recreate each day dependent on the ethical foundations of Islam, and also on the consciousness which keeps us awake so that we do not stray away from the true path.

VI.3. Selected Moments from the 'Self-Narratives' of Muslim Women

Why do they call us *Islamcı* [Islamist] Ayşe Hanım? It sounds something like *köfteci*.[23] Aren't we all Muslims? Why do they discriminate against us like that?

Although this cry was from a middle-aged university graduate, the mother of four children and married to a senior bureaucrat, who was working in a public lycée as a teacher of religion and had assumed the veil in her early twenties while attending the Faculty of Theology in Ankara, it well expresses the sentiments of many other women I encountered during my fieldwork. Another protest çame from a woman in her thirties, veiled since her lycée years in Istanbul, married to a civil servant, a graduate of both a vocational girls' lycée and Koran courses, who worked as a teacher at a private Koran course and occasionally tailored at home while looking after her three small children:

Do they think of us as stupid women who unquestioningly obey men? I tell you, if I were not a Muslim, I would be a feminist. But thanks be to Almighty God, who blessed me with an ability to see that my religion gave me all the rights a woman could wish for. Those people think we are only concerned with headscarves. It is true that our headscarf is the flag of Islam but it is not the whole of our faith. It is just a part of it.

The next quotation is from a primary school graduate housewife in her fifties, married to a well-off merchant and the mother of four grown-up children. What she told about her personal development, shaped by her marriage, sheds some light on what these so-called Islamist women expect from life in general:

> When I first met my husband I liked his beard, but I didn't know that it was Islamic. We both came from conservative families and I only covered my head when I was going out shopping and the like. After we married I saw that he was truly a pious man. Actually, he was not as conscious about Islam as he is now. We have both learned our religion together. But if I am a Muslim woman now, I owe it to him, to his love and affection which made me conscious of my religion. You have been among us for a long time, so you must have noticed that it is not an easy task to observe Islam properly. This is especially so for a beginner when you have to perform ritual prayers five times a day, get up early in the morning and so on. But each time my husband saw me praying he heartily thanked me for filling our house with the holy light of Islam. He even brought me some small gifts. Later on, he also took me on the Hac. You can see how happy a woman I am now. Throughout our marriage, we have helped each other and raised our children together, though he seems a very authoritarian guy on the surface. He is, of course, a strong man, but I am not a weak woman either. We have respected each other's authority. I've never bothered him with little family problems and he's never tried to control my behaviour, but whenever I need him, he never lets me down. May God be with him.

The same woman, an adherent of a branch of the Nakşibendi order, was among those who cheerfully showed me photographs from their '*Cahiliye* (ignorance) periods'. They would make fun of their arrogance, and tell stories about the unhappy marriages of their rich, well-educated relatives who did not lead their lives according to Islam, pointing out how they could have harmonious marriages by following the Islamic way of life.

The last, but perhaps the most 'ideological', quotation is from a relatively young university graduate with a master's degree who taught in an Imam Hatip lycée. When I interviewed her she was about to marry an official security officer. What she told about her personal history might very well be the story of any young urban lower or lower-middle class woman from a semi-urbanized, conservative family encountering recent Turkish politico-cultural networks:

> In my middle school and lycée years I had so-called leftist friends, although I didn't know anything really about Marxism and so on. I just read Aziz Nesin, Orhan Kemal and Nazım Hikmet, and listened to Zülfü Livaneli. But my friends and I all felt anger at the inequalities and unjust nature of the system and so on. We were young, insecure, unsatisfied and without guidance. In the meantime, my father got involved in politics. He became a fervent follower of Necmettin Erbakan and participated in the party's propaganda activities. One day he threw all those authors' books into the stove and told me I could only attend university if I went to the Faculty of Theology. You can't imagine how much I cried. I thought this would be the end of my life. I protested to him and stayed at home for a year. However, quite interestingly, he never forced me to cover my head. Actually since the last years of my lycée education I had started to become more and more cognizant of how our family life had changed after my father had become a party member. Before, when he was just a religious officer, he had even beaten my mother. After he joined the party, he started to become a decent man, as did my brothers. I must admit that my brothers had always been respectful and affectionate to me since I was the only daughter in the family. My mother also has always been tender to me. But you know her, she is an illiterate, silent peasant woman. She never questioned my father's authority, though she always tried to protect me. It really makes me glad to see her happy and confident in her marriage now. She can go out freely to join her friends for Friday prayers, as well as visiting her relatives and so on. Besides, my brothers help her around the house much more than me since, for the young generation of Muslim men, sharing house chores is not a big deal. In fact, they see it as their duty.
>
> Anyway, during that year I stayed at home, I read a lot. My father did not try to control what I read, so I read whatever I could find, but more importantly, I discovered Necip Fazıl Kısakürek.[24] His sincerity and sense of authenticity really impressed me. In the end, I decided to agree to attend the Faculty

of Theology, in the hope of having a chance to change faculty. But, believe me, once I started there, I really found the curriculum very interesting. I also liked the whole atmosphere of the school and had nice friends. I studied hard. It was not an easy education. I also started to receive private lessons in Arabic. In the meantime, I read about Marxism and world political history. What I learned was that no secular system of thought could explain fate and that no religion was better suited to women than Islam. It was then that I veiled myself. Now, I am grateful to God for letting me know my true religion. Yet I know a lot of veiled women who don't know what Islam is all about. They think that by veiling themselves they automatically become proper Muslims. Unfortunately, most of them are just false Muslims and I feel really sorry when people judge Islam by looking at them.

Now, as you know, I am going to marry a friend of my brother's and leave Ankara, since he has been appointed to East Anatolia. My fiancé is also a good Muslim, but I am afraid he is not as conscious as I am. I hope my knowledge will help both of us to make our marriage Islamic. I am aware of my rights as a Muslim woman and I hope my husband will respect them. But, of course, we'll see. For my part, I wish to be a good wife and a devout mother and be happy. Then I'll see if I can continue to work in the East. Now I need some rest and calm. I hope I won't face much hostility in the East for being a veiled woman. You might find this a little bit strange, but sometimes I really feel a little bit tired of life at the moment. However, I believe my all-merciful God will help me.

This story can be read as a story of 'indoctrination' as well as a story of a life struggle which culminated in conformism. But the effort she put into bringing the pieces of her life together, using the available resources to develop an identity and build a way of life, should not be underestimated. Moreover, the fact that the path she followed was chosen rather than imposed should not be ignored. More recently, many other women with similar educational and cultural backgrounds have been prompted to take much more risk than she took and have changed the direction of their lives. Here the point at stake is the positive sense of change that she experienced within the social milieu in which she lived, and thus the sense of trust she developed in the moral superiority of her way of life. Last, but not least, is the sense of continuity that the Islamic 'idiom' can provide in the way of upward mobility, both in philosophical and substantial terms, without forcing people to make a total break with the set of culturally given frames of conduct which shape their daily lives. This reflects what Mardin argues for, the pervasiveness of Islamic 'idiom': 'it covers all aspects of life in society and . . . it is shared more equally by upper and lower classes of society than its equivalents . . . in the West' (1989a, p. 6).

But if life as a veiled professional woman can be quite a stressful experience in Turkey, conformity can turn out to be self-defeating. More importantly, the so-called Islamic way of life is a life politics which needs constant effort for its actualization, much more than others, to the extent that, on the one hand, this occurs in the hegemonic context of a westernized secular order and, on the other, it has to be differentiated from the so-called secular paths which cannot, at least in terms of their cultural patterns and structures, be completely distinguished from the so-called Islamic ones.

VI.4. Between Hope and Despair: Demarcation of Muslim Women's Identity

Apart from individual prayers and conventional worship practices, such as getting together for Friday prayers, *tefsir* studies and *kandil* celebrations, the women had developed other methods of learning and actualizing Islam and Islamic ideologies. During their home visits and receptions, while they drank their tea they read passages from the Koran, or other religious books teaching tradition, and answered practical questions regarding daily life. They organized small groups to discuss specific issues such as Masonic guilds, feminism or women's rights in Islam. They frequently organized seminars and panels to discuss the role of women in Islam and current political issues affecting their social position. Through these inventive and dedicated activities they created an intellectually active milieu which aimed to facilitate the consolidation of an alternative Islamic lifestyle and strengthen their faith in Islam. They brought together many Muslim women from different intellectual levels around one ideal and perpetuated the sense of Islamic equality.

More importantly, this type of activity, involving seminars and panels, and so on, as well as the virtual transformation of women's reception days[25] into reading days, implies a new understanding of the position of Muslim women. Tapper observed in her study on women's *ziyaret* (visiting) patterns in a small Turkish town that men's ideals, beliefs, and actions are usually placed above those of women. Religious activities common among women, such as visiting shrines, organizing *mevlûd* recitations[26] and going to religious charity meetings, distinguished women from men and reinforced the construction of female inferiority (N. Tapper, 1990, p. 237). Here, however, Muslim women had the opportunity to take part in activities similar to those of men. These activities made their efforts as valuable as men's, and provided them with a public image of active, intellectual Muslim women. At issue here was not simply the comparison of the value of their activities with those of men and competition with them but, more significantly, the attainment of the status of 'person' in the community. This lay behind their efforts to be recognized as playing a significant and legitimate social role in the development of the community in addition to the role they played in family life. This coincides with what both Eickelman and Mardin have observed about the supremacy of personhood against individuality in the Islamic realm of identity formation: 'person' refers to cultural concepts that lend social significance to the individual, whose loyalty to the community should take precedence over individualistic concerns, though a considerable amount of responsibility and autonomy is allocated to the person (Eickelman 1991, pp. 37–8; Mardin 1989a, pp. 163–71).

The same activities also enabled these Muslim women to develop ideas about the position of women in Islam, and to compare this with the position other ideologies accorded it. In this context, they had a close interest in feminism, since feminism questions the position of women in any given social order and aims to transform the conditions under which women have been oppressed. It was in this area that Muslims claimed to have gained ground. To the extent that feminism challenges a specific form of patriarchal order thought to have been imported into Turkish society from the West, that is, the forms of patriarchy which emerged in Western capitalist societies, it becomes a worthy opponent of Islamic reviv-alism. But feminism in their view was nothing but an extremist ideology unacceptable to various sections of Turkish society and for them it was just a means of attacking what they saw as the despicable status accorded to women by modern Western thought.

The way in which feminism is construed also helps to describe what Islam provides for Muslim women. Feminism was a movement which emerged in the West as a result of the secondary position accorded to women in Christianity. It was argued that Islam had recognized women as equal to men in the sight of God at a time when Christians were still debating whether women had souls or not. Thus women under Islam enjoyed civil rights while Christians still questioned their humanity. Women in Muslim society were protected and enjoyed an exalted status, while by contrast women were used as objects of male sexuality in the Christian world. Later, in the name of individualism, capitalism began to force women out of their homes and use them as a source of labour. Moreover, in the name of sexual freedom, capitalism also turned women into sex objects to be exploited for profit. Women in the West began to rise up against this multi-faceted exploitation, a revolt which would come to nothing unless the social system was radically transformed. This reading of feminism allowed these Muslim women to conclude that feminists were barking up the wrong tree when they demanded equality because all they were really demanding was the chance to be like men, thus denying the importance of motherhood. Feminists, they believed, thought that they were working for the emancipation of women, but all they had managed to achieve was economic independence through work. This could not save women from becoming sexual objects and, through their very negation of the essence of womanhood, they became uneasy in their souls.

In contrast to Western women, Muslim women had been given the right to choose whether they wanted to stay at home or go out to work. In this world, God wanted woman to obey her man but not men. Men were not to decide what women's rights were. It was God, who is above human beings, who determined women's rights and duties. That was why these Muslim women thought that in veiling themselves they were not conforming to men's demands, rather they were obeying God's commands, which thus did not amount to accepting women's subordination to men. Likewise, men were responsible for taking care of and protecting their own women but were not able to control other women's behaviour

and as such nobody could force women into work, including
housework. A woman could not even be forced to nurse her own
child or serve her husband's family. But, since God had created
women with a motherly heart, they had the elevated attributes of
sensitivity and affection which made them tender towards all weak
creatures, and thus they would of course look after their children.
These attributes also made women fragile and even somewhat
vulnerable, not only in physical terms but also in terms of being
compassionate in comparison to men. On the other hand, God
had given men the responsibility of ruling social life according to
His will, that is, according to Islamic principles. They were therefore the guardians of the Islamic social order and the heads of
families. Although the nature of man was not depicted in full, as
was woman's, there was a strong implication of the strength, both
in physical and social terms, necessary to make wise and logical
decisions and carry them out to rule society. This duty to decide
for others could even make men harsh and uncompromising.
Women's nature, invested with motherly mercy and the instinct
to nurture, was unable to emulate such necessary ruthlessness. On
the contrary, their compassionate nature could help men to be
merciful towards the weak, something which would also help them
to behave justly and tactfully.

Men were not superior to women. Superiority could only be
obtained by *taqwa* (*takva*, piety) that is, by getting closer to God
through worship and being always conscientious in the application
of His rules. Thus, the relationship between men and women was
based on neither superiority nor equality; rather it was complementary, being defined by their respective natures. God had created
men and women with different natures to fulfil different functions
on earth. Each was called upon to obey the divine principles of
God and to behave according to their *fitra* (*fitrat*, nature), their
innate characteristics. However, this did not mean that there could
not be women endowed with a superior mental capacity who
exceeded men's ability in social and religious matters – in fact, the
history of Islam was 'full' of such women.

In spite of the effort to define the relationship between the social
conditions of existence and religious precepts, the codes of this
discourse were construed as simply a matter of faith by these
Muslim women. A belief in God and the Koran as His word,
logically implied acceptance of all His judgements without ques-

tion. People should strive to develop a better understanding of the wisdom of His judgement. After all, they said, who could know better than Him what is good and what is not for human beings, all of whom were created by Him? They had the same attitude towards the rules of veiling and segregation of the sexes. These were all conceived as rules for the establishment of a better social life for human beings in accordance with their nature, something which could not be attained by other Muslim societies such as Iran, Egypt or Algeria. Hence, Turkish Muslims should lead the *umma* as they had before: they believed that the best Islamic social order could be established by the Turkish Muslims and would be based on their experience inherited from their Ottoman past.

In line with this somewhat uncompromising stance, I never came across any woman who implied that women were the source of *fitna*, that is, social disorder and anarchy. On the contrary they all asserted that it was not only women who had to cover their '*awra* (*avret*, private parts) and act in accordance with Islamic *adab*: men also had to follow the same rules and be modest. However, they did not elaborate upon why women's hair, necks and arms are considered to be private parts but men's are not. They rather tended to conceive of 'those parts' of women's bodies as their *zina* (*ziynet*, in vernacular usage, ornament, adornment), referring to the twenty-fourth Sura of the Koran, 'Nur', in which women were called upon not to show their *zina*. An extremely intelligent, well-educated and influential woman preacher explained the situation in a different way, not only to me but also to many other women, as I observed on several occasions such as in Koran courses and *irshad* (*irşad*, guidance) meetings. According to her, God had placed love between man and woman to allow them to live in peace and harmony, and human beings, men and women, were responsible for saving and nurturing this emotional bond. It was true that God had first created Adam as *insan* (human), and then paired him with another human, Eve (in Turkish, *Havva*, desire,[27] in her own words the 'source of desire'), and placed them on earth to realize His will. Thus woman was the very source of life, without whom man could not fulfil God's will on earth. That was why men were usually so anxious to protect their women, and it was also the responsibility of a woman to not let anybody, including herself, misuse this divine gift of being the source of life.

This preacher, of course, never pointed out the power struggle which was inherent to her story, a struggle whereby whoever had the power to control women, the source of life, would also fulfil the first condition to exercise power over society. Nevertheless, through her interpretation, women were seen as invaluable creatures responsible for their own dignity and, more importantly, women were not objects of desire but sources of desire, and thereby sources of life. Nor was the sole purpose of sex for Muslim women, as in Sirman's conviction, the production of future generations (Sirman 1989, p. 26). On the contrary, romantic love was so important a topic in the Islamic imaginary that it formed part of the core of the Islamic regime of truth which set the order of life; the 'regime of truth' is used here in the sense that Foucault uses it, that is, 'the ensemble of rules according to which the true and false are separated and the specific effects of power attached to the true' (Foucault 1980, p. 131). However, most of these Muslim women understood the moral of this and similar interpretations, which were designed to convey the importance of women, as, simply, that women were so valuable that it was normal for them to be under the protection of those who were stronger.

The effort to cover the bitter connotations of power struggles between men and women in this discourse of complementarity faced certain difficulties when Islamic historical realities came into discussion. Thus, this discourse, like any other, had some blind spots. It could not, for example, explain polygyny, nor could it deal with the 'right' of husbands to punish their wives by beating them, 'even though softly', and to control their physical movements and the circumstances under which they might receive visitors. When pressed to answer, Muslim women immediately resorted to 'ifs' and 'buts', always bringing up the conditions under which such controls could become necessary. At best, they maintained that such issues could be solved through conviction rather than protest. However, I observed that monogamy was the norm and even the women who could not have children seemed to be unlikely to accept their husbands' taking a second wife. Likewise, in my experience, Muslim women also seemed very conscious of the violence used against women and children in family relations. Although mothers saw themselves, to some extent, as having the right to punish their small children physically up to the age of puberty, the right of husbands to beat their wives was neither approved nor exercised. This point becomes very important when it is considered that the beating of women is widespread in every section of Turkish society regardless of social stratum.[28]

The necessarily protective nature of men might sometimes prevent them from tolerating women's legitimate demands for the freedom accorded them by religion. In this case, a good way to convince a recalcitrant husband was to provide examples from the Prophet's life and words. Men, they argued, could only be convinced as long as women remained within the boundaries of Islam. Similarly, men also had to submit to Islamic rules. They had to concede on such issues, and be good providers and faithful to their families. Any deviation from the norm was explained away in terms of 'tradition', a term which mainly referred to traditions 'typical of Turkish culture' and 'folk Islam', as opposed to God's words encoded in the Koran. But this point should not be understood as entailing a clear-cut distinction for them between 'scripturalist' and popular religiosity.[29] On the contrary, the Muslim women tried to include local customs and practices in the 'scripturalist' discourse while 'purifying' them of 'irrational' aspects incompatible with Islam. For instance, visiting shrines to seek help was not thought of as requesting a favour from a dead person. Rather, since these 'saints' were the beloved friends of God they could be expected to convey mortal people's wishes to God more effectively. Similarly, without totally rejecting the importance of modern psychology, for instance, they also believed that a şeyh or a veli could help people to solve their personal and family problems as usefully as a psychologist could. Here again, religious practices tended to be combined with 'modern' mechanisms of social survival. Since they condemned resorting to sorcery and fortune telling, they thought their attitude much more modern than that of other urban educated women who commonly believe in such 'superstitious' practices.

However, these women did not seem prepared to produce their own arguments about the meanings of certain hadiths, such as, 'Those who entrust their affairs to a woman will never know prosperity' or 'I [the Prophet Muhammad] took a look at paradise, and I noted that the majority of the people there were poor people. I took a look at hell, and I noted that there women were the majority'[30] which put women in an inferior position not only in the construction of social life but also in the sight of God. Although deeply suspicious of such hadiths, they had very mixed feelings about the ways in which they had come into being. They were unsure whether they were the words of God's messenger and indicative of the wrongdoings of women or whether misogynistic men, who had destroyed the original sayings of the Prophet, had invented them.[31]

Similarly, they also tried to give 'reasonable' explanations for the rules in Islamic law which prevent women from being judges or imams and equate two women's testimony to that of one man. These explanations generally stressed the emotional side of women but made no reference to their supposed lesser mental capacity. Here the physiological characteristics of women also entered the discourse as a handicap. Roles such as judge or imam should be fulfilled by persons in a state of ritual purity in an ideal Islamic social order. If women are excused from even their routine religious observances during menstruation, how would they be able to perform such roles? However, I observed that they tended to justify these restraints as benefits reducing women's heavy responsibilities in this mortal world. This justification was an overall part of what I call a discourse of gratitude: they used this to offset the uneasy effects of Islamic rules which restricted the scope of their behaviour and self-actualization in a modern social context where women were expected willingly to take part in every sphere of public life. Their selective participation in public life had been strongly criticized by the secular urban élite and this had created a sense of resentment among them; the discourse of gratitude evolved as an extension of the strategy developed to cope with this resentment. It was based on Koranic concepts of *shukr* (*şükr*, thankfulness), which is another attribute of 'faith', the lack of which corresponds to *kufr*, unfaithfulness.[32] Therefore, for some Muslim women, also including some well educated, working women, too much questioning of men's authority in worldly affairs might be sinful. Men should not oppress women and should respect their spheres of authority, but nor should women attempt to destroy the harmony of Islamic life. This did not mean that women could not participate in political activities, receive higher education or follow their professions, but in doing so they should continue to be modest. Others, however, who were mostly well educated and had urban backgrounds, saw nothing wrong in questioning the limits of men's authority as long as such questioning served to eradicate the effects of traditional restrictions imposed upon women in the name of Islam. This slowly unfolding difference between the Muslim women was revealed in the labelling of the former group as 'narrow-minded' as opposed to the latter who were 'open-minded'. This was ironic considering the way in which Muslim women are differentiated from their secular counterparts, in that the major distinction marking the Muslim women is that their bodies are 'closed' whereas those of the secularist women are 'open'.

I have tried to describe the major strategies of resistance and containment used by Muslim women to cope with dominant discourses, both religious and secular. I have emphasized how they reorder and recontextualize these dominant discourses in their everyday life through the medium of reflexive action. What needs to be kept in mind, however, is that Muslim women, like any other dedicated believers, primarily saw this world as a transitory place. Whatever they did was directed towards winning God's favour in the next world. The effort they spent to lead their lives according to Islamic ideals not only rendered Islam a living practice but also created an ethics for the quotidian designed above all to help them prepare for the next world and assure eternal life in God's heaven. In the process of constituting a Muslim identity, then, 'the third', the superaddressee in the Bakhtinian sense, was ultimately God. Hence the deeds and thoughts of Muslim women as well as men were shaped a priori by an image, God, whose fair and responsive understanding was presumed. After all, Muslims are people who stand before God 'torn between hope and despair'.

Notes

[1] When this *site* was established, some of the important founders of the cooperative (some of whom still live in the *site*) who were adherents of Zahid Kotku did not become followers of Esat Coşan on Kotku's death, though they showed him considerable respect. Likewise, people who are strong supporters of the WP and not adherents of his sect also respect his authority in spite of certain political differences. The same was also true for the followers of the ANAP who either lived in the *site* or had close relationships with some of its inhabitants.

[2] Ayşe Güneş-Ayata makes similar observations for the fundamentalist trends of the discourse of Islamic revivalism in Turkey, arguing that it revolves around the axes of fundamentalism, modernism and traditionalism/neo-traditionalism (1991, p. 256).

[3] For an exceptional study examining the ways in which upwardly

mobile lower and lower-middle class urban people in Ankara decorate their houses and use domestic space in accordance with their understanding of modernity, cultural norms of privacy, hospitality, respect, etc., all of which shape their image of social status, see Ayata (1988).

[4] The theme of rejection of Western-inspired celebrations often underpinned the most important points of the preaching during *kandil* gatherings. The women who formed the congregations were constantly warned by the preachers not to indulge themselves with even the smallest 'joy' or non-Islamic habits in such celebrations and were encouraged to reject them totally and instead adopt Islamic behaviour and conduct to gain the mercy of God.

[5] Mardin builds this argument on Luhmann's discussion of the differences in the formation of trust in modern and 'traditional' societies: Niklas Luhmann, *Trust and Power*, ed. T. Burns and G. Poggi (Chichester and New York: John Wiley, 1979), p. 46, cited in Mardin (1989a, p. 218).

[6] Giddens sees no congruity between the formation of trust and risk in pre-modern and modern cultures. See the chart he proposes to show the distinction: 'Environments of Trust and Risk in the Pre-Modern and Modern Cultures' (1990, p. 102). See also 'Trust in Modernity' and 'Trust in Ontological Security' (pp. 81–3 and 92–100). It is true that, in order to be able to analyse the place of trust and risk in today's societies, one has to see the impacts of the organizational peculiarities of modern societies on the formation of modern conditions of being-in-the-world and the self-placement of people in social processes. However, as well as the structural differences which mark modern society, to see the congruity of meanings prevalent in modern societies, whether it stems from 'pre-modern' times or is invented in the course of shaping modern cultures, it is also necessary to be able to analyse the place of trust and risk in the formation of modern cultures if we are not to constantly relegate 'kinship relations', 'local community', 'religious cosmologies as modes of belief', etc., to pre-modern times, as if they were nothing to do with the modern human being's ways of comprehending how 'things work themselves out in our lives'.

[7] 'Trust in abstract systems does not presuppose any encounters at all with the individuals and groups who are in some way "responsible" for them. But in the large majority of instances such individuals or groups are involved, and I shall refer to encounters with them on the part of lay actors as the *access points* of abstract systems. The access points of abstract systems are the meeting ground of face-work and faceless commitments. . . . *The nature of modern institutions is deeply bound up with the mechanisms of trust in abstract systems*, especially trust in expert systems (Giddens 1990, p. 83, emphasis original). For instance, a doctor, dentist or travel agent may be the representatives of what Giddens calls abstract systems.

[8] To lie down to sleep (after performing duties of worship) in the hope that God will show what is best in a dream.

[9] The same woman also showed me photographs from her university years where she and her friends covered their heads in a style known as *sıkmabaş* or *Şulebaşı*, referring to the name of the first female student who wanted to enter the Faculty of History, Geography and Language in the University of Ankara in the 1960s. In those pictures, they were wearing fairly short skirts and tight waistcoats while their heads were covered in this style, which was actually a turban.

[10] I met this lady many times and she participated in two focus group discussions, though I did not specifically interview her. She also came to visit my home. She was one of the constant figures in the *kandil* celebrations and in many *tefsir* study sessions, as well as various seminars and panels I participated in. She was known as a very influential teacher and was usually called *hoca*. She later on established her own private school for girls which includes both primary and secondary levels. Her style of attire and that of other female members of her family was certainly noteworthy for the quality of silk and other fine fabrics used in their fashionably tailored costumes.

[11] Later on I learned that by 'those people', she was referring to people she found 'different', in her case some Nurcu (another Sufi brotherhood) families who left the *site* towards the end of the 1980s. For others, 'different people' could be Iranian Shi'i families or people adhering to rather rigid branches of the Nakşibendi order with Eastern origins. In general, for the individuals who agreed to be interviewed or who showed some interest in this study, people who displayed a highly secluded attitude, even towards the other inhabitants of this *site*, and had minimum interaction with them were usually seen as 'different' or 'unusual', although care was taken not to be too critical of them. In other words, people were expected to be sociable in their interaction with others as well as tactful, at least to a certain extent to count them as 'us'.

[12] She was not only criticized for her outspokenness. Although no one gossiped about it to me, I could see that her indoor dress and jewellery also attracted the attention of other women. In addition, although she tried not to show off and decorated her house rather modestly, the social facilities she had access to, such as yachting in summer and going to the mountains in winter, etc., were completely outside the experience of many in this complex. Similarly, she could also make plans to move to England for a while, not only for her husband's academic career but also for her daughter's education because of the restraints on covered female students in Turkey. This was because, according to her, her ambition to become an architect had been hindered by the ban on headscarves in Turkish universities, which was harsher in her time than it is today.

However, she also admitted that she should have completed her lycée education instead of leaving it in her last year (because of the headscarf ban) and tried to enter the Faculty of Architecture; only then would it be meaningful to use such arguments. On the other hand, the worry she had felt over the possible humiliation she would have been subjected to as a covered university student cannot be underestimated, especially considering the fact that many families hesitated to send their daughters to university during the 1970s because of the anarchic atmosphere in the universities.

[13] According to Goffman this 'hate stare' is exemplified by the behaviour of white people towards black people in the past in the Southern United States. The 'hate stare' was directed at black people in public settings to reflect a rejection of their rights to participate in orthodox forms of day-to-day interaction with whites (Goffman 1963, cited in Giddens 1990, p. 81).

[14] For example, Mottahedeh's fictitious protagonist Ali says that he was amazed in his childhood (he was the son of an honourable seyyid family, descendants of the Prophet's family) to observe how often the only protection for privacy was foot-shuffling and the clearing of throats for both women and men in their home life in the city of Qom in Iran. In addition, coughing was a common way to make one's presence felt by others, a way of getting permission to join other people (Mottahedeh 1985, p. 29). I am sure this type of behaviour will not sound unfamiliar to many Turks.

[15] Supererogatory night service in the month of Ramadan performed immediately after the fifth obligatory ritual worship of the day, yatsı namazı, that is, the prayer performed by Muslims two hours after sunset. Teravih is a rather long prayer consisting of twenty genuflexions with an interval for rest and breathing after each two or four acts. Though not obligatory, it is accepted as one of the sunnas of the Prophet.

[16] Sherifa Zuhur shows how the early women of Islam, especially the wives and descendants of the Prophet, are crucial referents for the Muslim oppositionist images of modern women. She also shows how the 'archetypes of Middle Eastern women' work to build linkages between the contemporary intellectual and spiritual environment and the early Muslim community by which modern Muslims search for authenticity, morality, equality and new solutions for political authority and gender issues (1992, pp. 27–57).

[17] Mardin tried to explore how military valour and hero-worship, as intermingled with Islamic religious history, myths and legends, played a significant role in the process of forming the folk traditions of the culture of the masses both in Ottoman and republican Turkish society, as well as forming the behaviour of university students in modern Turkey in the 1970s (1969, pp. 107–16 especially p.115; 1974, pp. 403–6; 1978; 1989a,

p. 5f). One example Mardin uses to show how Islamic idioms could have informed the 'ego ideals' of Turkish men I find most illuminating. It concerns a Turkish psychiatrist who wrote in the daily *Cumhuriyet*: 'The theme he developed was that in his boyhood spent in a Central Anatolian village, he had only known "ego ideals" derived from Islamic religious history, the sword of Ali "cutting fifty heads when it swung right, seventy heads when it swung left . . . the justice of the Chalif Umar"' (1989a, p. 230). On the concepts of honour, *namus* and *şeref* (one associated with female sexual purity and the other with the social honour of men) with which 'a *şerefli* (honourable) person protects the *namus* of his family and reacts aggressively against those who either threaten or stain it', see Magneralla (1974, p. 396). There is no need to mention that the same is also valid for the *namus* of community or *mahalle*.

[18] Unfortunately I did not have the opportunity of meeting her husband. I think it might have been very interesting to talk with him: she told me that her husband had said that if she wished she could wear two-piece suits instead of long loose overcoats when they went to see his schoolmates and professors, though he did not want her to go out in the same attire in the *site*. However, although she seemed to have suffered through being labelled *kara öcü* (black monster), because she believed that the covering of women was God's command, she refused to follow his suggestion.

[19] Both mean 'good morning': *hayırlı* connotes religious 'good' in the sense of 'blessed' but *günaydın* has no religious connotation. Islamic circles in Turkey deliberately replace new terms with religiously loaded ones.

[20] An Islamic formula meaning 'May God commend and salute him!' and used after mentioning the name of the Prophet Muhammad, usually abbreviated in writing as S.A.S. In fact she still could not pronounce it correctly when she told me this, just as she could not repeat many other Islamic formulae that even I had learned to repeat correctly in the course of my fieldwork.

[21] A Farsi word, the Arabic equivalent of which is *salah*.

[22] It is not only recorded in my notes but it is also quite fresh in my memory that at this moment his wife strongly opposed him and invited him to show respect for my way of life and my decisions about how I raise my children. She also stressed the difficulties she had faced when raising their daughters, while he participated in *irşad* meetings, political propaganda activities, etc. She added: 'The Islamic environment does not mean everything, husbands should also help their wives to raise their children. But you men think of your endeavours to earn your families' livings as your selflessness, but of women's housework as their duty. It is neither fair, nor Islamic.' She also criticized him quite strongly for daring to play on my motherly feelings and asked him: 'Do you want other people to say the same thing to your daughters when they leave their children to go out

to follow their professions? Or what will you do if their husbands do not permit them to work? Did I make all that lace and earn money to make contributions to our daughters' school expenses just for them to become mere housewives? Wasn't it you who always told them they should have a profession to raise the honour of Muslim women?' After all those criticisms, he tried to clarify his point by saying that insofar as the schools, the people, and the environment, etc., to which I entrusted my children were not Islamic, I could not be sure that they were safe; otherwise he had no objection women working. However, his wife did not seem satisfied with this and continued to maintain that his comments were not fair in any way. She was a semi-literate woman, who had only been able to attend primary school for a while but had had some religious education through Koran courses, and she contributed to the family budget by making and selling works of embroidery. She was said to be a very devoted mother and suffered so much when her daughters went abroad that she even had a sort of psychological breakdown due to the longing she felt for her children, and required medical help. She also told me at one point in our interview that I must see myself as blessed by God in being the mother of twins.

[23] In Turkish the suffix '-cı' or '-ci' refers to a seller or producer. Thus, for instance, a *köfteci* is someone who sells *köfte* (a Turkish food). This Muslim woman's humorous utterance shows the incongruity in the usage of the term *Islamcı*, as if they were selling Islam.

[24] A famous Turkish poet known as the founder of the 'Ideal of the Great East'. He has usually been seen as the right-wing counterpart of Nazım Hikmet.

[25] For a comparison of the functions and purposes of women's *kabul* days (women's systematic visiting) in Turkey, see Aswad (1979, pp. 478–9) and N. Tapper (1983).

[26] *Mevlûd* is a poem written by Süleyman Çelebi depicting the birth of the Prophet Muhammad, sung only by special singers. It is also defined as the chanting of the nativity poem.

[27] For the figure of Havva (Eve) as portrayed in the Koran, in Islamic tradition and in contemporary Muslim writings, see Haddad and Smith (1982). For the meaning of Havva as desire see, for example, Mernissi (1991, p. 152).

[28] See, for example, the booklet published after the protest against the battering of women in May 1987 entitled *Bağır Herkes Duysun* (Shout and be Heard); see also Sirman (1989, p.19).

[29] The ways in which in the context of the Mediterranean and the Middle East much cultural practice might very well be informed by religious orthodoxy intermingled with local customs, and vice versa, even

among different religions, is a point which was also aptly observed by Sami Zubaida (1994, pp. 163–85).

[30] Translations of these *hadiths* are from Mernissi (1991, pp. 1 and 76).

[31] It was quite interesting for me to come across almost the same stories told by Fatima Mernissi (1991). She traces the roots of *hadiths* referring to women and attributed to the Prophet, most of which were probably fabricated after the death of the Prophet by Muslim men who opposed the rights and freedoms maintained for women by Islam but who did not dare to oppose the Prophet while he was alive.

[32] For these Koranic concepts see, for example, Izutsu (1966, p. 200). However, Izutsu does not distinguish belief and faith and uses the terms coterminously.

CHAPTER VII

Conclusions

Before the results of the municipal elections of 27 March 1994, which were won by the WP, I could have terminated this study by stressing the theme of the sense of what Sennett (1971) calls distantiation. This was prevalent among the inhabitants of the *site*, as well as among others who either have strong religious affiliations or call themselves conscious Muslims. Their sentiments and the way in which they expressed their ideas about national political matters such as democratization, the development of human rights, problems of national identity caused by secularization and westernization, as well as economic problems such as the causes of underdevelopment, the inadequacy of the capitalist market economy, the integration of Turkey into the European Economic Community, could all be collected under the heading of distantiation. Alienation from the general cast of modern Turkish culture and society seemed evident. Their attitude in approaching all these matters, as well as environmental problems, was one of emotional and cultural distance. The current social system and socio-cultural morality were resented. But because of their Islamic faith, they consciously avoided hopelessness about the future and the appearance of pessimism. They preserved their hope for the amelioration of social and environmental matters by the establishment of an Islamic order. They continued, however, to be critical of the prevailing social order, but this did not prevent them from committing themselves to Islamic ideals and believing that one day, no matter how long off, divine order would imbue this otherwise blind and meaningless world with its reason and meaning. This attitude showed itself at the end of almost all the interviews: 'I'm optimistic about the future, but it seems everything goes from bad to worse in Turkey.' But in view of the recent political empowerment of Islamic circles in Turkey, this sense of distantiation seems likely to transform itself into an enthusiasm for participation and a thirst for political power.

However, besides distantiation, the other two discursive components of the Islamic politics of resentment (the discourse of justice developed against the oppression of Muslims, and the discourse of faith which determines Islamic political activism) still continue to dominate the oppositional discourse of Turkish Islamic circles in general, and the political discourse of the WP in particular.

Thus distantiation usually went hand in hand with another aspect of the sentiment of resentment and, through this, different versions of the uses of the discourse of justice dominated the interviews and group discussions. Here, justice, of which God was the ultimate source, was seen as something which should be constantly sought in order to realize 'truth' in the course of social life. In the discourse of justice, the idioms were constructed around the concepts of 'truth' *haqq* (*hak*), which in Izutsu's (1966) analysis of the ethico-religious concepts of the Koran, for instance, represents the objective side of reality as opposed to 'vanity' or 'falsehood' *batil* (*batıl*), which corresponds to unreality. In this discourse, then, insofar as God was the absolute *haqq*, 'truth' meant something pre-eminently real, a living force operating in the very process of life and death (Izutsu 1966, pp. 97–8). Thus, the ultimate way of coping with the perceived oppression of people with religious affiliations was to take their complaints to God. This search for justice became the part of WP's political programme known as the 'just order', a propaganda tool second only to the differentiation of 'secularized' and 'non-secularized/conscious' Muslims.

The third component of this politics of resentment, after distantiation and justice, is the discourse of faith: all the social and political actions of these Muslims could be explained as a consequence of striving for the mercy of God. 'Being torn between hope and despair in the face of God' is the definitive feature of the faith dimension of Islamic revivalism, and it is the way in which people who aim to become conscious Muslims perceive their lot in this world and the next. Within the framework of Islamic faith, however, striving for the mercy of God always brings the hope of having a relationship of 'reciprocity' with God. Thus, in this specific dialogical relation, where 'the third' in the Bakhtinian sense is ultimately God, God responds to the strivings of His subjects by promising to reward them in Heaven, as indicated in the Koran: 'This [Heaven] in truth is your recompense and the acceptance of your endeavors' (76:22, al-Qur'an 1984, p. 515). The discourse of the Day of Judgement, which bridges this world and the next, therefore also appears as a very important aspect of the faith dimension of Islamic revivalism: it gives rise to the desire for harmony between this world and the next and Islamic activists are thus urged to dedicate themselves to realizing the will of God in this temporary, mortal world in order to gain an eternal life in Heaven. This also constitutes the departing point of the discourse of moral transformation, the socio-political content of which is determined according to ongoing power struggles in societies where Islamic activists try to gain political ground. Moreover, the faith dimension of the Islamic movement provides the basis of its socio-political legitimacy, as well as making its followers vulnerable to certain types of political impact, which can hardly be challenged by other sources of legitimacy, those of the secular democratic system for example, as long as its religious loyalty is sustained to mobilize it for political ends. In this respect, the most important aspect of the Islamic project is how people from different sections of society and cultural backgrounds become followers. I have tried throughout this study to make the point that this process cannot be explained merely by indicating the likely economic benefits of attaining political power. Whether or not this plays a part, the ways in which people persuade themselves of the nature of their lives, as well as the dialogical imaginations used for this, should be studied to give a sociological explanation for their involvement in Islamic activism.

At the moment, it appears that the broader social structures proposed by Turkish activists for their Islamic society are not radically different from those maintained by the prevailing republican socio-economic system. In fact, the Islamic movement's success is likely to rest on its efficient use of the existing political, social and economic mechanisms in accomplishing its so-called Islamization of society. Here Islamization appears to mean a pragmatic project of civilization, the basic components of which are organized around a political project to set the moral standards of society according to Islamic precepts. The effort to build an Islamic way of life is the major enterprise in this overall project, in that if Islam is the legitimizing force in social life, the result will be the means of exercising ruling power over society. On the other hand, insofar as the republican project of civilization was associated with the republican nation-state building project, and also insofar as it was seen as an indispensable part of the political moves of the state, any social movement taking the centralist nation-state as its political target tended to be seen in the politico-cultural tradition of Turkish society as the representative of democracy and civil society, often without regard to whether or nor these movements were capable of proposing a cultural and/or moral pluralism. More importantly, in the context of the social projects of these so-called civil society movements, there often seems no room to question the moral premises of patriarchy, whether they be dominated by secular or by religious male-ordered cultural codes. This, I believe, constitutes the common denominator of all sexist political ideologies. As a result the emancipation of women has been given secondary importance to democratization, development and the advancement of society, all of which, regardless of the method, have been ulti- mate social goals. The problem, then, for Islamic movements in general, and the WP in particular, is to try and resolve this difficulty within the parameters of a rather romantic discourse of comple- mentarity, in which the position of both men and women in society is conceived as an unchallengeable ontological matter. Thus, the supposed equality of men and women in an ideally imagined equal society and its exemplars turns out to be a question of equity sustained according to the rules of an assumed Islamic divine order. In Turkey, equality between men and women has been mainly provided by legal codes regulating the public sphere, but a similar sort of equality has not been fully maintained, in either legal or civil terms, in the private sphere. Here the Islamic discourse of complementarity, sentiment and intimacy has dominated the every- day philosophy of the majority of people, and thus it becomes difficult to discriminate between secular and Islamic patriarchal moralities. This would not necessarily be problematic if, within the secularization project, Islamic, as well as secular, cultural codes had been incorporated into the new social life. Putting the problem the other way round, in the Turkish polity and society the ethics and morality of secularization did not become an area of sensible sociological inquires (in the sense of making social scientific researches on the meanings, symbols and functions of the forma- tion of secular culture and asking how the secular culture of

Turkish society developed, what sorts of patterns of cultural transformation made the secularization process possible, and how this
was experienced by people in different sections of society). Thus
the place of Islam and its different versions in Turkish culture has
usually appeared to be a matter of social conflict and contradiction
and, more strangely, a matter of sympathy or antipathy directed
towards religion and religious matters.

This situation is important in many ways. First, it has prevented
an understanding of secularization as a way of life rather than just
as a matter of state regulation. Second, it has entailed an evaluation
of culture and tradition as if both were remnants of the past and
had nothing to do with the present and future characteristics of
social life or the question of modernity in which the place of
religion could not be eradicated as an important cultural construct.
Third, seeing religion as an untouchable matter of private conscience has made religious tradition an important prop for patriarchal codes and practices in the private sphere, and has thus hindered
the modernization of common religious understanding. Therefore,
when religious precepts have been used as a source of legitimation
and as the model for an alternative way of life, it has led to a
reaction in secular circles, the target of which was not patriarchy
but religion. Before the rise of Islamic activism, the place of religion
in the cultural realm was not a common object of inquiry. This
omission should also be seen, however, as the result of not taking
women into account as social and political actors, as well as a
misreading of the importance of the private sphere and its quotidian
in the instillation of secular ethics in society. Therefore, not surprisingly, the basic perception of the place and function of women in
society in both the secular and Islamic discourses has been primarily as mothers, as the bearers of culture. In the context of Islamic
revivalism, women are responsible for the education of new generations of faithful Muslims ready to struggle for the progress of
Islam. This is indeed a very similar responsibility to that vested in
women both at the time of the Ottoman reforms and under the
Republic. However, while westernizing reformers expected women
to educate the nation in the name of national progress, a Muslim
woman was to educate others to establish God's system on earth.
Similarly, in the making of an Islamic way of life, as observed in
this case-study, the formation of the ethos of an Islamic middle
class woman becomes essential: without her efforts it is not possible

to form either the strategies for a new way of life or the tactics of its quotidian in building 'ways of operating'. That is why the position, identity and also the image of women become so important in the formation of this particular life politics through which answers have been sought to the question 'How should we live?' and which first and foremost has entailed the control and regulation of the private space organized by women.

However, simultaneously trying to realize an Islamic way of life and challenge the secular ethics of modernity is not an easy task, since such a project cannot remain in its purified form as it can at the ideological discursive level. This is because, in the actualization of an Islamic way of life, modernity functions as an index in which the objective givens of social life are indicated whereas Islamic thought serves as a lexicon from which the meanings of these objective givens can be discerned. Thus, the strategy of containment and resistance that 'conscious Muslims' develop for the secular ethics of modernity in Turkey is based on a rather simplistic belief that the more they can learn about that index, the more knowledge they can acquire to alter it. They therefore disregard the fact that the index of modernity is also the product of a variety of ideologies flourishing from within specific discursive formations, and they forget that these ideologies, like all other ideological discourses, are nothing but semantic systems of coding reality. Thus coded, 'reality' as lived experience cannot be separated from its ideological definitions and modernity is no exception. Seen from this perspective, it should also be argued that Islamic ideologies can also inform that index, but to what extent they can transform it obviously depends on their ability to displace its referential context, basis of legitimacy, social norms and idioms. This is not a matter of political power struggle in the strict sense of the term. It is rather a matter of seeing power as something which is, in the Foucauldian sense, exercised from the bottom up rather than merely possessed by a group of rulers. So far, the relative success of Islamic activists in Turkey seems to have depended on their ability to grasp this aspect of power and apply it to their political programme. This forms the basis of life politics and the effort to actualize an Islamic way of life that has enabled Islamic circles to represent themselves as one of the strongest representatives of civil society against the groups supporting the social ideals put forward by the republican nation-state. However,

I maintain that the relative failure of Islamic activists in Turkey will also depend on the degree of political power attained, since I believe they have also succumbed to an understanding of the state shared, in general, by the secularists: that is, the state is understood as an overarching, unshakeable agent possessing repressive power, rather than as a particular form of power constantly shaped and reshaped by those who have managed to gain access to it. This, I believe, is the consequence of a broader problem related to the question of civil society in the popular political discourse of Turkey. In this, the content of civil society is emptied by assigning to it all aspects of social regulation that are thought to remain outside state practices, and the state is seen as a source of authoritarian power. In this understanding, since the inseparability of the state and the citizenry is disregarded, i.e., it is strangely forgotten that without a state there can be no citizenship, civil society is also likely to be construed as outside the boundaries of that relationship. Therefore, the necessary critical distance between state and society is reduced to a situation where there might as well be a civil society without the existence of a democratic state and vice versa. Hence civil society is seen as the victim of the state instead of any attempt being made to maintain the democratization of the state as well as that of civil society. Thus, just as a civil society movement which does not offer a moral and cultural pluralism (like Islamic activism) cannot contribute to the democratization of the state apparatus, a state which is organized to keep society under its strict regulatory power may jeopardize its social legitimacy in the eyes of other culturally accepted sources of legitimation such as religion. Moreover, it may end up as the competitor of religion – as has been the case so long in Turkey. Secularization is the first step to overcome this difficulty, and the consolidation of secular culture seems the only way to reorganize the state and the law to provide the necessary communication between state and society. However, I think the major problem that Turkish society and social science face is how to view the existing parameters of secularization not as something developed outside state regulations, but rather as a living culture and tradition. Because the question of how secular culture has developed and been accepted in Turkey did not become a matter for social inquiry, but instead was only seen as something imposed on society by the state and thus accepted as it was, the ways in which people become part of Islamic revivalism has been construed merely as a reaction to the existing state and its social order. Thus, I believe, the present study, the aim of which has been to comprehend the parameters of lived Islam as it occurs in the daily experiences of so-called conscious Muslims and within a particular Islamic dialogical imagination, can open a meaningful discussion if it creates an interest in understanding the parameters of secular culture in Turkey as it is found in the experiences of the people who form the majority of Turkish society, and who want to actualize a pluralist, democratic national society, but who, however, do not really acknowledge the fact that without social equality between men and women such a goal will be unattainable.

APPENDIX I

The Survey Form

Ayşe Saktanber
Department of Sociology
METU/ Ankara

'Islam in Urban Life and the Cultures Created'
The Survey Form for the Doctoral Study

The questions below try to explore the lifestyles and the culture of a group of people who have preferred to live in a close neighbourhood to experience and share similar religious and cultural values as a way of life. This study aims to understand the influence of religion and religious values in a suburban context in developing lifestyles and world-views for life.

The present study aims to collect data from various families by using two different techniques. In the first phase of the study, the data about the demographic and socio-economic structures of the families will be collected by the questionnaire method. The second phase will be conducted as in-depth-interviews to explore the cultural structures of the families. Additionally, if it will be possible, participant observation techniques will be used. The identity of the interviewees will be concealed, and nobody else will be allowed to use the raw data except for the researcher, this data will not be used either except for academic purposes. In addition, the interviewees will not be allowed to know information about each other or the information gathered from each interviewee and from their families separately.

Data about the Demographic and Socio-economic Structure of the Family

I) Data about the Household

For the Spouses:

1) Date of birth
2) Place of birth
3) Years of marriage
4) First spouse?
5) If any, kinship relation between spouses
6) Education
7) Professional life
   a) Profession
   b) Present occupation
   c) Previous occupation
   d) Reason for quitting previous job
   e) The status in the present job

For the Children

1) Sex
2) Date of birth
3) Place of birth
4) Education
5) If any, extra-school courses, sports and other leisure time activities that children participate in
6) Occupation

For the Others in the Household

1) Sex
2) Date of birth
3) Place of birth
4) Marital status
5) Type of affinity with the family
6) Occupation
7) How long has s/he been in the household

For the Children out of the Household

1) Sex
2) Date of birth
3) Place of birth
4) Education
5) The reason for leaving the household
6) The time when s/he left the household
7) Marital status
8) If married, the occupation of the spouse
9) If there are any, his/her children
   a) Sex
   b) Age
   c) Education

II) Residency

1) The period of residence in Ankara
2) If there are any, the previous places of residence and the time of residency
3) The places lived in in Ankara and the periods of residency
4) The period of residency in the present residence
5) The owner(s) of the house
6) The area of the residency in square metres
7) The number of rooms in the residence

III) Level of Income

1) Average monthly income of the family
2) Sources of income
3) The number of people contributing to the family income
4) The proportion of their contribution
5) Own a car or not?
6) If there is one, who drives it?
7) The electrical appliances at home
8) Do they have a maid at home?

Data about the Cultural Background of the Family

This part of the survey will be conducted by in-depth interviews with family members. The subtopics of the interview are listed below:

- The daily life activities of the family.
- General ideas about the family as a social unit.
- Division of labour in the family: The roles and responsibilities of spouses and children toward each other.
- Attitudes and ideas about child-rearing practices and education.
- The reading habits of the family member. The newspapers, magazines and books read by the family member.
- The habits of watching TV and listening to radio.
- The leisure time activities of the family.
- The attitudes of the family toward neighbourhood, social network and mutual support within the neighbourhood.
- The norms and values of the family on special occasions like birth, death, marriage and circumcision.
- The habits and ways of conduct for religious days and holidays.
- The habit of the family for the religious worship.
- The relationship of the family with various social organizations (e.g. educational, health, vocational).
- The perspective of the family on economical and political issues.
- The general evaluations of the family about their future.

Tables

Table 1: Level of Education Attained by Men and Women

	Men (25)	Women (25)
Postgraduate (2 Ph.D. candidates, 1 assistant professor, 1 associate professor)	4	
University	10	4
College (Institute of Education)	5	
Higher Vocational Training School		3
Lycée diploma (Imam Hatip school)	4	2
Left lycée		2
Middle School diploma	1	1
Left Middle School		2
Primary School diploma		9
Left Primary School		2
Medrese (Muslim theological school, not available in republican Turkey)	1	

Table 2 : Type of Profession for Men and Women

Type of Profession	Men (25)	Type of Profession	Women (25)
Higher level bureaucrat	8	Housewife	14
State University	3	Occasional home-based tailoring	3
Private University	1	Marketing clothing accessories at home	1
		Preacher	2
Religion teacher at lycée level	3	Koran course teacher	2
Religious functionary	1	Secondary School teacher (English, religion)	2
Construction business (1 employee, 1 self-employed contractor)	2	Private teacher (maths and sciences, Koran recitation)	1
Accountant (1 employee, 1 self-employed)	2		
Merchant	1		
Journalist	2		
Retired (military and parliament)	2		

Table 3: Distribution of Children among Families

Number of Families (25)	Number of Children (56)
8	3
6	2
4	1
4	4

Table 4: Level of Education and Type of School: Children Living with their Families

Level of Education and Type of School	Boys (24)	Girls (23)
Faculty of Theology (MA)		1
Imam Hatip School graduate	1	1
Imam Hatip School (Lycée level)		2 (including 1 dropped out)
Vocational Lycée	1	
Public Lycée	2	
Public School graduate		1 (external student)
Private Lycée*	2	2
Imam Hatip School (Middle School level)	3	4
Public Middle School	1	3
Private Middle School*	2	1
Local Primary School	7	4
Private Primary School	1	
Nursery School	1	2
Not attending any school (pre-school age)	3	2

*Private school providing education in accordance with religious ideals in addition to compulsory curriculum.

Table 5: Level of Education of Children away from Home

Level of Education	Men (4)	Women (5)
Faculty of Theology	2	
Faculty of Law	1	
Faculty of Applied Science	1	
Faculty of Economics (MA abroad)		1
Vocational lycée		3 (including 1 who studied Arabic abroad)
Imam Hatip school (Middle School level)		1

Table 6: Place of Birth of Parents and Children

Place of Birth (name of city by region)	Mothers (25)	Fathers (25)	Children (56)
Marmara (north-west Turkey)			
Balıkesir		1	
Bursa	1	1	1
Çanakkale		1	
Istanbul	1		
Central Anatolia			
Ankara	4	2	45
Bolu		1	
Çorum	2	1	2
Eskişehir	2		
Kayseri	2		
Kırıkkale	1	1	3
Kırşehir	1	2	
Konya	3	3	
Yozgat	3	2	4

Table 6: Place of Birth of Parents and Children (*cont.*)

Place of Birth (name of city by region)	Mothers (25)	Fathers (25)	Children (56)
Black Sea (north and north-east Turkey)			
Amasya		1	
Ordu		1	
Rize	2	1	
Samsun		2	1
East and South-East Anatolia			
Bayburt		1	
Erzurum		1	
Diyarbakır	1	1	
Mardin	1	1	
Muş	1	1	

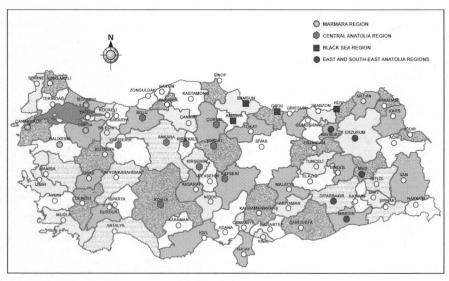

Map showing Place of Birth of Parents and Children

Bibliography

Abadan-Unat, N. 1991. 'The Impact of Legal and Educational Reforms on Turkish Women'. In *Women in Middle Eastern History*, ed. N. Keddie and B. Baron. New Haven and London: Yale University Press.

Abu-Lughod, L. 1986. *Veiled Sentiments*. Berkeley: University of California Press.

Acar, F. 1990. 'Türkiye'de İslamcı Hareket ve Kadın'. In *Kadın Bakış Açısından 1980 'ler Türkiye' sinde Kadınlar*, ed. Ş. Tekeli. Istanbul: Iletişim.

———. 1991. 'Women in the Ideology of Islamic Revivalism in Turkey'. In *Islam in Modern Turkey*, ed. R. Tapper. London: I. B. Tauris.

———. 1993. 'Islam in Turkey'. In *Turkey and Europe*, ed. C. Balkır and A. M. Williams. London and New York: Pinter Publishers.

Afshar, H. 1987. 'Women, Marriage and the State in Iran'. In *Women, State and Ideology*, ed. H. Afshar. London: Macmillan.

———. 1988. 'Behind the Veil: The Public and Private Faces of Khomeini's Policies on Iranian Women'. In *Structures of Patriarchy*, ed. B. Agarwal. London: Zed.

Ahmad, F. 1977. *The Turkish Experiment in Democracy*. Boulder, Colorado: Westview Press for the Royal Institute of International Affairs, London.

———. 1991. 'Politics and Islam in Modern Turkey', *Middle Eastern Studies* 27 (1), 3–22.

Ahmed, L. 1982. 'Feminism and Feminist Movements in the Middle East. A Preliminary Exploration: Turkey, Egypt, Algeria, People's Democratic Republic of Yemen', *Women's Studies International Forum* 5 (2), 153–68.

———. 1992. *Women and Gender in Islam*. New Haven and London: Yale University Press.

Akşit, B. 1985. 'Ortakentte Toplumsal Farklılaşma ve Siyasal-

Kültürel Çatışma'. In B. Akşit Köy, Kasaba ve Kentlerde Toplumsal Değişme. Ankara: Turhan Kitapevi.

——. 1991. 'Islamic Education in Turkey: Medrese Reform in Late Ottoman Times and Imam-Hatip Schools in the Republic'. In Islam in Modern Turkey, ed. R. Tapper. London: I. B. Tauris.

Algar, H. 1985. 'Der Nakşibendi Orden in der republikanischen Turkei'. In Jahrbuch zur Geschichte und Gessellschaft des Vorderen und Mittleren Orient, ed. J. Blaschke and M. van Bruinessen. Berlin: Express.

——. 1990a. 'A Brief History of the Naqshbandi Order'. In Naqshbandis: Historical Development and Present Situation of a Muslim Mystical Order. Proceedings of the Sèvres Round Table 2–4 May 1985, ed. M. Gaborieau, A. Popovic and T. Zarcone. Istanbul: Isis.

——. 1990b. 'Political Aspects of Naqshbandi History'. In Naqshbandis: Historical Development and Present Situation of a Muslim Mystical Order. Proceedings of the Sèvres Round Table 2–4 May 1985, ed. M. Gaborieau, A. Popovic and T. Zarcone. Istanbul: Isis.

Anderson, B. 1990. Imagined Communities. London and New York: Verso. First published in 1983.

Arat, Y. 1990a. 'Islamic Fundamentalism and Women in Turkey', Muslim World 80 (1), January, pp. 17–23.

——. 1990b. 'Feminism ve Islam: Kadın ve Aile Dergisinin Düşündürdükleri'. In Kadın Bakış Açısından 1980ler Türkiyesinde Kadınlar, ed. Ş. Tekeli. Istanbul: Iletişim.

——. 1993. 'Women's Studies in Turkey: From Kemalism to Feminism', New Perspectives On Turkey 9 (Fall), 119–35.

Aren, M. 1980. Türk Toplumunda Kadın Bibliyografyası. Ankara: Türk Sosyal Bilimler Derneği.

Arjomand, S. A. 1984. 'Introduction: Social Movements in the Contemporary Near and Middle East'. In From Nationalism to Revolutionary Islam, ed. S.A. Arjomand. Albany: State University of New York Press.

Arkoun, M. 1994. 'İslam Tarihinde Yöntem Sorunu', trans. by C. Erdem and Y. Aktay, Tezkire no. 6, Winter, 49–70.

Aslanoğlu, I. 1984. '1928–46 Döneminde Ankara'da Yapılan Resmi Yapıların Mimari Değerlendirmesi'. In Tarih İçinde Ankara, ed. E. Yavuz and Ü. N. Uğurel. Ankara: Orta Doğu Teknik Üniversitesi.

Aswad, B. C. 1979. 'Women, Class, and Power: Examples from the Hatay, Turkey'. In *Women in the Muslim World*, ed. N. Keddie and L. Beck. Cambridge, Mass: Harvard University Press.

Ayata, S. 1988. 'Statü Yarışması ve Salon Kullanımı', *Toplum ve Bilim* no. 42, Summer, 5–25.

——. 1993a. 'The Rise of Islamic Fundamentalism and Its Institutional Framework'. In *The Political and Socioeconomic Transformation of Turkey*, ed. A. Eralp, M. Tünay and B. Yeşilada. Westport: Praeger.

——. 1993b. 'Continuity and Change in Turkish Culture: Some Critical Remarks on *Modern Mahrem*', *New Perspectives on Turkey* 9 (Fall), 137–48.

——. 1996. 'Patronage, Party and the State: The Politicization of Islam in Turkey', *Middle East Journal* 50 (1), 40–56.

Ayubi, N. 1991. *Political Islam: Religion and Politics in the Arab World*. London: Routledge.

Azari, F. 1983. 'Islam's Appeal to Women in Iran: Illusion and Reality'. In *Women of Iran: The Conflict with Fundamentalist Islam*, ed. F. Azari. London: Ithaca Press.

Al-Azmeh, A. 1993. *Islams and Modernities*. London and New York: Verso.

Badran, M. 1991. 'Competing Agenda: Feminists, Islam and the State in 19th and 20th Century Egypt'. In *Women, Islam and the State*, ed. D. Kandiyoti. Hong Kong: Macmillan.

Baker, R. W. 1990. *Sadat and After: Struggles for Egypt's Political Soul*. Cambridge, Mass: Harvard University Press.

——. 1991. 'Afraid for Islam: Egypt's Muslim Centrists. Between Pharaohs and Fundamentalists', *Daedalus* 120 (3), 41–68.

Bakhtin, M. 1986. *Speech Genres and Other Late Essays*, ed. C. Emerson and M. Holquist and trans. V. W. McGee. Austin: University of Texas Press.

Balamir, N. 1983. *Kırsal Türkiye'de Eğitim ve Toplum Yapısı*. Ankara: ODTÜ Mimarlik Fakultesi.

Bartky, S. L. 1990. *Femininity and Domination*. New York and London: Routledge.

Bayraktar, M. F. 1992. *Eğitim Kurumu Olarak Kuran Kursları Üzerne Bir Araştırma*. Istanbul: Yıldızlar Matbaası.

Behar, B. E. 1992. *Iktidar ve Tarih: Türkiye'de 'Resmi Tarih' Tezinin Oluşumu (1929–1937)*. Istanbul: Afa Yayınları.

Bellah, R. 1970. *Beyond Belief: Essays on Religion in a Post-Traditional World*. New York: Harper and Row.

Berger, P. L. 1967. *The Sacred Canopy: Elements of Sociological Theory of Religion*. Garden City, NY: Doubleday.

Berkes, N. 1978. *Türkiye'de Çağdaşlaşma*. Istanbul: Doğu-Batı Yayınları.

Berman, M. 1982. *All That Is Solid Melts into the Air: The Experience of Modernity*. New York: Simon and Schuster.

Beyer, P. B. 1991. 'Privatization and Public Influence of Religion in Global Society'. In *Global Culture: Nationalism, Globalization and Modernity*, ed. M. Featherstone. London and Newbury Park, California: Sage.

Bhabha, H. K. 1990. 'DissemiNation: Time, Narrative, and the Margins of the Modern Nation'. In *Nation and Narration*, ed. H. K. Bhabha. London and New York: Routledge.

———. 1998. 'Culture's In-Between'. In *Questions of Cultural Identity*, ed. S. Hall and P. du Gay. London and Thousand Oaks, California: Sage. First published 1996.

Binder, L. 1988. *Islamic Liberalism: A Critique of Development Ideologies*. Chicago: University of Chicago Press.

Bingöllü, B. (B. Toprak). 1979. 'Türk Kadını ve Din'. In *Türk Toplumunda Kadın*, ed. N. Abadan-Unat. Ankara: Türk Sosyal Bilimler Derneği Yayınları.

Boğaziçi Üniversitesi Türk Müziği Klübü. 1980. *Atatürk Devrimleri Ideolojisinin Türk Müzik Kültürüne Doğrudan ve Dolaylı Etkileri*. Istanbul: BÜTMK Yayınları.

Bolak, H. 1990. 'Aile İçi Kadın Erkek İlişkilerinin Çok Boyutlu Kavramlaştırılmasına Yönelik Öneriler'. In *Kadın Bakış Açısından 1980ler Türkiyesinde Kadınlar*, ed. Ş. Tekeli. Istanbul: İletişim.

Bourdieu, P. 1977. *Outline of a Theory of Practice*. Cambridge, England: Cambridge University Press.

———. 1989. *Distinction: A Social Critique of the Judgement of Taste*, trans. R. Nice. London: Routledge.

Bozdoğan, S. 1994. 'Architecture, Modernism and Nation-Building in Kemalist Turkey', *New Perspectives on Turkey* 10 (Spring), 37–55.

Byod, W. and E. King. 1952. *The History of Western Education*. London: Adam and Charles Black.

Çakır, R. 1991. *Ayet ve Slogan*. Istanbul: Metis Yayınları.

———. 1994. *Ne Şeriat Ne Demokrasi: Refah Partisini Anlamak.* Istanbul: Metis Yayınları.

Çakır, S. 1992. '1980 Sonrasında Türkiye'de Kadın Araştırmaları Bibliyografyası'. In *Türkiye'de Kadın Olgusu*, ed. N. Arat. Istanbul: Say Yayınları.

Campo, J. E. 1991. *The Other Side of Paradise.* South Carolina: University of South Carolina Press.

Caplan, P. 1988. 'Engendering Knowledge: The Politics of Ethnography', *Anthropology Today* 14 (5), 8–10 and 14 (6), 15–17.

Certeau, M. de. 1984. *The Practice of Everyday Life*, trans. S. F. Rendall. Berkeley: University of California Press.

———. 1988. *The Writing of History*, trans. T. Conley. New York: Columbia University Press.

Chatterjee, P. 1993. *The Nation and Its Fragments: Colonial and Postcolonial Histories.* Princeton, NJ: Princeton University Press.

Cherifati-Merabtine, D. 1994. 'Algeria at a Crossroads: National Liberation, Islamization and Women'. In *Gender and National Identity*, ed. V. M. Moghadam. London and New Jersey: Zed; Karachi: Oxford University Press.

Choueiri, Y. M. 1990. *Islamic Fundamentalism.* Boston: Twayne Publishers.

Coser, L. 1970. *Men of Ideas: A Sociologist's View.* New York: Free Press. First published 1965.

Coward, R. and J. Ellis. 1979. *Language and Materialism.* London, Boston and Henley: Routledge and Kegan Paul.

Crapanzano, V. 1992. *Hermes' Dilemma and Hamlet's Desire: On the Epistemology of Interpretation.* Cambridge, Mass: Harvard University Press.

Delaney, C. 1991. *The Seed and the Soil.* Berkeley: University of California Press.

Dessouki, A. 1987. 'Official Islam and the Political Legitimation in the Arab Countries'. In *The Islamic Impulse*, ed. B. F. Stowasser. London and Sydney: Croom Helm.

Dilipak, A. 1988. *Bir Başka Açıdan Kemalizm.* Istanbul: Beyan Yayınları.

———. 1989a. *Cumhuriyet'e Giden Yol.* Istanbul: Beyan Yayınları.

———. 1989b. *İnönü Dönemi.* Istanbul: Beyan Yayınları.

———. 1990. *Menderes Dönemi.* Istanbul: Beyan Yayınları.

———. 1991. *İhtilaller Dönemi.* Istanbul: Beyan Yayınları.

Dodd, C. H. 1990. *The Crisis of Turkish Democracy*. Huntingdon, England: Eothen Press.

Doğramacı, E. 1992. *Türkiye'de Kadının Dünü Bu Günü*. Ankara: İş Bankası Kültür Yayını.

Douglas, M. 1991. 'The Idea of a Home: A Kind of Space', *Social Research* 58 (1), 287–307.

Duben, A. 1982. 'The Significance of Family and Kinship in Urban Turkey'. In *Sex Roles, Family and Community in Turkey*, ed. Ç. Kağıtçıbaşı. Bloomington, Indiana: Indiana University Press.

Dubetsky, A. 1976. 'Kinship Primordial Ties and Factory Organization in Turkey: An Anthropological View', *International Journal of Middle East Studies* 7, 433–51.

Durakbaşa, A. 1988. 'Cumhuriyet Döneminde Kemalist Kadın Kimliğinin Oluşumu', *Tarih ve Toplum* 9 (52), 167–71.

Eickelman, D. F. 1978. 'The Art of Memory: Islamic Education and its Social Production', *Comparative Studies in Society and History* 20, 485–516.

———. 1987. 'Changing Interpretations of Islamic Cultures'. In *Islam and the Political Economy of Meaning*, ed. W. Roff. Berkeley and Los Angeles: University of California Press.

———. 1991. 'Traditional Islamic Learning and Ideas of the Person in the Twentieth Century'. In *Middle Eastern Lives*, ed. M. Kramer. Syracuse: Syracuse University Press.

El-Guindi, F. 1981. 'Veiling Infitah with Muslim Ethics: Egypt's Contemporary Islamic Movement', *Social Problems* 28 (4), 465–85.

Elias, N. 1991. *The Society of Individuals*, trans. E. Jephcott. Cambridge, Mass.: Basil Blackwell.

Elliott, A. 1992. *Social Theory and Psychoanalysis in Transition: Self and Society from Freud to Kristeva*. Oxford: Blackwell.

Enayat, H. 1982. *Modern Islamic Political Thought*. Austin: University of Texas Press.

Ertürk, Y. 1991. 'Convergence and Divergence in the Status of Muslim Women: The Cases of Turkey and Saudi Arabia', *International Sociology* 6 (3).

Esposito, J. L. 1991. *Islam: The Straight Path*. New York: Oxford University Press.

———. 1992. *The Islamic Threat*. New York and Oxford: Oxford University Press.

Fallers, L. 1974a. *The Social Anthropology of the Nation State.* Chicago: Aldine.

———. 1974b. 'Notes on an Advent Ramadan', *Center for Middle Eastern Studies Reprint Series 7.* University of Chicago.

Fallers, L. and M. C. Fallers. 1976. 'Sex Roles in Edremit'. In *Mediterranean Family Structures*, ed. J.G. Peristiany. Cambridge, England: Cambridge University Press.

Fischer, M. J. M. and M. Abedi. 1990. *Debating Muslims: Cultural Dialogues in Postmodernity and Tradition.* Madison, Wisconsin: University of Wisconsin Press.

Foucault, M. 1977. 'Nietzsche, Genealogy, History'. In *Language, Counter-Memory, Practice: Selected Essays and Interviews by Michel Foucault*, ed. D.F. Bouchard, trans. D. F. Bouchard and S. Simon. Ithaca, NY: Cornell University Press.

———. 1979. *Discipline and Punish.* New York: Vintage Books.

———. 1980. *Power/Knowledge*, ed. C. Gordon. New York: Pantheon Books.

Friedmann, Y. 1971. *Shaykh Ahmad Sirhindi.* Montreal: McGill University, Institute of Islamic Studies

Gardiner, M. 1992. *The Dialogics of Critique.* London: Routledge.

Geertz, C. 1960. *The Religion of Java.* New York: Free Press.

———. 1968. *Islam Observed: Religious Development in Morocco and Indonesia.* Chicago and London: University of Chicago Press.

Gellner, E. 1983a. *Muslim Society.* Cambridge, England: Cambridge University Press.

———. 1983b. *Nations and Nationalisms.* Ithaca, NY: Cornell University Press.

———. 1992. *Postmodernism, Reason and Religion.* London and New York: Routledge.

Gibb, H. A. R. 1963. 'The Community in Islamic History', *Proceedings of the American Philosophical Society* 107 (2), 173–6.

Giddens, A. 1990. *The Consequences of Modernity.* Stanford, California: Stanford University Press.

———. 1991. *Modernity and Self-Identity: Self and Society in the Late Modern Age.* Stanford, California: Stanford University Press.

Gilsenan, M. 1982. *Recognizing Islam.* London: Croom Helm.

Goffman, E. 1963. *Behavior in Public Places.* New York: Free Press.

Gök, F. 1990. 'Türkiye'de Eğitim ve Kadınlar'. In *Kadın Bakış Açısından 1980 'ler Türkiye 'sinde Kadınlar*, ed. Ş. Tekeli. Istanbul: İletişim.

Göle, N. 1991. *Modern Mahrem*. Istanbul: Metis Yayınları.
——. 1996. *The Forbidden Modern: Civilization and Veiling*. Ann Arbor: University of Michigan Press.
——. 2000. *Islam'ın Yeni Kamusal Yüzleri: Islam ve Kamusal Alan Üzerine Bir Atölye Çalışması*, ed. Nilüfer Göle, Kenan Çayır, et al. Beyoğlu, Istanbul: Metis Yayınları.
Gündüz, İ. 1984. *Gümüşhanevi Ahmed Ziyaüddin*. Istanbul: Seha Neşriyat.
Güneş-Ayata, A. 1990–1. 'Gecekondularda Kimlik Sorunu, Dayanışma Örüntüleri', *Toplum ve Bilim* 51/52, 89–101.
——. 1991. 'Pluralism Versus Authoritarianism: Political Ideas in Two Islamic Publications'. In *Islam in Modern Turkey*, ed. R. Tapper. London: I. B. Tauris.
——. 1992. *CHP: Örgüt ve Ideoloji*. Ankara: Gürdoğan.
Gürdoğan, E. 1991. *Görünmeyen Üniversite*. Istanbul: Iz Yayıncılık.
Haddad, Y.Y. and J. I. Smith. 1982. 'Eve: Islamic Image of Women', *Women's Studies International Forum* 5 (2), 135–44.
Hale, S. 1987. 'Women's Culture/Men's Culture', *American Behavioral Scientist* 3 (1), 115–34.
Harding, S. 1986. 'The Instability of the Analytical Categories of Feminist Theory', *Signs* 11 (4), 645–64.
Hatem, M. 1991. *The Demise of Egyptian State Feminism and the Politics of Transition (1980–1991). The G. E. von Grunebaum Center for Near Eastern Studies Working Paper No. 3*. Los Angeles: University of California.
——. 1993. 'Toward the Development of Post-Islamist and Post-Nationalist Feminist Discourses in the Middle East'. In *Arab Women*, ed. J. Tucker. Bloomington, Indiana: Indiana University Press.
Heck, M. C. 1980. 'The Ideological Dimension of Media Messages'. In *Culture, Media, Language*, ed. S. Hall et al. London: Hutchinson.
Hentsch, T. 1992. *Imagining the Middle East*. Montreal and New York: Black Rose Books.
Heper, M. 1981. 'Islam, Polity and Society in Turkey: A Middle Eastern Perspective', *Middle East Journal* 35 (3), 345–63.
——. 1985. *The State Tradition in Turkey*. Beverley, North Humberside, England: Eothen Press.
Heyd, U. 1954. *Language Reform in Turkey*. Jerusalem: Israel Oriental Society.

Hodgson, M. G. S. 1974. *The Venture of Islam*. 3 vols. Chicago: University of Chicago Press.

Hoffman-Ladd, V. 1987. 'Polemics on the Modesty and Segregation of Women in Contemporary Egypt', *International Journal of Middle East Studies* 19, 23–50.

Hourani, A. 1980. 'Western Attitudes Towards Islam'. In *Europe and the Middle East*, ed. A. Hourani. Berkeley and Los Angeles: University of California Press. First published 1974.

———. 1991. *Islam in European Thought*. Cambridge, England: Cambridge University Press.

İlyasoğlu, A. 1994. *Örtülü Kimlik*. Istanbul: Metis Yayınları.

Inalcık, H. 1978. 'The Heyday and the Decline of the Ottoman Empire'. In *The Cambridge History of Islam*, ed. P.M. Holt, A. K.S. Lambton and B. Lewis. Vol. 1A, 324–53. Cambridge, England: Cambridge University Press.

Izutsu, T. 1966. *Ethico-Religious Concepts in the Quran*. Montreal: McGill University Press.

Jaschke, G. 1972. *Yeni Türkiye'de Islamlık*, trans. H. Örs. Ankara: Bilgi Yayınevi.

Juergensmeyer, M. 1993. *The New Cold War? Religious Nationalism Confronts the Secular State*. Berkeley: University of California Press.

Kağıtçıbaşı, Ç. 1981. *Çocuğun Değeri: Türkiye'de Değerler ve Doğurganlık*. Istanbul: Boğaziçi Üniversitesi Yayınları.

———. 1982. 'Introduction'. In *Sex Roles, Family and Community in Turkey*, ed. Ç. Kağıtçıbaşı. Bloomington, Indiana: Indiana University Press.

———. 1984. 'Aile-ici et kileşme ve ilişkiler: Bir aile değişme ,modeli önerisi'. In *Turkiye'de* Ailenin Değişimi: Toplumbilimsel İncelemeler. Ankara: Turk Sosyal Bilimler Derneği Yayinlari.

Kandiyoti, D. 1982. 'Urban Change and Women's Roles in Turkey: An Overview and Evolution'. In *Sex Roles, Family and Community in Turkey*, ed. Ç. Kağıtçıbaşı. Bloomington, Indiana: Indiana University Turkish Studies.

———. 1984. 'Aile yapısında değişme ve süreklilik: Karşılaştırmalı bir yaklaşım'. In *Türkiye'de ailenin değişimi: Toplumbilimsel İncelemeler*, ed. T. Erder. Ankara: Türk Sosyal Bilimler Derneği Yayını.

———. 1987. 'Emancipated but Unliberated? Reflections on the Turkish Case', *Feminist Studies* 13 (2), 317–37.

———. 1988a. 'Bargaining with Patriarchy', *Gender and Society* 2 (3), 274–90.

———. 1988b. 'Slave Girls, Temptresses, and Comrades: Images of Women in the Turkish Novel', *Feminist Issues* 8 (1), 37–49.

———. 1989. 'Women and the Turkish State: Political Actors or Symbolic Pawns?' In *Women-Nation-State*, ed. N. Yuval-Davis and F. Anthias. London: Macmillan.

———. 1991a. 'End of Empire: Islam, Nationalism and Women in Turkey'. In *Women, Islam and the State*, ed. D. Kandiyoti, Hong Kong: Macmillan.

———. 1991b. 'Islam and Patriarchy: A Comparative Perspective'. In *Women in Middle Eastern History*, ed. N. Keddie and B. Baron. New Haven and London: Yale University Press.

Karpat, K. 1963. 'The People's Houses in Turkey. Establishment and Growth', *Middle East Journal* 17 (1/2), 55–67.

———.1976. *The Gecekondu: Rural Migration and Urbanization*. London: Cambridge University Press.

———.1991. 'The Republican People's Party, 1923–1945'. In *Political Parties and Democracy in Turkey*, ed. M. Heper. London and New York: I. B. Tauris.

Keddie, N. R. 1979. 'Problems in the Study of Muslim Women', *International Journal of Middle East Studies* 10 (2), 225–40.

———. 1991. 'Introduction'. In *Women in Middle Eastern History*, ed. N. Keddie and B. Baron. New Haven and London: Yale University Press.

Kepel, G. 1985. *The Prophet and Pharaoh: Muslim Extremism in Egypt*, trans. Jon Rothschild. London: Al Saqi Books.

Keyder, Ç. 1988. 'Class and State in the Transformation of Modern Turkey'. In *State and Ideology in the Middle East and Pakistan*, ed. F. Halliday and H. Alavi. Hong Kong: Macmillan Education.

———. 1989. *Türkiye'de Devlet ve Sınıflar*. Istanbul: Iletişim Yayınları.

———. 1993. 'The Dilemma of Cultural Identity on the Margin of Europe', *Review* 16 (1), 19–33.

Kıray, M. 1976. 'Changing Roles of Mothers: Changing Intra-Family Relations in a Turkish Town'. In *Mediterranean Family Structures*, ed. J. Peristiany. London: Cambridge University Press.

———. 1982. 'Women in Small Towns'. In *Women in Turkish Society*, ed. N. Abadan-Unat. Leiden. E. J. Brill.

———. 1991. 'Introduction. A Perspective'. In *Structural Change in Turkish Society*, ed. M. Kıray. Bloomington, Indiana: Indiana University Turkish Studies.

Kriegel, A. 1971. *The French Communists: Profile of a People*, trans. Elaine P. Halperin. Chicago: University of Chicago Press.

Lakoff, G. and M. Johnson. 1980. *Metaphors We Live By*. Chicago and London: University of Chicago Press.

Lapidus, I. M. 1992. 'The Golden Age: The Political Concepts of Islam', *American Academy of Political and Social Science, Annals* 524 (November), 13–25.

Lawrence, B. B. 1989. *Defenders of God*. San Francisco: Harper and Row.

Lazreg, M. 1988. 'Feminism and Difference: The Perils of Writing as a Woman on Women in Algeria', *Feminist Studies* 14 (1), 81–107.

———. 1990. 'Gender and Politics in Algeria: Unravelling the Religious Paradigm', *Signs* 15 (4), 755–80.

Levi, A. 1991. 'The Justice Party, 1961–1980'. In *Political Parties and Democracy in Turkey*, ed. M. Heper. London and New York: I. B. Tauris.

Lewis, B. 1968. *The Emergence of Modern Turkey*. London, Oxford and New York: Oxford University Press.

———. 1985. 'Preface'. In G. Kepel, *The Prophet and Pharaoh*. London: Al Saqi Books.

———. 1991. *The Political Language of Islam*. Chicago and London: University of Chicago Press.

Luckmann, T. 1967. *The Invisible Religion: The Problem of Religion in Modern Society*. New York: Macmillan, 1967.

Magneralla, P. 1974. *Tradition and Change in a Turkish Town*. New York: John Wiley.

Marcus, J. 1992. *A World of Difference: Islam and Gender Hierarchy in Turkey*. London and New Jersey: Zed.

Mardin, Ş. 1960/1961. 'Some Notes on an Early Phase in the Modernization of Communications in Turkey', *Comparative Studies in Society and History* 3, 250–71.

———. 1966. 'Opposition and Control in Turkey', *Government and Opposition* 1 (3), 375–87.

———. 1969. *Din ve Ideoloji*. Ankara: Ankara Üniversitesi SBF Yayınları.

———. 1971. 'Ideology and Religion in the Turkish Revolution', *International Journal of Middle East Studies* 2 (3), 197–211.

——. 1973. 'Center-Periphery Relations: A Key To Turkish Politics?' *Daedalus* 102 (1), 169–90.

——. 1974. 'Super-Westernization in Urban Life in the Ottoman Empire in the Last Quarter of the Nineteenth Century'. In *Turkey: Geographic and Social Perspectives*, ed. P. Benedict, E. Tümertekin and F. Mansur. Leiden: E. J. Brill.

——. 1977. 'Religion in Modern Turkey', *International Social Science Journal* 29 (2), 279–97.

——. 1978. 'Youth and Violence in Turkey', *Archives européennes de Sociologie* 19 (2), 229–56.

——. 1981. 'Religion and Secularism in Turkey'. In *Atatürk. Founder of a Modern State*, ed. A. Kazancıgil and E. Özbudun. London: C. Hurst and Company.

——. 1983a. 'Religion and Politics in Modern Turkey'. In *Islam in the Political Process*, ed. J. P. Piscatori. Cambridge, England: Cambridge University Press.

——. 1983b. 'Batıcılık', *Cumhuriyet Dönemi Türkiye Ansiklopedisi* vol.1, 245–50.

——. 1984. 'A Note on the Transformation of Religious Symbols in Turkey', *Turcica* 16, 115–27.

——. 1989a. *Religion and Social Change in Modern Turkey: The Case of Bediüzzaman Said Nursi*. Albany, NY: State University of New York Press.

——. 1989b. 'Culture and Religion Towards the Year 2000'. In *Turkey in the Year 2000*, Turkish Political Science Association. Ankara: Sevinç Matbaası.

——. 1990a. 'Yenileşme Dinamiğinin Temelleri ve Atatürk'. *Türkiye'de Toplum ve Siyaset*. Istanbul: Iletişim. First published 1984.

——. 1990b. 'Islamic "Fundamentalist" Perspectives: Egypt and Turkey'. Paper presented to the Conference on Socio-Economic Transformation, State and Political Regimes: Egypt and Turkey, July 26–28, Istanbul.

——. 1991a. 'The Just and the Unjust', *Daedalus* 120 (3), 113–29.

——. 1991b. 'The Nakşibendi Order in Turkish History'. In *Islam in Modern Turkey*, ed. R. Tapper. London: I. B. Tauris.

——. 1992. *Ideoloji*. Istanbul: Iletişim. First published 1976.

Mardin, Ş., ed. 1994. *Cultural Transitions in the Middle East*. Leiden: E. J. Brill.

McCarthy, J. 1983. *Muslims and Minorities: The Population of Ottoman Anatolia and the End of the Empire*. New York: New York University Press.

McLuhan, M. 1965. *The Gutenberg Galaxy*. Toronto: University of Toronto Press.

Meeker, M. E. 1976. 'Meaning and Society in the Middle East: Examples from the Black Sea Turks and Levantine Arabs, Parts I and II', *International Journal of Middle East Studies* 7(2), 243–70 and 7(3), 383–423.

———. 1991. 'The New Muslim Intellectuals in the Republic of Turkey'. In *Islam in Modern Turkey*, ed. R. Tapper. London: I. B. Tauris.

Mernissi, F. 1975. *Beyond the Veil*. New York: John Wiley.

———. 1991. *The Veil and the Male Elite*. Reading, Mass.: Addison Wesley Publishing Company.

Mills, C. W. 1951. *White Collar: The American Middle Classes*. New York: Oxford University Press.

Moghadam, V. M. 1988. 'Women, Work and Ideology in the Islamic Republic', *International Journal of Middle East Studies* 20, 221–43.

———. 1991. 'Islamist Movements and Women's Responses in the Middle East', *Gender and History* 3 (3), 268–84.

———. 1992. 'Patriarchy and the Politics of Gender in Modernising Societies: Iran, Pakistan and Afghanistan', *International Sociology* 7 (1), 35–53.

Mottahedeh, R. 1985. *The Mantle of the Prophet*. New York: Pantheon Books.

Nader, L. 1989. *Orientalism, Occidentalism and the Control of Women*. Leiden: E. J. Brill.

Najmabadi, A. 1987. 'Iran's Return to Islam: From Modernism to Moral Order', *Middle East Journal* 41 (2), 202–17.

———. 1991. 'Hazards of Modernity and Morality: Women, State and Ideology in Contemporary Iran'. In *Women, Islam and the State*, ed. D. Kandiyoti. Hong Kong: Macmillan.

Nispet, R. A. 1973. *The Sociological Tradition*. London: Heinemann.

Norton, A. R. 1993. 'The Future of Civil Society in the Middle East', *Middle East Journal* 47 (2), 210–16.

Olson, E. A. 1985. 'Muslim Identity and Secularism in Contemporary Turkey: "The Headscarf Dispute"', *Anthropological Quarterly* 58 (4), 161–72.

————. 1991. 'Of Türbe and Evliya: Saints and Shrines as Environments Facilitate Communication and Innovation'. In *Structural Change in Turkish Society*, ed. M. Kıray. Bloomington, Indiana: Indiana University Turkish Studies.

Ong, A. 1990. 'State Versus Islam: Malay Families, Women's Bodies, and the Body Politic in Malaysia', *American Ethnologist* 17 (2), 258–76.

Ortaylı, İ. 1987. *Imparatorluğun En Uzun Yüzyılı*. Istanbul: Hil Yayınları.

Özbay, F. 1979. 'Türkiye'de Kırsal/Kentsel Kesimde Eğitimin Kadınlar Üzerinde Etkisi'. In *Türk Toplumunda Kadın*, ed. N. Abadan-Unat. Ankara: Türk Sosyal Bilimler Derneği Yayını.

Öztürkmen, A. 1994. 'The Role of People's Houses in the Making of National Culture in Turkey', *New Perspectives on Turkey* 11 (Fall), 163–81.

Parla, T. 1989. *Ziya Gökalp, Kemalism ve Türkiye'de Korporatizm*. Istanbul: Iletişim.

Perry, J. R. 1985. 'Language Reform in Turkey and Iran', *International Journal of Middle East Studies* 17, 295–311.

Piscatori, J. P. 1986. *Islam in a World of Nation States*. Cambridge, England: Cambridge University Press.

al-Qur'an. 1984. Transl. by Ahmed Ali. Karachi: Akrash.

Rahman, F. 1984. *Islam and Modernity: Transformation of an Intellectual Tradition*. Chicago and London: University of Chicago Press.

Reed, H. A. 1954. 'Revival of Islam in Secular Turkey', *Middle East Journal* 7 (2), 267–82.

————. 1956. 'Religious Life of Modern Turkish Muslims'. In *Islam and the West: Proceedings of the Harvard Summer School Conference on the Middle East, July 25–27, 1955*, ed. R.N. Frye. 's-Gravenhage: Mouton.

Rhode, D. L., ed. 1990. *Theoretical Perspectives on Sexual Difference*. New Haven and London: Yale University Press.

Robertson, R. 1991. *Mapping the Global Condition: Globalization as the Central Concept in Global Culture*, ed. M. Featherston. London, Newbury Park, New Delhi: Sage Publications.

Roff, W. R. 1987. 'Islamic Movements: One or Many?' In *Islam and the Political Economy of Meaning*, ed. W. R. Roff. Berkeley and Los Angeles: University of California Press.

Rogers, S. C. 1978. 'Women's Place: A Critical Review of Anthropological Theory', *Contemporary Studies in Society and History* 20, 123–62.

Rosenau, P. M. 1992. *Post-Modernism and the Social Sciences*. Princeton, NJ: Princeton University Press.

Roy, O. 1994. *The Failure of Political Islam*, trans. C. Volk. Cambridge, Mass: Harvard University Press.

Rustow, D. A. 1956. 'Politics and Islam in Turkey 1920–55'. In *Islam and the West*, ed. R. N. Frye. 's-Gravenhage: Mouton.

Rykwert, J. 1991. 'House and Home', *Social Research* 58 (1), 51–62.

Said, E. 1987. *Orientalism*. Rickmandsworth, England: Penguin. First published 1978 Routledge and Kegan Paul.

Samim, A. 1981. 'The Tragedy of the Turkish Left', *New Left Review* 126, 60–85.

Sarıbay, A. Y. 1985a. 'Türkiye'de Siyasal Modernleşme ve İslam', *Toplum ve Bilim* 29–30, 45–64.

———. 1985b. *Türkiye'de Modernleşme, Din ve Parti Poltikası: MSP Örnek Olayı*. Istanbul: Alan Yayıncılık.

Sayarı, S. (B. Toprak). 1979. 'Turkiye' de Dinin Denetim İskvi' Ankara Üniversitesi Siyasal Bilgiler falcültesi Degisi, vol. 33, nos. 1–2.

———. 1992. 'Turkey: The Changing European Security Environment and the Gulf Crisis', *Middle East Journal* 46 (1), 7–21.

Schick, E. C. 1990. 'Representing Middle Eastern Women: Feminism and Colonial Discourse', *Feminist Studies* 16 (2), 345–80.

Schimmel, A. 1986. *Mystical Dimensions of Islam*. Chapel Hill: University of North Carolina Press. First published 1975.

———. 1989. *Islamic Names*. Edinburgh: Edinburgh University Press.

Scott, R. B. 1965. 'Turkish Village Attitudes Towards Religious Education', *Muslim World* 55 (3), 222–9.

———. 1971. 'Qur'an Courses in Turkey', *Muslim World* 61 (4), 239–55.

Sennett, R. 1971. *The Uses of Disorder*. London: Allen Lane.

———. 1992. *The Fall of Public Man*. New York and London: W. W. Norton and Company. Originally published 1976.

Sennett, R. and J. Cobb. 1973. *The Hidden Injuries of Class*. New York: Vintage.

Sichtermann, B. 1986. *Femininity: The Politics of the Personal*, ed. Helga Geyer-Ryan, trans. John Whitlam. Cambridge, England: Polity.

Siebers, T. 1988. *The Ethics of Criticism*. Ithaca, NY: Cornell University Press.

Sirman, N. 1989. 'Feminism in Turkey: A Short History', *New Perspectives On Turkey* 3 (1) (Fall), 1–34.

———. 1990. 'Köy Kadınının Aile ve Evlilikte Güçlenme Mücadelesi'. In *Kadın Bakış Açısından 1980ler Türkiyesinde Kadınlar*, ed. Ş. Tekeli. Istanbul: İletişim.

Sivan, E. 1985. *Radical Islam: Medieval Theology and Modern Politics*. New Haven and London: Yale University Press.

———. 1992. 'Islamic Resurgence: Civil Society Strikes Back'. In *Fundamentalism in Comparative Perspective*, ed. L. Kaplan. Amherst: University of Massachusetts Press.

Smith, W. C. 1981. *On Understanding Islam*. The Hague: Mouton.

Stirling, P. 1958. 'Religious Change in Republican Turkey', *Middle East Journal* 12 (4), 395–409.

Stowasser, B. F. 1987a. 'Religious Ideology, Women and the Family: The Islamic Paradigm'. In *The Islamic Impulse*, ed. B. F. Stowasser. London and Sydney: Croom Helm.

———. 1987b. 'Liberated Equal or Protected Dependent? Contemporary Religious Paradigms on Women's Status in Islam', *Arab Studies Quarterly* 9 (3), 260–83.

Sunar, I. and B. Toprak. 1983. 'Islam in Politics: The Case of Turkey', *Government and Opposition* 18 (4), 421–41.

Tachau, F. 1964. 'Language and Politics: Turkish Language Reform', *Review of Politics* 26 (2) 191–204.

Tapper, N. 1983. 'Gender and Religion in a Turkish Town: A Comparison of Two Types of Formal Women's Gathering'. In *Women's Religious Experience*, ed. P. Holden. London: Croom Helm.

———. 1985. 'Changing Wedding Rituals in a Turkish Town', *Journal of Turkish Studies* 9, 305–13.

———. 1990. 'Ziyaret: Gender, Movement, and Exchange in a Turkish Community'. In *Muslim Travellers*, ed. D. Eickelman and J. Piscatori. Berkeley: University of California Press.

Tapper, R., ed. 1991. *Islam in Modern Turkey: Religion, Politics, and Literature in a Secular State*. London and New York: I. B. Tauris.

Tapper, R. and N. Tapper. 1987a. ' "Thank God We're Secular!" Aspects of Fundamentalism in a Turkish Town'. In *Aspects of Religious Fundamentalism*, ed. L. Capan. London: Macmillan.

——. 1987b. 'The Birth of the Prophet: Ritual and Gender in Turkish Islam', *Man* n.s. 22 (1), 69–92.

——. 1991. 'Religion, Education and Continuity in a Provincial Town'. In *Islam in Modern Turkey: Religion, Politics and Literature in a Secular State*, ed. R. Tapper. London, New York: I. B. Tauris.

Taşkıran, T. 1976. *Women in Turkey*. Istanbul: Redhouse.

Thomas, L. V. 1952. 'Recent Developments in Turkish Islam', *Middle East Journal* 6 (1) 22–40.

Tibi, B. 1990. *Islam and the Cultural Accommodation of Social Change*, trans. C. Krojzl. Boulder, Colorado: Westview Press. First published 1985.

Timur, S. 1972. *Türkiye'de Aile Yapısı*. Ankara: Hacettepe Üniversitesi Yayınları.

Timur, T. 1987. 'Atatürk ve Pozitivizm', *Cumhuriyet Dönemi Türkiye Ansiklopedisi* vol.1, 94–6.

Todorov, T. 1992. *Mikhail Bakhtin: The Dialogical Principle*, trans. W. Godzich. Minneapolis: University of Minnesota Press.

Toprak, B. 1981. *Islam and Political Development in Turkey*. Leiden: E. J. Brill.

——. 1984. 'Politicisation of Islam in a Secular State: The National Salvation Party'. In *From Nationalism to Revolutionary Islam*, ed. S. A. Arjomand. Albany, NY: State University of New York Press.

——. 1988. 'The State, Politics, and Religion in Turkey'. In *State, Democracy and the Military: Turkey in the 1980s*, ed. M. Heper and A. Evin. Berlin: de Gruyter.

——. 1990a. 'Emancipated but Unliberated Women in Turkey: The Impact of Islam'. In *Women, Family and Social Change in Turkey*, ed. F. Özbay. Bangkok: Unesco.

——. 1990b. 'Religion as State Ideology in a Secular Setting: The Turkish-Islamic Synthesis'. In *Aspects of Religion in Secular Turkey*, ed. M. Wagstaff. Durham: University of Durham, Centre for Middle East and Islamic Studies.

——. 1994. 'Women and Fundamentalism: The Case of Turkey'. In *Identity Politics and Women. Cultural Reassertions and Feminisms in International Perspective*, ed. V. M. Moghadam. Boulder, Colorado: Westview Press.

Tunaya, T. Z. 1991. *İslamcılık Akımı*. Istanbul: Simavi Yayınları.

Vergin, N. 1985. 'Toplumsal Değişme ve Dinsellikte Artış', *Toplum ve Bilim* 29/30, 9–28.

Voll, J. O. 1982. *Islam, Continuity and Change in the Modern World*. Boulder, Colorado: Westview Press.

Waines, D. 1983. 'Through a Veil Darkly: The Study of Women in Muslim Society', *Contemporary Studies in Society and History* 3, 642–59.

Wallace, A. F. C. 1956. 'Revitalization Movements: Some Theoretical Considerations for their Comparative Study', *American Anthropologist* n.s. 58 (2), pp. 264–81.

Watt, W. M. 1960. 'The Charismatic Community in Islam', *Numen* 7, 77–90.

Wuthnow, R. 1991. 'Understanding Religion and Politics', *Daedalus* 120 (3), 1–20.

Yalman, N. 1969. 'Islamic Reform and the Mystic Tradition in Eastern Turkey', *European Journal of Sociology* 10, 41–60.

———. 1979. 'The Center and the Periphery: The Reform of Religious Institutions in Turkey', *Current Turkish Thought* 38.

Yeatman, A. 1990. 'A Feminist Theory of Social Differentiation'. In *Feminism/ Postmodernism*, ed. L. J. Nicholson. New York: Routledge.

Zubaida, S. 1994. *İslam, Halk ve Devlet*. Istanbul: İletişim. First published in English: *İslam, the People and the State: Essays on Political Ideas and Movements in the Middle East*. London and New York: Routledge.

Zuhur, S. 1992. *Revealing Reveiling: Islamist Gender Ideology in Contemporary Egypt*. Albany, NY: State University of New York Press.

Index